Levinas and the Postcolonial

To the everyday blessing that is Marisa and Miles

Levinas and the Postcolonial

Race, Nation, Other

John E. Drabinski

EDINBURGH UNIVERSITY PRESS

© John E. Drabinski, 2011

Transferred to digital print 2012

Edinburgh University Press Ltd
22 George Square, Edinburgh

www.euppublishing.com

Typeset in 11/13 Adobe Sabon
by Servis Filmsetting Ltd, Stockport, Cheshire, and
printed and bound by CPI Group (UK) Ltd
Croydon, CR0 4YY

A CIP record for this book is available from the British Library

ISBN 978 0 7486 4103 1 (hardback)

ents

Acknowledgements

Parts of Chapter 4 were published as 'Future Interval: On Levinas and Glissant,' in *Totality and Infinity at 50*, ed. Diane Perpich and Scott Davidson. Pittsburgh: Duquesne University Press, 2010.

I wrote this book, like my previous one, in the pauses and breaks of my work and personal life. Of course, one always imagines books written in long, sustained periods of meditation, alone, in the library, weary but steeled against the body, and so on. We have all seen the paintings. The reality is that books are written alongside the buzz of daily life. For me, that makes it all the more satisfying when it is done and sent off to the publisher. I think I wrote this one without being an altogether terrible partner, friend, brother, colleague, and father. And for that, I have a bunch of people to thank. So, here are some words of acknowledgement.

Two anonymous referees for Edinburgh University Press provided insightful criticisms and suggestions, and I hope this book reflects how those comments improved my ideas.

In many ways, the thoughts about this book began after hearing a talk at Hampshire College. The speaker trotted out a few of the uglier occasional remarks by Levinas for a bit of cheap outrage. As a Levinas scholar, I heard a lot about those remarks from colleagues in the days that followed. What struck me was how we were invited by the speaker to think with shallowness and lack of analysis about Levinas's rather nasty comments, as if it were all a matter of gossip and moralizing gasps (which, in its own way, instrumentalizes the degraded and insulted Other). Surely something more needs to be said, I thought. And pleaded. In particular, after explaining and discussing some of my concerns with my colleagues Omar Dahi and Margaret Cerullo, I thought, yes, a book needs to be written about Levinas, difference, and postcolonial theory. So, here we are.

I want to thank some of the people who have been exceptionally supportive of my position at Hampshire College, then Hampshire and Amherst College jointly, and now Amherst College permanently. A

ne thing. A job that allows space for research, supports travel,
ierally values inquiry and writing – that is another thing, and
ok was only possible because of my time at Hampshire and
t. My gratitude is real and deep: Alan Goodman, Aaron
l, Susan Tracy, Christoph Cox, Monique Roelofs, Margaret
, and *especially* Barbara Yngvesson, to whom I owe so, so
hank yous. Folks at Amherst College deserve that same kind
iks: Karen Sanchez-Eppler, Greg Call, Rhonda Cobham-
, Hilary Moss, Tom Dumm, Anston Bosman, Judy Frank,
'arker, Barry O'Connell, and Jeff Ferguson. Many others.
SAWG writers from summer 2010. Most of all, thanks to
)ole, who has been an important and always hilarious friend.
ist-coffee-chat-headphones-writing. That sequence with Chris
'er these pages. I will even include two of my sisters here, Katie
ski and Emily Drabinski, whose sense of humor and patience
y ranting or rambling phone calls is most appreciated.
students have meant a lot to me. I have been able to test my
1 the classroom and in conversation, which has made me a
writer and clearer thinker. I am thinking of all the theses I
ll the casual and formal chatting about Levinas, postcolonial
ts, and many other related ideas with Jay Rosenberg, Adrian
1, Quanita Toffie, Jay Cassano, Aminah Hasan, Seth Wessler,
ost especially, Desirée Ramacus-Bushnell. Many others.
side the colleges, so many colleagues and long-standing com-
s. The Levinas Research Seminar is always so fun. Thanks to
you for being patient with the sometimes cantankerous and
ent development of my project. I have been debating a lot of
iff for years with old friends like Claire Katz, Diane Perpich,
uffer, Jim Hatley, Bettina Bergo, and Oona Eisenstadt, as well
'er friends who have engaged me critically (and with sympa-
)ver the past years, in particular Michael Paradiso-Michau,
vhom I have had a number of great conversations about the
of Levinas's work. Perhaps most of all, yet another thank
my dissertation director (it has been fifteen years!) and now
Robert Bernasconi for opening up so many different paths in
s's work and reminding European philosophers that the Other
from many geographies of reason.
thelle Huynh, my research assistant, was so incredibly helpful
later stages of this project. Thanks, Michelle, for the hard work
anization and tracking down so many primary and secondary
s. All of those tiny bits of research help made such a difference.

In the end, my biggest thanks go to the two people I see every day: Miles Henry (my beautiful little boy) and Marisa Parham (love of my life). I remember the exact moment I decided to write this book, and the memory reminds me of how such things are often decided in inconsequential moments. Because she is a brilliant and creative thinker, one might imagine the moment to be a profound or searching conversation. Actually, not this time. Marisa and I were unpacking groceries. I was rambling on at her about Spivak and Levinas, maybe about Bhabha too, and she said, with her head in the refrigerator, 'Yeah, you should write about that.' Well, I went ahead and did that.

: is sacred in its alterity with respect to which, in an unexcep-
onable responsibility, I post myself deposed of my sovereignty.
aradoxically, it is qua *alienus* – foreigner and other – that man is
ot alienated.

Emmanuel Levinas, Otherwise Than Being

'his is a freedom that does not demand universal frames or syn-
hronous knowledges but that will allow the silence to inscribe the
aveling and unraveling between the psychic body and its political
/eight.

Homi Bhabha, 'On the Irremovable Strangeness
of Being Different'

Preface

Every significant writing project begins with some sort of anxiety. Perhaps about a philosophical problem, a matter of particular political or cultural urgency, or, as with the present project, concern about the fate of a thinker.

The origins of this project are really quite simple. It begins with a worry about Levinas scholarship, a worry that he, like so many others in the European tradition, labors with too much locality and too little interest in the transnational context of culture, politics, and, indeed, the whole of social reality. A worry that the religious dimensions of Levinas's work only condemn his insights to an even more insular world of ideas. A worry that his legacy might go the direction of nationalists and defenders of the myth of Europe and, more recently, Israel. These worries come from trends in scholarship, to be sure. They have to do with articles, books, conferences, and institutes, where the associations of a name with places on the conceptual and political map are formed. But these worries also come from the conflicted and conflicting aims of Levinasian theory. Levinas's work is caught between two very different, very tense aspirations. There is, on the one hand, the language of first philosophy, subjectivity-time-space-embodiment *as such*, and so on. Whatever the emphasis on the singular, Levinas is genuinely talking about the drama of *the* interhuman, how *the* intrigue of our lives with others structures *the* meaning of thinking and being at – with all due caveats in place – its very foundations. Levinas's work clearly aspires to a certain kind of universality. *This is what it means to come to moral consciousness.*

On the other hand, there is the emphatic specificity of Levinas's work, which is rooted in the drama of European history and the Western tradition of navigating ideas. He works from the canon of ancient and modern thinkers, situating even moments of radical break within the unfolding of ideas across Occidental history. Levinas is a European through and through. As well, and perhaps most importantly, Levinas is concerned with the meaning and future

ism. For Levinas, Judaism is both internal to the very meaning
ɔpe and always outside the prerogative of European ideas,
s, politics, and culture. Levinas's concern with the meaning
ure of Judaism seals his work, especially when combined with
ɔpeanness, in the particularity of a geography of ideas.
ɪt does this tension between aspirations mean for Levinas's
How are we to assess the broadly philosophical sense of his
his interest in universal themes) in relation to the sociologi-
nic, and culturally driven preoccupation with the Judaic (his
: in a particular geography of ideas and people)? This is no
uestion. In the question, the enduring and endurable relevance
nas's work is explicitly at stake. Is Levinas to be relegated to
fic historical moment and global space? Or is his work rel-
cross borders? We will never form a systematic answer from
;'s texts, unfortunately. The question does not seem to have
:d to him and, in the end, Levinas seems to have had very little
: in world affairs. For all the outrage – and I remain suspi-
f the actual sincerity of much of it – about Levinas's scattered
s across a handful of decades on the Chinese, 'everything else
e,' and the often mis-reported statement about Palestinians, it
s simply true that he demonstrates almost no interest or par-
y incisive insights into contemporary global affairs. Instead,
; the sense, probably entirely true, that Levinas was concerned
very small part of Europe and its future. It is up to commenta-
explore the limits and possibilities of Levinas's work on the
and companion issues.
the task of the commentator is no after-thought, nor is it
supplementary intellectual activity. Commentators carry a
'. Of course they do. Perhaps one would want to imagine ideas
o be capable of the difficult work of making an intellectual
ːven tradition. Perhaps the fantasy of the great thinker consists
ing that an articulation of a world-historically important idea
·ry across historical experience, language, geography, and all
e other markers of difference. That is a lot to ask of a thinker
ːlea, and yet it seems that many of the institutions of scholar-
rn on, then defend, that very vision of the world of ideas. But
not how writerly life operates. For what it is worth, I believe
t thinkers. I believe that big, great ideas come from brilliant
writing at important moments in history, and that certain
ːlave world-historical importance. There is something called
nsight or even, to use a fraught term, *genius*, which becomes,

when registered in full analytical significance, genuinely transformative. I also believe that no single thinker, each of whom is of course
only a person, always saturated with finitude, is capable of understanding the ultimate meaning and significance of his or her innovations. There is always much more to be said. That might even be the
mark of genius – to be *fecund* at the same moment as one is edifying
and declarative and aspiring to say it all. If the fecundity of an idea or
constellation of notions is (at least in part) the mark of genius, then
commentators carry a thinker by demonstrating the productive and
enduring (across history, borders, and otherwise) meaning of those
ideas, notions, and so on.

Levinas offers a particularly interesting example of building an
intellectual trend or tradition. His notion of 'the Other' changes and
has changed so much of contemporary European philosophy. If he
is right about the trajectory of the Western tradition, and I think he
is, Levinas's work contests the heart of European violence with a
thought of the most fragile who is most high. The Other is outside
language, outside conceptualization, outside notions of teleology,
and all of those various strategies devised for neutralizing difference. This is what is meant by the qualifier 'radical' in the claim that
Levinas's work concerns *radical difference*. Levinas's aim is above
all with a sense of difference uprooted from all of those roots – we
can just call them *comparisons* – according to which the language
of difference is conventionally rendered. Difference, for Levinas, is
only genuinely radical when it is thought outside its distinction from,
which invariably means *derivation* from, identity. The infusion of
this insurgent notion of difference with the language of the ethical
only radicalizes and extends the problematic. It is not simply the
case that difference is different than the play of identity and difference. Radical difference signifies a relation of obligation, a sense of
responsibility that exceeds my grasp and my comprehension, yet at
the same time weighs upon me and makes me the subject I am. To be
is to be in the accusative: the direct object, named by the Other. In
the accusative, I am responsible as a matter of my very being. Radical
difference indeed – and a difference that makes all the difference in
the world.

So, the infusion of the language of difference with the ethical
deepens the Levinasian problematic. Levinas is not simply a thinker
of the ethical, even though that has come to be something of his
calling card. Levinas has interventions in epistemology, the ontology
of the subject, theories of time and space, notions of embodiment,

: meaning of the political and politics for life. Each of these
ts in Levinas's work is awash in obligation, the infinity of
iibility. It is therefore all the more jolting to read Levinas's
failings at reckoning with alterity in a transnational context.
, Levinas's human prejudices are odd and jarring when they
not because his work sets some sort of standard up to which
to live (though that is often the tone of polemical critics), but
: part of Levinas's racism or anxiety about national difference
ls from an explicit articulation of the Other's difference. And
n as that difference is given a gesture and words, the Other is
h cultural prejudice and chauvinism. This Other to Levinas's
and he is by no means alone in this failing – is what I will
ply 'the other Other.' An other Other, that is, who appears as
and alien, but does not register as obligating. An Other who
' than the meaning of Other in Levinas's writings; epistemo-
distance is opened up, then responsibility fails to arrive on the
low is this possible? And what needs to be done to Levinasian
g to intervene in this strange scene of (radical) difference
t responsibility?

present project centers on the work of Levinas. For that
these questions are posed to his work and the constellation of
iat comprise his notions of difference and ethics. I want to ask
questions of Levinas's epistemological, ontological, ethical,
itical work in order to do what commentators do: explore the
tive and creative potential of Levinas's thought. At the same
ie present work is motivated by a simple observation. Just as
; developed his notion of difference and immediately in the
f that, theorists from the historical and cultural place of his
ither theorized radical difference, but in a different tone, with
it resonance, and so with different consequences. From Frantz
to Gayatri Spivak to Homi Bhabha to Édouard Glissant to
: Dussel to Subcomandante Marcos, revolutionary work
irmer colonies asked (and continue to ask) very Levinasian
ns about epistemology, ontology, and politics. What does it
) be on the margins of the knowable and the known? What is
l in terms of epistemic force when there is a retreat from the
iy of knowing? What does it mean to *be* between two or more
es, two or more languages, and so two or more historical
nces? How does thinking, being, creating, and acting *as* and
e position of the Other transform the meaning of the thought
iginary of each?

And what would it mean to infuse these postcolonial explorations of difference with the language of the ethical?

In other words, what would it mean to transmit and engage Levinas across borders of history, culture, and experience?

This sort of work has barely begun in Levinas scholarship. Levinas's commentators have not carried him in this direction. Quite the contrary, Levinas's work has remained fixated on Europe and matters of European culture, even as that imagined place – let us never forget that it is not actually a continent, but a cultural imaginary – is increasingly diverse, transformed in ways loud and quiet by immigration, and has, for centuries, entangled with global culture. Colonialism, after all, is an old practice. Europe has been everywhere, for a long time, so transmitting Levinas beyond boundaries, borders, and old habits of scholarship *ought* to be quite natural. It is in the very orientation of work dedicated to the Other to seek out alterity without the prerogative of conquest. This is a point Derrida makes so convincingly in the second essay of *Rogues*. One need not go far in seeking out alterity, after all, for one of the primary functions of colonial relations is the production of otherness as proximate, even intimate. And, after the fall of colonial rule (and certainly before), the Other speaks back about otherness, its epistemology, its ontology, and of course its politics. Another future opens up. How could Levinas's work have remained closed to this other Other? And what has to be done to re-open that conversation? What does Levinasian thinking look like *after* that conversation? And so on. The following reflections aim to make sense of this encounter between languages of difference in the interest of making difference *radical* and, in the end, *ethical*.

                               *   *   *

Let me close this prefatory remark and begin the project with a comment addressed to the community of Levinas scholars. Scholarship on Levinas has undergone two major phases. The first phase, which is to be expected for any innovative and revolutionary thinker, was about exposition. Levinas's prose is dense, complex in both its meaning and implied references, and full of intriguing enigmas that require(d) a first reading in print. This kind of first wave of scholarship has accompanied the major thinkers of the twentieth century in Europe as well; I am thinking mostly of Edmund Husserl and Martin Heidegger, but also Jean-Paul Sartre, Maurice Merleau-Ponty, Gilles Deleuze, Michel Foucault, and others. Perhaps one of

ıracteristics of a great thinker is that s/he inspires this sort
ılarship – scholarly clarification that then leads to a next
f more exploratory scholarship dedicated to the implications
ınker's work. And so the second wave of Levinas scholar-
ırticularly that in the English language, attached itself quite
astically to the work of Jacques Derrida. This was no coinci-
Derrida's massively important review of *Totality and Infinity*
ıssay 'Violence and Metaphysics,' collected in *Writing and*
nce – had a clear impact on Levinas's work, inspiring impor-
anced changes to the language of difference, and also showed
ofoundly motivated Derrida's own work was (and continued
ıme) by Levinasian heterology, ranging from the critique of
ı-as-presence to the trace to the meta-critique of the West as
:d with totalitarian thinking. Reading Levinas with Derrida,
ın (albeit to a lesser extent) Derrida with Levinas, the force
ınas's work was nicely registered in relation to problems of
ʒe, figures of the feminine, and the strange, complicated legacy
 legger's work. There is surely much more of this sort of work
one; Derrida's last decade and a half has left an abundance of
ıve texts and occasions for re-reading Levinas with Derrida,
ı with Levinas.

r the first wave, and now after the deconstructive splash,
ʒ scholarship has widened. In this widening, it has to my mind
at a certain crossroads. Perhaps this crossroads is just another
ır possible shift) in scholarly emphasis, but I think something
nportant is at stake. When a thinker becomes a *great* thinker
ıands of a scholarly community – that is, when a community
ılars take his work to be transformative of how we think
ıurselves, others, and the world – a certain spell is cast. That
:ovokes great scholarship, to be sure, but it can also provoke
liar loyalty to the text. *Loyalty to the text* – by this I mean
that Levinas's word is taken as exceptionally instructive, even
cal, for thinking ethically about community, politics, and the
spectrum of what we call responsibility. As well, Levinas's
t in Judaism has taken a more prominent role over the past
. One can easily understand this emerging interest, as Levinas
of those utterly unique readers of important philosophical
o the same can be expected of his reading of religious texts.
ı recent turn, though, has an interesting and, to me, troubling
fect. While the textual basis for such an approach to Levinas is
nd wholly justifiable, the effect of this turn is to make Levinas

and Levinasian thinking ever more insular. I worry about this insularity. I worry about this insularity because I think it poses a real
danger to Levinas's legacy, consigning him to that group of thinkers whose significance lies mostly in a small group of commentators
who find so much truth in the text and have little interest in reading
outside that text's internal references. I also worry – and this is my
most emphatic concern – that such a turn in Levinas scholarship has
a much too conservative edge, appealing to a series of traditions and
coded concepts that edify themselves and are never fully put in question by what is other. One can see this in a number of sites. There
is the defensive posture taken toward Levinas's various xenophobic
and racist remarks, seeking to minimize or marginalize the importance of those statements. Such a posture fails to take seriously the
idea that Levinas might have very deep, well-established grounds
for indifference to issues of nation and race. There is the extension
of Levinas's thought into defending 'the West' and Europe in the
work of Philippe Nemo and Alain Finkelkraut. Perhaps Levinas's
ambivalent relation toward the West – at once a profound critic *and*
willing cultural operative – enables such thinking, or perhaps this
is a perversion of Levinasian ideas. This is a question that needs to
be decided, one that becomes exceptionally urgent when one hears
in those defenses of the West a closing of borders, cultural hegemony against immigrants, and, too often, a defense of Zionism and
Israeli violence. There is, as well, the revitalization of the religious
dimension of Levinas's thought, both Christian (largely Catholic)
and Jewish, which sees in his work a vigorous defense and extension of monotheism and the West's great theological-philosophical
tradition. To my mind, this is the most peculiar and difficult turn
in Levinas's work. The religious turn certainly leaves philosophy
proper, appealing to the authoritative voice of religious texts and
commentary, but that is merely a shift in legitimating language. Or
is it? I would in fact propose that legitimating language, those ideas
and phrases put forward as the basis for a series of claims about the
very meaning of responsibility, ought to be the most fraught and
expansive site for radical scholarship, a scholarship animated by
the Other. Legitimating language *ought* to be forever put in question, forever troubled by the Other who arrives unexpectedly – in
alternative ideas and phrases.

    For me, and this is my widest motivation for the present project,
Levinas scholarship needs to be more emphatically political. By this,
I do not mean simply (though I do also mean this) that we ought

sure Levinas's thought in relation to the pressing issues of
ation, immigration, and political violence. Rather, I mean to
t the implications of Levinasian thinking need to be explored
icized space. We need to ask difficult questions of Levinas's
s his thought deeply wedded to the idea of Europe? And what
at mean? Does the de-culturized notion of the face, posed in a
ive register (Levinas famously goes so far as to say one ought
ice the color of the Other's eyes), compromise the radicality
hinking, de-linking the thought of the Other from the cul-
ational, racial, and so political significations?[1] What are we
e of Levinas's Zionism? It is not enough to say that he means
n' in a philosophical sense. Is there something in Levinas's
: that makes him indifferent to the displacement of and vio-
against Palestinians? Perhaps the famous remark to Salomon
is not such a mistake or expression of political ignorance.
stly, we have to ask: what is Levinas's place in the ongoing
on of cultural and racial diversity, both in philosophy and
theoretical disciplines and in democratic societies? Does
guage of Other and responsibility speak to such matters?
evinasian thinking too provincial and insular for the global
er with the Other?

these last three questions, the present project begins. I want
bout the relevance of Levinas's work for questions of subal-
migration, the global margin, and alternative interventions in
d ante-national political life. I want to ask how theorizing-
e-other-place impacts Levinas's conception of the Other, but
v Levinas's work might add an important frame, subtext, and
o such theorizing. But I do not ask these questions innocently
natter of theory alone (though that is enough, I believe). I ask
estions because I want to explore – even insist on – the notion
rinas's work *must* become more politically engaged in order
in relevant to contemporary theorizing about the ethical, the
and the intrigue of the interhuman. *Commentators carry a*
I do not have delusions about the end of this work. It is only
ning. A beginning, though, that I hope will widen the scope of
scholarship to Levinas commentators, while at the same time
ing a sense and meaning of Levinas's ethics to those working
olonial theory and related fields. In this space, I hope, a better
: Levinas and the meaning of his work can emerge. And,
, a small, less violent bit of re-fashioning of the Other on the
cene.

Note

1. I have argued this point in a couple of places, in a largely suggestive manner, claiming simply that the Other needs to be re-situated in a wider political context. After all, are we not addressed by the Other in our own, and so the Other's, skin? Does that skin not carry with it wide and deep political significations? See of course Chapter 1 below, but also John E. Drabinski, 'The Possibility of an Ethical Politics,' *Philosophy and Social Criticism*, vol. 26, no. 4 (2000): 49–73 and 'Wealth and Justice in a U-topian Context', in Eric Nelson et al., *Addressing Levinas*. Evanston: Northwestern University Press, 2003, 185–94.

ıduction: Decolonizing Levinasian
ːs

'he Occident is not in the west. It is a project, not a place.
                    Édouard Glissant, *Le Discours antillais*

re many reasons to raise critical questions about the relation-
tween the ethics of Emmanuel Levinas and the wider intel-
reaches of colonialism. In fact, to begin, it might be worth
  over some interesting dates and their coincidences. The
vinas published *Existence and Existents* (1947) and the year
Time and the Other comes into print (1948), the wide-circu-
dition of Aimé Césaire's *Notebook of a Return to the Native*
ppears on the intellectual scene and Léopold Senghor pub-
ıe famous anthology of 'new black poetry,' *Anthologie de la*
e poésie nègre et malgache. Just after *En découvrant*, Frantz
publishes *Black Skin, White Masks* and the very same year
  drops *Totality and Infinity,* his first *magnum opus*, Fanon
es *Wretched of the Earth.* No doubt, Levinas wrote and lived
ɔled and troubling times for France. At once the hypostasis
ıubject *and* the volcanic force of the marvelous, at once the
ɔtion of metaphysical totality and the violent confrontation
lonial totalization – what a curious collision-which-was-not-
deas. I find these publication occasions curious for the simple
that, despite the books, voices, and movements exploding
him, Levinas seems utterly unaware of and unconcerned with
ɪsing face of the political. We could also mention Levinas's
 silence about anti-colonial struggle in Algeria – remarkable
:ime, given the French intellectual scene of his younger days.
ntion these few items, not to rehearse some now familiar
ɪ, I think, still under-theorized) criticisms about Levinas's
ty and general indifference to global affairs and suffering. As
lo not want simply to implicate Levinas in a sort of late colo-
adence in which one could think with some distance from the
ier – a term that refers of course to the overseas territories,

but firstly, historically, to those states conquered in the Crusades. I think those criticisms and hesitations about Levinas the man and the writer remain crucial for thinking about his place in twentieth-century intellectual history. One cannot praise the stranger as most high and expect nationally or racially troubling comments to pass by without notice and polemical critique. My concerns are slightly more generous, I hope. For I believe that Levinas's insight into the ethical, that sense of responsibility to the Other who accuses and obligates *without prior measure*, is critical for thinking in a postcolonial context. To the elaborate and nuanced postcolonial notions of discourse, subalternity, syncretism, interstitiality, and strategic identity formation, Levinas brings an ethical dimension that, I would like to suggest, lies at the heart of so much theory as an unthematized cornerstone. But there is also something at the heart of Levinas's thought that blocks any easy engagement across geographies: his idea of Europe. Thus, the title of this Introduction. The work of decolonizing Levinas's thought is crucial for the project of an ethical postcolonial cultural politics and, in order to register its force, must be uncoupled from a staggeringly naïve and problematic conception of Europe.

With these concerns in view, I want in the reflections that follow to set the groundwork for a simple pair of questions that animate the chapters below: what do a cluster of postcolonial ideas and thinkers have to say to Levinas and a Levinasian ethics? And, what does a Levinasian ethics have to say to postcolonial theory?

BIBLES, GREEKS, PROJECTS

An obvious question: why decolonization? That is, why raise questions of history, culture, and politics in the context of a thought committed to notions of singularity, interruption, and the otherwise than being? For Levinas's claim is really quite simple: the face of the Other exceeds all categories, pre-delineations, and anticipations. This is why the formulation 'beyond Being' is so critical for Levinas. According to Levinas, the ethical is only possible to the extent that our thinking is wrested free, by way of a pre-history of thought, of any metaphysical or epistemological fore-structure. Affects of guilt, regret, and so on serve at best only as clues to what lies beyond and before experience. The time-structure of moral consciousness is diachronic, marking a temporal distance between my experience and the an-archic, unconditioned condition of that experience. The Other is

-archy and unconditioned condition. Remote from conscious
nce, yet deeply embedded in it as the empty space of a fracture
nce, the Other obligates. To say that ethics is first philosophy
y, well, that nothing else comes first.
this firstness of the ethical that I would like to contest. This
o say that the ethical *should not be* or *is not* first, but rather
vinas's relation to conceptions of culture, history, and politics
∋s the ethical where it is most demanded – across geographies
ed by history. To be plain and blunt about my claim here:
∋'s conception of the ethical, while absolutely transformative
notion of obligation, remains tied to a kind of metaphysics,
also a kind of epistemology of alterity, both of which block
sian thinking from the sorts of geographical wanderings with
it *ought to be* engaged.
me turn to a well-known and exceptionally revealing comment
,evinas about Latin America and the concern with suffering. I
o begin with this particular remark rather than the now well-
 remarks by Levinas about the Chinese, 'everything is dance,'
estinian non-Other, and so on, not because such remarks are
ortant or not instructive, but because (and this is part of my
claim here) they express a deeper problem in Levinas's think-
ne remark I have in mind here is relayed by Enrique Dussel in
places, and it is one that Dussel claims changed his intellectual
ory and sensibility. The story goes this way: after being asked
is work only addresses the millions murdered in the Holocaust
ot the many more millions murdered in slavery, in conquest,
ider colonialism, Levinas tells Dussel simply 'that is for you to
about.' Rather than extend his own thoughts or meditations
ider sense of catastrophe, Levinas prefers to keep it local. And
s that Dussel do the same: you, Enrique Dussel, are charged
aking up the problem of theorizing the disasters that define the
ical experience of the Americas.
w, to be sure, one can imagine just why this remark was so edi-
for Dussel. For anyone familiar with Dussel's ever-growing set
ections on ethics and politics, the effect of Levinasian thinking
ious: Levinas gives liberation theology an important new ethical
nessianic dimension. And even a cursory glance at Gustavo
rrez's work, from *A Theology of Liberation* through *On Job*,
now the relevance of Levinas for a thinking that puts the poor
center of the world. So, the notion of ethics as first philosophy
ates quite easily with the theorization of liberation struggle in

Latin America, though, as Dussel makes clear and convincing, such resonance places Marx's work in the heart of any ethical politics. (I think this is a crucial advance on Levinas's thinking, which lacks a commitment to the materiality of suffering.) At the same time, Dussel is too generous to Levinas and Levinas fails to see the implications of the question at hand. That is, at the very moment Levinas makes the problem of thinking the trauma, loss, and ethical imperative of the Americas a problem for Americans, he reifies a colonial fantasy about the identity of Europe. I think there are enormous implications in Levinas's remark and how it reifies a terrible fantasy, so some clarity on his conception of Europe and the stakes of decolonizing that conception is paramount.

Levinas's conception of Europe is at once simple and complex. The simplicity lies in the terms of his description, a description that carries complex ideological formations within itself. For Levinas, Europe is of course not a unified entity. It is, rather, made a 'continent' (wholly cultural, since there is no purely geographical sense to the term 'the European continent') because of the constitutive tensions between the philosophical and religious elements of European identity. Europe is created and sustained by the zigzag movement of the universal and the singular – a continent as the *and*, as it were, of totality and infinity. The difference that makes identity is neither cultural nor historical, but rather an intellectual sensibility and double propensity toward Being and the Other. Levinas is plain when he writes:

> What is Europe? It is the Bible and the Greeks. The Bible: an ontological inversion? The original perseverance of realities in their being – the inertia of material objects, the enrootedness of plants . . . the war among 'owning and interested' men . . . is inverted in the man announced to humanity in Israel.[1]

At first glance, this definition is remarkably potent, capturing the tensions and unities – often at one and the same time – between the ancient and modern world, Judaism and Christianity, and the religious and the secular. Indeed, if we set aside the odd notion that Athens and Jerusalem were single-rooted sites of identity, rather than complex intersections of culture and history, then we can see how deeply Levinas thinks the internal differentiation of European identity without giving up the notion of a single philosophical culture.

The differentiation-which-is-unity Levinas calls Europe means that he is able to install the ethical into the heart of the continent.

the Hellenic sets up as a boundary and condition of exclu-
ne Hebraic welcomes without conditions. What the Hellenic
s into Sameness, the Hebraic sets free in Otherness. And so on.
: therefore becomes both the site and the possibility of respon-
. It is not simply that a European is a kind of being capable of
ding to the Other, I would argue; rather, one is a responsible
because one is European, made of the Bible and the Greeks.
s continues:

There is this possibility of a responsibility for the alterity of the other
person, for the stranger without domicile or words with which to
converse, for the material conditions of one who is hungry or thirsty,
or the nakedness of the defenseless mortal . . . The other, the one
separated from me, outside the community.[2]

tion and the outside – those terms that function so centrally
n *Totality and Infinity* and *Otherwise Than Being* – move
the constitutive forces of the continent's name. Outside the
unity becomes not just an occasion of, but something close to
ient condition for, the ethical. All of which is fundamentally
an, operating in the dynamics of cultural difference that make
ntity.

worth noting here that the evocation of the biblical and the
Greek is precisely where Levinas, within a few years of pub-
the short essay 'The Bible and the Greeks,' famously waves
rything else as 'dance' (as if dance were somehow abject or
resting). Levinas makes this remark after being asked, rather
rdly, by Raoul Mortley about racism, sexism, and the thought
Other, which then prompts Levinas to say again that the out-
r alien character of the Other makes ethical concern possible.
re,' Levinas says, 'in relation to the other, it is *because* he is
nat he is incumbent on me.'[3] And yet Levinas hesitates before
ich difference, preferring instead this peculiar notion of trans-
– the capacity of European thinking (here, colonial through
rough) to make of the other sorts of otherness a proper Other.
ntinues, in the now famous passage:

I often say, though it's a dangerous thing to say publicly, that
humanity consists of the Bible and the Greeks. All the rest can be
translated: all the rest – all the exotic – is dance.[4]

there is certainly much to be said here, not the least of
is a question about what else Levinas thinks, yet believes

is too dangerous to 'say publicly.' But the critical turn of phrase, to my mind, is the 'can be translated.' What could Levinas mean by translation? And how is translation related to the power of the Greek, even when disrupted by the Biblical? Or perhaps we should just understand Levinas to be saying this: every Other is a Jewish Other, oppressed and exploited by the same Same, which is always a Greek Same. That is, Europe is not just for Europeans. Europe is for the whole world, in the (wholly colonial) sense that Europe is the measure of every Other and every ethical demand.

We can take this sort of issue in a number of directions. We can chide Levinas (and perhaps shame Levinasians) by pointing out what these sorts of remarks say about Levinas the person, his character, and his judgement of the world in which his notion of ethics ought to have some purchase. We can write off such remarks, claiming that Levinas was an old-fashioned kind of guy, susceptible to sadly common prejudices and racisms, or perhaps even just oblivious to world affairs and larger issues of cultural difference. Or, as I would like, we could say that there is something presupposed in Levinas's conception of Europe that not only makes such racist and xenophobic utterances possible, but even makes them necessary. I do not think the problem is simply that Levinas deploys Europe as a measure (though that is problem enough). Rather, the very formulation of Europe as a continent underwrites the possibility of these sorts of utterances.

Let me return to Dussel in order to open up this claim. Dussel reports that Levinas tells him that the pain of slavery and conquest is for him and others to think about, think through, and perhaps thematize as a historical irruption of the ethical. Dussel takes this as a charge and, indeed, it becomes one of the signature turning points in his intellectual career, allowing him to infuse liberation theology with Levinasian sensibilities. No reader of Dussel can deny that this has produced genuinely profound and lasting insights, helping him theorize the hybrid cultural products of the continental Americas (and so not the Caribbean, it should be noted) and explore, along with Walter Mignolo, the limits and possibilities of delinking Europeanness from indigenous and mixed forms of life.[5] At the same time, though, Dussel is too generous to Levinas. Dussel takes from Levinas the imperative to think his own place (the Americas), much as Levinas had putatively thought through the meaning of his own place (Europe). It is here instructive to recall the epigraph above, suggesting that the Occident – Levinas's Europe, the Bible and the Greeks – is not a *place*, but a *project*. As a project, of course, one cannot thematize it without understanding the processes of valuation at work in projections and how the objects brought into focus (or even being) by those projections come to constitute the very meaning of the West.

What is Europe, really, without what Martinican theorist Édouard Glissant calls the *entanglements of modernity*? That is, is it really possible to conceive what we call Europe without the centuries of empire and all of the violence that came from it? Glissant's interpretation of the name 'Europe' presses on this insight repeatedly, an insight that, for him, not only implicates Europe in a moral relationship with the subjects of empire, but even more importantly, raises the question of how the entanglement of Europe with its others stakes out an *ontological* claim. The very being of Europe is already tied up with global conquest. This means, to twist Levinas back into the complex story Glissant weaves, that an ethical interruption does not lie on the margins or periphery of Europe, but rather in the heart of its being. Indeed, this is part of Dussel's own claim about the origins of modernity – viz., modernity as calculative and bureaucratic reason – in the essay 'The "World-System": Europe as "Center" and its "Periphery" Beyond Eurocentrism.'[6] The essay title tells much of the story. If we, with Glissant, think of Europe as a project and not a place, then we have to think about the relation of alleged *centers* and *peripheries* according to a logic of entwinement, rather than hierarchy and simple exercises of power. According to Dussel, this is already what it means to say *modernity*. The origin of modernity, he argues, does not lie in the works of theorists and writers in Europe, but instead in the managerial crisis that follows from Bartolomé de las Casas's convincing series of letters to the Spanish royals. In those letters, as we all know, Las Casas lays the foundation of the argument, largely theological, for freeing indigenous populations from the yoke of slavery. For Europe, this means a crisis of management – how can minerals and spices and related stuffs be extracted in the most volume, at the least cost? The answer of course is the trans-Atlantic slave trade. The *project* of European modernity begins at this moment; which is to say, Europe begins in what one *might* refer to as its elsewhere. But the New World is never really an elsewhere. The New World is rather Europe itself, an identity worked out not just in the constitutive tension of the Bible and the Greeks, but also and at the same time in the slave ship, on the plantation, and so in all of the violence of empire.

My point here, though, is not to reiterate the familiar, if again

under-theorized moral identity of Europe as – in Césaire's words
– *indefensible*. Instead, I want to insist that the entanglements of
empire and its aftermath constitute the very being of Europe. And so
to return to Dussel's report of Levinas's remark, one has to wonder
what sort of evasions are at work in Levinas's seemingly encouraging
comment. Why are the sufferings and deaths of the millions under
slavery and colonialism 'your concern'? Why are those concerns
not the concern of all under that identity-rubric – which is of course
Levinas's own claim? Decolonizing Levinas corrects that constrained
sense of identity, restoring the entanglement of empire back at the
center of identity talk. To see this sense of identity-as-entanglement,
we of course have to give up the fantasy of a Europe bound only to
itself, within its continent, constituted by two forces we also have
to imagine are not themselves globally entangled. That is a colonial
fantasy. It is the fantasy that imagines the elsewhere and the *outre-
mer* as separate from European identity, while also maintaining the
sorts of cultural and economic controls bemoaned by postcolonial
political critics. To decolonize Levinas begins at his home: there, in
Europe, re-entangling identity in the elsewhere, returning the other
Other to the Same and the Other of the Bible and the Greeks. In
taking that return seriously – and this is perhaps the most difficult
methodological pill for Levinasians to swallow – we see the return
of a repressed historical thinking, a sense of historical experience
that *ought to* inform our conceptualizing of methodological motifs
like 'Europe.' While this is a difficult and even unexpected turn for
Levinasian thinking, I would suggest or even insist that Levinas's
own work, like any repressed force, is always already entangled in
the prejudices of historical experience – something he seems to take
seriously only when it comes to the role of Judaism in thinking about
otherness. So, in the end, decolonizing Levinas really only reactivates
the repressed sense of historical experience and historicity of his
concept of Europe, a concept that gathers to it all the problematic
notions of empire under a repressed and repressive fantasy of dis-
entanglement. These repressed entanglements register with decisive
force when encountered, again, and yet as if for the first time, in the
globally entangled identity of this project called Europe.

DISENTANGLING LEVINAS, RE-ENTANGLING EUROPE

If we can convincingly relink the question of Europe, difference, and
obligation to the entanglements of empire, then suddenly Levinas's

work stands in a very different relationship to postcolonial theory. That is, if Levinas's work is not simply a model either exalted by how it champions the Other of totality or compromised by the racism of its author, and is instead already a broken theory of the limits of globally totalizing thinking, then I think the ethical can be readdressed – albeit in importantly modified forms – both by and to the postcolonial experience of otherness. What would this readdress look like? A few remarks.

Let us set aside for a moment the problem of Europe and its identity. Whatever the problems we might want to explore in Levinas's evocation of the Bible and the Greeks, there is also the thought of the Other. And that thought, though I want to hold close to the particular way in which it resonates in his work, exceeds whatever Levinas may say about singularity, the incomparable, and the sorts of questions the Other raises in the face of domination and exploitation. Levinas's work has long made a significant impact on European philosophy, shifting so many of the conversations about being and knowing away from what he calls the obsession with totality, toward the enigmatic and interruptive function of alterity. The consequences of this shift are enormous, and indeed one is hard pressed to imagine the contemporary European philosophical scene without Levinas's transformative interventions. At the very same time, numerous other engagements with the deconstructive function of alterity in aesthetics, cultural studies, and postcolonial theory have developed alongside Levinas's work. Yet there has been no sustained conversation between Levinas scholars and these developments, even as questions intersect with intriguing resonances and important differences. How is the language of otherness altered by transnational and transcultural contact, underwritten by a newly re-entangled conception of Europe and Levinasian thinking, with all of the ideological formations at stake in that exchange? How does the experience of historical violence (subjugation, enslavement, colonialism) change the meaning of speaking and silence, the said and the saying? How does the experience of cultural mixture open up the complex interstitial or creolized space of an identity affirming, rather than obscuring, radical difference? What is the meaning of a politics that puts difference first and keeps always resistant to the hegemony of identity *even as hegemony is formulated and exercised?* What does Levinasian thinking have to say to companion and parallel accounts of alterity, singularity, and difference? How do those accounts challenge the Levinasian prerogative? These are the questions that structure any encounter between

Levinas and postcolonial theory. Thus, such an encounter will have to stay committed to exploring the zigzag movement of how a distinctively Levinasian concern with the Other gains nuanced insight from cultural studies and postcolonial theory, just as the latter stand to gain so much normative purchase from Levinas's work.

The significance of revisiting Levinas *after* postcolonial theory in the present work does not lie in adding yet another rehearsal of the already numerous renderings of transcultural contact, subalternity, and hybridity. As well, the aim is neither to reinvent Levinas as a postcolonial thinker nor simply to critique his work as Eurocentric. Rather Levinas's work needs to be creatively reread across geographies – literal and figurative – in order to think more rigorously about the question of the Other as an *ethical, cultural,* and *political* question. Transcultural contact, subalternity, and hybridity retain the cultural and political force articulated by innovators of the terms, of course, but that force, by way of a conversation with Levinas, gains two crucial features: an important phenomenological mode of legitimation, rooted in an account of embodiment, and the claim of the ethical in difference. Such a rereading of Levinas and the postcolonial thereby labors between multiple modes of discourse about race, nation, and the Other. This is a conversation about alterity, silence, responsibility, and (ultimately) the paradox of thinking identity and difference at the same time. This conversation gathers together so many urgent questions – questions that transcend academic trends, disciplines, and traditions by asking the very Levinasian question: what does it mean to *be* in a world structured by difference? And what are the possibilities for at least a little bit of *goodness* in that world? For there is always the Other – that jewel, however small, who still adorns the earth.

Let me briefly summarize four sites of contact between Levinas and the postcolonial that orient the following chapters.

To begin, the first chapter addresses a general methodological problem: how do we begin Levinasian thinking? I argue that Levinas's thought is best understood as the deployment of a method that entwines intentionality with embodiment. From that entwinement, we have a sense of incarnation as the site of subjectivity's formation, deformation, and reformation. We also end up with a site exposed to the decolonizing work of history; I call this the problem of 'incarnate historiography.' If incarnate historiography undoes the centering of subjectivity – generally as a theory of the subject, specifically as the European expression of body and relation – then Levinas, at least as a possibility, becomes a thinker of the transnational. That is, if history is written on the body (my central claim), then the entangled history of transnational contact is written into the very method of the ethical. A very different sense of difference, and so a different kind of Levinas, emerges from this transformation of method. Thus, the four sites of transnational contact that follow are natural developments of the opening of method *after* decolonizing Levinas's work.

In the second chapter, 'Epistemological Fracture,' we shift emphasis from the question of method and embodiment in a transnational context to the question of the relationship between the Levinasian Other and subalternity – in particular, Gayatri Spivak's treatment of the gendered subaltern. A leading question: is Levinas's Other compatible with the gendered subaltern, or does the subaltern challenge Levinas's claim to have given a first philosophy of alterity? I argue that Spivak's account of the subaltern exposes Levinas's failure to think about otherness in a transnational, transcultural context, and also that the rhetoric of subalternity needs the Levinasian nuance of the ethical in order to retain its political and other purchase. Subalternity questions the character of Levinasian alterity, engaging *l'autrui* with cultural, gendered, racial, national, and political matters, which in turn leads to the question of the third chapter: how are we to think about identity *after* the irreducible character of difference? Or, in a blending of theories, the sharper question: what is an ethical sense of *hybridity*? So, in the third chapter below, entitled 'The Ontology of Fracture,' we consider how Homi Bhabha's reflections on interstitial space and the problem of nation, narration, and counter-narration provide important occasions for thinking through these questions. With Bhabha, we see how the urgency of the postcolonial situation pushes matters of collectivity and migration to the fore, even as difference is posited as intractable. Levinas's truncated treatment of history and historicity meets its limits in conversation with Bhabha, to be sure; the denucleated subject, arguably Levinas's most important innovation in *Otherwise Than Being*, never quite comes to terms with mixed identities, even as subjectivity is understood, as it crosses from the ethical to the worldliness of politics, as *creaturely*. At the same time, we can see how, from the perspective of the Levinasian prerogative, the urgency of the question of hybridity depends on a sense of the ethical. The force of difference in the hybrid and hybridizing identity of Bhabha's subject fundamentally alters, yet remains engaged with, the fragile force of ethical life.

Subalternity and hybridity – those two signature ideas of the postcolonial – suggest a sense of subjectivity bound to the Other in nuanced ways, challenging the often atomistic or dyadic formulations we find in Levinas's work. 'Ethics of Entanglement,' the fourth and penultimate chapter below, revises this language of otherness with Glissant's account of entanglement. The problem of entanglement – which generates a compelling and complex notion of globalization for Glissant – is treated in this chapter at its foundations: the question of beginning. What does it mean to begin after catastrophe? How do we conceive a future after radical, destructive, disastrous violence? For both Levinas and Glissant, this is a pressing question. If we read Levinas as a post-Shoah thinker, seeing his work as an attempt to reckon with the devastation of European Jewish life and to conceive a future after catastrophe, then it opens up important points of contact and contrast with Glissant's treatment of the Middle Passage, trauma, and the Caribbean problem of beginning. In particular, I argue that a rereading of fecundity and futurity in *Totality and Infinity* exposes a nascent sense of continuity in Levinas's thought – a sense of continuity we do not, and indeed cannot, find in Glissant's account of the Middle Passage and the absolute gap it opens in memorial and historical time. The difference between these accounts of beginning mark the European character of Levinas's work, but the decolonization of that character – the re-entanglement with the transnational other – begins an important discussion, with Glissant, about the ethics of entanglement and global poetics.

The final chapter, 'Decolonizing Levinasian Politics,' raises the question of how alterity transforms the political. With some important work of decolonization accomplished, it is worth revisiting a famously fraught question in Levinas's work: what remains of politics and the political after 'ethics as first philosophy'? Meditations on violence, loss, subalternity, hybridity, and entanglement gather to the political question, which allows us to draw productively on Levinas's method. If we conceive history as broken apart by difference, and if the urgency of a cultural and political future registers without qualification, then how does the body of the political subject – an altogether under-theorized aspect of Levinas's thinking – signify political obligation(s)? And how does that signification prescribe certain ways of thinking about community and hegemony? In addition to Spivak, Bhabha, and Glissant, the political writings of the Zapatista movement, specifically in how those writings enact a practice of Glissant's description of the rhizome, challenge Levinasian thinking in the formulation of a notion of community *in and as difference.* In particular, engagement with this cluster of thinkers allows us to begin articulating a sense of political community motivated by an ethically infused sense of solidarity. The innovation in this reading of a Levinasian politics lies in the saturation of now familiar questions of ethics and politics with issues of historical and cultural experience across geographies, and so across the traumas and losses that generate political senses of responsibility.

Emerging from these sites of contact with postcolonial theory, I hope, is a Levinasian thinking that engages historical experience with a transnational and transcultural sensibility. The alterity of *kinds* of historical experience is set out as the fundamental imperative of a Levinasian thinking after decolonizing the ethical. In the end, I would like to claim that this sort of engagement, guided by *another* imperative of difference, is necessary in order to ensure that – or even to begin to articulate how – Levinas's conceptions of the Other, difference, and infinite responsibility make deep claims in a global context.

FANON AND AFTER

By way of transition, and to cast the project even more widely, let me make a short, speculative remark or two. Decolonizing Levinasian ethics widens the scope of alterity by lifting the colonial provincialism of a fantasied Europe; decolonized, Levinasian thinking is entangled, rather than insular and withdrawn from the world. The entanglement of the ethical has a zigzag effect for the central trends in the postcolonial theory we consider in the present work. In particular, I have in mind how the political confrontation with discourse, subaltern difference, interstitial subjectivity, and a politics of material difference is infused with Levinas's strange sense of the ethical (zig). Such postcolonial notions also move Levinas across borders in important ways (zag). This movement is motivated both by a reformed conception of what it means to think through the idea of Europe – a conception in which global entanglement recasts the global political Other as immanent to European political identity – and by an imperative to take companion theoretical notions of alterity seriously. *A postcolonial Levinas,* concerned with race, nation, and all senses of the Other.

As well, and this may seem a bit abrupt or even surprising, I think one could read the task of decolonizing Levinas and an ethics as a matter of deciding something of the legacy of Fanon's work.

Interpretations of Fanon's work have been dominated by a mixture of urgent revolutionary concerns and a kind of reformed Sartreanism. Rightly so, for Fanon writes not only *Wretched of the Earth*, but also a whole host of minor and important essays in response to anti-colonial struggle in North Africa. The book and essays have a sense of militancy and commitment to tactics that are both textually undeniable and practically crucial for imagining, then enacting, revolutionary liberation. In *Black Skin, White Masks*, we find a different sort of Fanon, one obviously engaged in anti-colonial struggle, but here a struggle addressed to the psychological and other dynamics of the formation of subjectivity. Bhabha's quirky, yet hugely important reading of Fanon turns to these passages for theorizing the cultural anxieties of migration and dislocation. Fanon's Sartreanism, which entails a significant rewriting of Sartre's conception of the Other, the gaze, and so on, inheres in the motifs listed in the conclusion to *Black Skin, White Masks*: to be free of the prison of history and to become a question.

But, for me, the critical and unnerving impasse in that book is the short meditation on Hegel and the problem of recognition in Chapter 7, 'The Black Man and Recognition.' To recall, what troubles Fanon in subsection 'B' of that chapter is how the Hegelian dialectic of recognition seeks – if not presupposes – the very item of identity formation from which Fanon seeks to gain such distance: comparison. Fanon concludes that we need very different notions of dialectic, confrontation, and subsequent recognition. That difference gets only a hint and a gesture, as Fanon so quickly works his way to the long musing on history and self-assertion in the Conclusion. What is necessary in the dialectic of recognition, in a postcolonial context, is a confrontation that disrupts the under- and over-determining gaze of anti-black racism, but, unlike a conventional notion of dialectical recognition, Fanon does not come to this relation with a pre-formed identity. This is one of the consequences of a reformed Sartreanism that grows out of a rejection of Negritude. For, were Fanon to have taken up the project of Negritude, one could imagine this dialectic moving very differently and very decisively: *recognize my Africanness, my civilization that explodes through my culture, and then we have moved well beyond the colonial gaze and relation.* Césaire's essay, 'Culture and Colonization,' delivered in 1956 at the 1st International Congress of Black Artists and Writers (Fanon read 'Racism and Culture' at the same gathering), makes exactly that sequence of claims, claims that in many ways express the best and boldest ideas of the Negritude movement. Fanon does not have these sorts of resources when he comes to the dialectical event of Chapter 7 in *Black Skin, White Masks*. And so it results in something of an impasse, giving way to the final prayer and plea of the Conclusion.

That dialectic is made complex by its goal: to overcome the narcissism of whites and blacks that results from colonial psychological, ontological, and epistemological hegemony. As well, since Fanon does not bring a force so powerful as Negritude to the dialectical scene, and since he in some way reckons with how the experience of the Americas changes everything about the experience of blackness, he cannot appeal to *re*-cognition. There is no prior cognition of mutuality to recall in the moment of confrontation. Rather, there is the impossibility of any relation whatsoever, so long as the dialectical opponents are locked in mutual narcissism. And it is here that Levinas's work has special significance. Levinas, of course, puts transformation of relation at the center of his conceptions of subjectivity and the face-to-face. What is transformed is egoism: I no longer put myself at the center of the world. Rather, decentered, I 'cognize' the Other in another sort of way, a way that does not seize upon the Other with my gaze or pre-established categories of knowing, being, or value. There is instead a new relation that is responsible and obligating, while still not turning to dialectic, recognition, and invocation of measure. In other words, a putting in question that makes of both the Me and the Other *a question*. Perhaps something close to the very sort of question we hear in Fanon's final prayer. That final prayer – the suggestive and at times mesmerizing conclusion to *Black Skin, White Masks* – contests egoism without a pre-established model, without an idea of postcolonial subjectivity that is to come. The future is open, indeterminate, and undetermined. Like Levinas's, Fanon's work has so much modesty at the very moment – the interval between the traumatic past and an open future – that one might expect bombastic words. And this is an interval in a non-resolving dialectic of relation with the Other. What can be said about this stalled dialectic and the quirky idea of the future upon which it opens? *What method translates us into the new?*

I will conclude here, then, by wondering if Fanon's impasse is not the opening of Levinasian thinking for postcolonial theory. For it is precisely this impasse and thinking through new models of knowing, being, and valuing that sit at the heart of postcolonial thinking about philosophy, culture, and politics. The infusion of this moment with the gravity of the ethical is not just illuminating, but also, in a final utopian gesture, an expression of a fundamental goodness – so hope – in the space of encounter. And who would not want a little bit of that?

Notes

1. Emmanuel Levinas, 'La Bible et les Grecs,' in *À l'heure des nations*. Paris: Minuit, 1988, 155; 'The Bible and the Greeks,' trans. Michael B. Smith, in *In the Time of Nations*. Bloomington: Indiana University Press, 1994, 133.
2. Ibid.
3. 'Emmanuel Levinas,' in *French Philosophers in Conversation*, ed Raoul Mortley. New York: Routledge, 1991, 18.
4. Ibid.
5. See, for example, Nelson Maldonado-Torres, *Against War: Views from the Underside of Modernity* (Durham: Duke University Press, 2008, Part III) for an interesting and largely convincing account of Dussel's relationship to Levinas's thought. Like Dussel, Maldonado-Torres lets Levinas's space of theorization stand, without raising the question of entanglement.
6. Enrique Dussel, 'The "World-System": Europe as "Center" and its "Periphery" Beyond Eurocentrism,' trans. Eduardo Mendieta, in *Beyond Philosophy: Ethics, History, Marxism, and Liberation Theology*. Oxford: Rowman & Littlefield, 2003.

CHAPTER 1

Incarnate Historiography and the Problem of Method

> The humanity of *conscience* is definitely not in its powers, but in its responsibility: in passivity, in reception, in obligation with regard to the other. It is the other who is first, and there the question of my sovereign consciousness is no longer the first question.
>
> Levinas, 'Philosophy, Justice, and Love'

What does it mean to put the Other first – to enact the simple 'after you!' of politeness in which I remove myself from the center in order to clear space for the Other's movement and life – as a fully developed theory of knowledge, ethics, and politics? What does it mean to claim, as Levinas does, to have overturned the force and power of two and a half millennia of Western philosophy with what is weakest and most vulnerable? What can be done with a philosophy whose most generous reading puts everything on the most precarious foundations imaginable? That is, *what does Levinas's work ultimately mean for philosophy?*

Levinas's work has been received in a few different registers. There is, of course, first and foremost the astonishing power of ethical language and the evocation of the Other as the anchor of moral consciousness. Difference, for Levinas, is not simply a random or marginal exception to the general rules of experience. While the Other surely stands out as exceptional in the synthetic flow of egoic life, that exceptionality functions as a foundational claim, even as Levinas carefully distinguishes his sense of originary or foundational from the fantasies of the tradition. The exceptional character of the Other is also violent, disruptive, and unruly. The Other speaks an interdiction on violence, but only after having dismantled the pretensions of egoic life in every aspect of that life: time, space, place, language, history, memory, and all notions of virtue and duty. Jacques Derrida rightly described this in his 'Violence and Metaphysics' as the recurring and relentless crashing of waves on the shoreline of thinking, an image that nicely captures the sense of the ethical as a force that clears what might stand before it, leaving us always to begin – to the extent that that is even possible – again. Each crash of a wave, each interruption of subjective life by the Other, drags the pretensions and aspirations of conventional and traditional theorizing, metaphysics, epistemology, and every other sort of thinking of totality out into the sea. And it is not coming back. This much is clear in Levinas's suggestive treatments of the theme of beginning, usually in the language of response and positive politics, where the infinity of infinite responsibility is manifest in the never-enough character of giving, gesture, and charity. The moment of accusation is a transformation of subjectivity. That transformation is irreversible.

The religious character of this sort of account has not been lost on Levinas scholarship. The sorts of passivity described in his later work, especially in the context of embodiment discussed below, couple with Levinas's volumes on Talmudic reading and extrapolation to comprise a compelling account of election. Election, though a largely Jewish term in his writings, expresses the monotheistic orientation – one might even say meta-foundation – of Levinas's work. Monotheism permeates so much of the rhetorical appeal of that work, resonating in a particularly European sense and, in that tradition, as a subconscious appeal evidenced in its intuitiveness. So we should not be surprised that one of the dominant receptions of Levinas's work is the religious context, whether that be the Christian appropriations of love and sacrifice or Jewish links to sacred texts and traditions of commentary. Now, the precise role of religious sources in Levinas's philosophical work remains open to debate, with the discussion ranging from claims that the religious writings only make philosophical sense as examples, subsuming them to the phenomenological or post-structuralist modes of legitimation and delegitimation, to seeing religious inspiration as the very basis of his work and insight. I am sympathetic to the former side of the debate, having argued in many places that Levinas's work can only make sense in a phenomenological context. And it is worth noting in this context that if one argues for a religious foundation to Levinas's work, then that only intensifies the imperative to decolonize his work. For religion is part of how cultural hegemony is articulated; perhaps only second to language, the religious structures and destructures in ways we cannot but see as chauvinistic, even just plainly violent, in a transnational context. Condemning everything as 'just dance,' after all, is not free of religious underpinnings; it might be blatantly so, in fact. But the same goes for phenomenology, as we shall see, for the sedimentations of habit and phrasing exceed what one might *explicitly* declare in a work or series of meditations. Levinas's own critical work on phenomenology has long explored the implications of operative concepts and historical habits in the practices of reduction and description. With another frame, we rehearse the spirit of that critical work here. Decolonizing Levinas is both an ante-phenomenological and anti-religious (which, despite protests to the contrary, is always a kind of religiosity) interpretative labor.

On the margins of these two trends in reception we find work on pre-Levinasian philosophy, seeking relations between Levinas and important thinkers of difference before him, ranging from the obvious candidates in Plato, Plotinus, Augustine, Descartes, and others to unexpected connections with Kant, Schelling, Wahl, Marcel, and others. This sort of work seizes upon something very interesting and, arguably, hitherto undocumented in the history of philosophy. Despite claims of a 'unity of tradition' and 'basic Western orientation,' Levinas's work on difference and the opening of closed systems has uncovered the peculiar, nascent tendency of the West to interrupt its own narrative. This sort of work, though still only emerging in Levinas scholarship, has been enormously important for understanding Levinas as both a reader and member of the philosophical tradition in the West, as well as appreciating his place among contemporaries. At the same time, as I hope to have shown above in our Introduction, the contradictions and ruptures that Levinas finds in the West are none the less points of surprise and interruption, and therefore, while outside lived experience, still a part of a bordered and boundaried place he calls Europe. Contradictions and ruptures are levied *against* the tradition *by* the tradition, which means, for Levinas, that it is still one and the same *project* masquerading in his thought as a *place*.

What has not been fully thematized, and perhaps with good reason, is the problematic of method. Levinas scholarship has paid very little attention to the question of *how* he arrives at his claims as a matter of philosophical approach and framing, preferring instead, for the most part, to illuminate traces of the texts and ideas of others in the Levinasian text. Now, there are surely legitimate reasons for setting aside or even critiquing the idea of a Levinasian methodology. To begin, Levinas's work has been, from the beginning, about the concreteness of encounter where the Other exceeds my grasp, placing all of those items of stability, control, and solidification in the an-archic and the trace. For all of the humility and austerity of Levinas's writing, there is a genuine wildness to the theme that surely puts any sort of methodology in question. Where would something like the question of method take root? Is the incessant recurrence of the anarchic in the concrete not a stake *against* methodology? How could a Levinasian subject, denucleated before it comes to itself, formulate something so stable and encompassing as philosophical method? So, alongside this hesitation, one might also ask if the problematic of method is not a fundamental category mistake. Are we not asking the wrong question when we ask about methodology? The ethical is above all the question of responsibility and response, whereas thinking about methodology places philosophy outside that sort of call, aligning the thinker with preparatory work rather than the drama and *mise en scène* of moral consciousness. Or maybe the question of methodology is just a bit too old-fashioned. Or less inspired and literary than the rhetoric of the Other in *Totality and Infinity* and *Otherwise Than Being,* not to mention some of the more exploratory essays. Is methodology ill suited to Levinas's philosophy or even just foreign to its expository sensibility? And what would we mean if we claimed his work ill suited? What demonstrates *that* claim?

At the same time, Levinas himself continually returns to the question of method, albeit with his characteristically suggestive and evocative turns of phrase. We find gestures toward certain phenomenological concepts, rather than patient elaboration of method and descriptive-analytical technique. So, the work is ours to do, taking Levinas's texts as a leading clue. Seeking this clue, it is most noteworthy that, in each case of describing his general philosophical approach, Levinas identifies Edmund Husserl's description of intentionality as the ground of method. Sometimes Levinas will pair an *inspiration* with his sense of method – as when he refers to Franz Rosenzweig as 'too present' in *Totality and Infinity* to cite – but the difference between method and inspiration is crucial. Method allows a certain repetition of approach, seeking (or demonstrating again) evidence for one and the same claim, whereas inspiration is more akin to personal testimony. If intentionality functions as the methodological principle for Levinas's thought of the Other, then we can revisit the structure of relation in search of the other Other, documenting the shifts and modifications along the way. Intentionality is deformalized in description, as we shall see, and this deformalization opens the necessary space for historical experience. Inspiration, on the other hand, links one to tradition more intimately and with all attendant insularity. If Levinas's work deploys intentionality as method, then we can repeat that sense of relation, infused with historical experience, and thereby generate proliferations of notions of difference against insularity.

Now, there is much to be said about the function of intentionality in Levinas's work and how that function draws continually and in increasingly novel ways on Husserl's work.[1] For now, though, it is enough to say, as a preliminary claim, that the phenomenological method is crucial for understanding not just Levinas's texts, but also how we might approach the question of what a 'Levinasian thinking' might look like. The preliminary question, of course, is how intentionality functions in Levinas's texts, but that initial query is ultimately in the service of a broader question of how to think *with* Levinas, even if our thinking with him takes another direction altogether. Intentionality makes this sort of thinking-with possible because, as the methodology of Levinasian thinking, it makes repetition *and* difference possible. That is, the question of method and the function of intentionality allow us to begin thinking about how Levinas's work is open to extension and critique from the outside at the very same moment that that work puts the ethical at the heart of theory. *A Levinasian thinking. A Levinas thought across borders.* This is a difficult task – the task of the entirety of this book, in fact – and securing the question of method is critical for theorizing Levinas after postcolonial critique rigorously.

I want to begin with an exposition of method, which will then be brought to bear on the problem of embodiment. The problem of the body, as we shall see, exposes Levinas's work – and so any future Levinasian thinking – to the sense in which the body carries memory and history into the encounter. If the body carries memory and history into the encounter, then the ethical cannot be described, as Levinas describes it, as entirely outside being. In this register, being intensifies and widens responsibility, rather than, as Levinas would have it, neutralizing the for-the-Other of subjectivity. The task of methodology lies in demonstrating the concreteness of this claim so that being is no longer understood as a construction and invasive, neutered force. With that in view, then, my aim here is two-fold. First, I would like to demonstrate how Levinasian thinking exceeds, of necessity, the articulation of the ethical in Levinas's work. The opening to the Other in Levinas's famous for-the-Other of subjectivity demands critique from the outside as a matter of methodological practice. This is the foundation of thinking *with*, yet *beyond*, Levinas's texts. Levinas's accounts of intentionality and embodiment say more than his own analysis can contain. Second, once we saturate methodological practice with the language of ethics and vulnerability, Levinasian thinking takes on an important urgency. It is not enough to document my obligation to the familiar Other. The other Others, the unfamiliar and unanticipated Others, the Others of historical experience, the alien *in every sense* of alien, and the critical practice of conceiving an approach to such other Others – these are the complex imperatives of Levinasian thinking. And, further, the opening of method to the Other as such and widely conceived – rather than what is, in Levinas's texts, an utterly familiar stranger – deeply implicates Levinasian thinking in the project of decolonization and a globalization of the ethical. Vulnerable to the outside, directed by the imperative of attending to the Other, Levinasian thinking is tasked with seeking out and crossing the very borders that define Levinas's work in its Eurocentric manifestation. Our Introduction above has already drawn attention to this, of course. The ethical brings the crucial nuance and regulative function: a seeking out and border-crossing that is exposed and vulnerable, and so never imperial *again* in its approach. So is the aspiration of a decolonized Levinasian thinking.

THE DESIRE OF RELATION

How do we think about the problem of methodology in Levinas's work?

This is a complicated question. Indeed, there are many reasons to resist the question, points of resistance rooted in nothing less than the fundamental insight of Levinas's work; the face is concrete and interrupts life, so the apparatuses developed in a philosophy of consciousness – arguably the ground of the question of method – are already late to the scene. Asking the question of method may in fact miss the point. Or perhaps this is just not Levinas's question, in which case one already exceeds Levinas's text when raising methodological questions. Or, worse, perhaps those structures set out in the methodological orientation only reiterate the violence to the Other, marginalizing or erasing the capacity to contest with fragility and weakness. Is the question of method not already imperial?

These suspicions say too much. To be sure, the ultimate purchase of Levinasian thinking lies in the notions of interruption and responsibility. Such notions overturn long-held beliefs about the nature of normativity, the status of rules and virtues and habits in moral thinking, and the order of priority in thinking about knowing and being. But even with that ultimate purchase fully in view, Levinas is always concerned with the structure of justification. Without a strong sense of justification, without asking about how to legitimate certain claims about difference, and so on, Levinasian thinking risks being reduced to a series of intuitions and speculative beliefs held in common by those sharing, well, ungrounded intuitions and speculations. That is not enough. After all, Levinas is a philosopher and has philosophical aspirations. Philosophical aspirations mean a couple of things in this context. First, it means that an assertion remains merely assertion pending a consideration of the structure of legitimation. Dogmatics are in fact part of the problem against which the an-archy of the ethical is deployed; the very idea of rules or justification by external authority is put in question – and exposed as fundamentally violent – by the concreteness of the face-to-face and the material exposure of sensibility. Second, philosophical aspiration indicates a largely under-appreciated aspect of Levinas's thought: his impact on questions of epistemology, ontology, and aesthetics. To be sure, we know a lot about his *criticism* of philosophy's major areas of investigation, but Levinas also has a fully complex and compelling epistemology and ontology of his own, and there are enormously important implications for aesthetics in his work. Levinas's work contains enigmatic and often experimental epistemologies and makes quasi-ontological claims, and the fact that such concerns animate his work reflects an aspiration to be *philosophical* in his work. Levinas's descriptions of responsibility are not merely personal reports. They are claims made about what it means to know and be under obligation and how affect is transmitted through these radically reworked notions of knowing and being. Time, space, place, and other such issues serve as legitimating structures for the Levinasian descriptions of responsibility, embedded as they are in the experience and accounts of accusation, *mise en question,* and the infinite work of justice.

All of this is to say that Levinas's work is animated by phenomenology, its methods, and its imperatives. The question of method in Levinas is inseparable from the question of phenomenology. In a peculiar twist, too, the question of phenomenology always begins the process of decolonization.

Now, it should be said that Levinas's relationship to the phenomenological movement is a complicated matter for independent study and debate. Nevertheless, a few things can be said here about that relation.

The juxtaposition of the ethical and phenomenology is easy enough, with Levinas's embrace of transcendence without immanence set against Husserl's reduction of all transcendence to a transcendence-in-immanence. This has led many commentators to see Husserl as Levinas's foil. But the historical and textual evidence is considerably more complicated. Historically, of course, Levinas translated Husserl's *Cartesian Meditations* and wrote a number of short, summary-like articles reporting on the meaning of phenomenology, beginning in the last years of the 1920s and into the early 1930s. Jean-Paul Sartre is reputed to have found Levinas's *Theory of Intuition in Husserl's Phenomenology* by chance on a Paris bookstore shelf and, upon perusing it, was revolutionized as a thinker. As well, and more importantly, Levinas attended Husserl's lectures on phenomenological psychology delivered in 1928. These lectures were a rereading of the notes from 1925 – published as *Phenomenological Psychology* in *Husserliana IX* – but the Husserl-Archiv contains important notes that supplemented the 1928 re-lectures, including an important excursus on what Husserl termed 'the intersubjective reduction.' It is no surprise, then, that we find that very same phrase at the end of the body of *Theory of Intuition,* where Levinas writes that 'the works of Husserl published so far make only very brief mentions' of the idea of intersubjective reduction and a phenomenology of the interhuman.[2] Levinas takes the meaning of this reduction in many different directions, of course, making phenomenology into a very different endeavor than Husserl would have ever anticipated, and yet it is important to note here that Levinas begins at the outer reaches of Husserl's work.

Where, then, to begin with Levinas and phenomenology? As a legitimating methodology, Levinas begins where Husserl always begins: the irreducible relationality of intentionality. '[T]he presentation and the development of the notions employed,' Levinas writes of the project of *Totality and Infinity,* 'owe everything to the phenomenological method. Intentional analysis is the search for the concrete.'[3] What could Levinas mean by this? For Husserl, famously, every consciousness is a consciousness-of something, which is to say, we cannot think of subjectivity without the formation of the subject in relation. Phenomenology begins with this insight. *Phenomenology and intentionality* – in that coupling, deformalized in the ethical relation, everything is changed for Levinas as a philosopher. The methodological orientation of Husserlian phenomenology is stretched to such a point that Levinas cannot reconcile relationality with the (allegedly) reflective, cognitive terms of its formulation in transcendental idealism. Indeed, Levinas's break with classical phenomenology revolves around the question of idealism. The relation with the Other, by definition, cannot be contained within the boundaries of active, constituting subjectivity. The constitution of (not by) subjectivity must flow in a different direction or directions. And yet the relation with the Other *does* constitute subjectivity, making a certain kind of subject out of that relation, so there is relationality even as that relationality breaks with the formulation in Husserl's work. Irreducible relation, intentionality, is what makes Levinasian thinking possible *after* a break with idealist traditions and strains.

Far from anti-intentionality, then, Levinas's methodological approach is largely a radicalization of the problem of relation. Radicalization, in this context, consists in uprooting the flow of relation from the idealist subject and replacing the source of that flow of meaning with the an-archic figure of the Other. We see this conception of intentionality and method at work in the Preface to *Totality and Infinity*. Levinas's remarks in the Preface describe the methodology deployed in the body of that text, but, in so doing, also evoke and build further on the work done in a series of fascinating essays from the late 1950s. In those essays, Levinas argues that the *ruin* of representation, by which he means the internal decomposition of representational renderings of particular sorts of exteriorities, is the outcome of a concrete practice of phenomenological description rather than the imposition of external prerogatives or external sets of philosophical claims.[4] Intentionality itself is disruption; it is wholly unstable in relation, as the mixture of subjectivity and its 'object' quickly becomes destabilized by this zigzag relationship. The other of the intentional relation, that part of intentionality said to be constitut*ed*, may in fact function as constitut*ing*. Husserl's elaborate philosophical labor aims at stabilizing the play of the object-side of relation through the transcendental turn, but his insight says more than his texts can handle. Representation *ruins* and *becomes a ruin* in representation. The process of gaining distance from the dynamism and resistance of the exterior builds ruin into representation from the outset, initiating the strange, alienated temporality of consciousness. This is a process internal to phenomenological description because the object of relation – the correlate of consciousness in consciousness-of – exceeds or even opens a breach in what *wants to be* a seamless relation. The ruination of representation therefore breaks with the perceptual model of grasping and seizing up on object of perception. In *Totality and Infinity*, Levinas writes that

> [t]he experience of morality does not proceed from this vision – it *consummates* this vision; ethics is an optics. But it is a 'vision' without image, bereft of the synoptic and totalizing objectifying virtues of vision, a relation of an intentionality of a wholly different type – which this work seeks to describe.[5]

From this remark, Levinas turns to the familiar refrains of thinking against Being, against war, and so on in the name of the possibility of ethical life. Those refrains draw life from the wholly different intentionality that works against objectification by liberating the perceived from the totalizing gaze. Decentered, subjectivity encounters, in *Totality and Infinity*, an excessiveness that signifies without the context of the gaze and its history. Such signification keeps relation in place; the Other does not signal itself from itself (*kath auto*) without putting the subject *held fast to relation* under a relation of responsibility. Even in its overturning, intentionality is irreducible.

Levinas's work undergoes a number of radical rethinkings after *Totality and Infinity*, and some of the most interesting scholarly work on his thought documents that rethinking by noting the increasing relevance of the Shoah, a revisiting of Husserl's work, the impact of Derrida's critical commentary, the new role of Talmudic readings on Levinas's philosophical reflections, and so on. Yet, throughout these shifts and twists and turns in thinking, Levinas's work remains committed to the problem of intentionality. Indeed, one can see this in how Levinas develops his new – and genuinely radical – language of *trace* on the basis of a reconsideration of Husserl's work on intentionality and the primal impression in essays like 'Intentionality and Sensation' and 'Notes on Sense.' The problems of time, trace, sensation, and sensibility in general culminate in the reformulation of the language of alterity in *Otherwise Than Being*. In that work, Levinas shifts from the language of excess in *Totality and Infinity* toward a more austere, desert landscape generated by a subject who comes late to itself. Intentionality persists as the methodological key, even in this (at times) dramatic shift. At the close of *Otherwise Than Being*, in the sub-section entitled simply 'Outside,' Levinas makes a clear and decisive affirmation of intentionality as method. And, again, the critical context is perception and the gaze. He writes:

> Our presentation of notions proceeds neither by their logical decomposition, nor by their dialectical description. It remains faithful to

intentional analysis, insofar as it signifies the locating of notions in the horizon, a horizon unrecognized, forgotten or displaced in the exhibition of an object, in its notion, *in the look absorbed by the notion alone.*[6]

Faithful to intentional analysis. With that turn of phrase, Levinas, here at the close of his second great work, rejoins Husserlian phenomenology, not as a mimic of doctrine, but as a practitioner of method. The method yields very different results, of course, reversing the flow of sense and meaning. This reversal discloses what Levinas repeatedly calls the 'forgotten horizon' of intentionality – the Other of relation. The horizon is forgotten precisely because it is part of the meaning of subjectivity embedded within Husserl's overriding prejudice in favor of sovereign consciousness. The method remains the same. And so Levinas makes it clear that, even in the wake of the radical work of *Otherwise Than Being* and despite his enormous rhetorical and theoretical distance from classical phenomenology, Husserlian philosophy has been 'restored to its rank of being a method for all philosophy.'[7] That is serious praise!

The lesson to be drawn is important for Levinasian thinking. Methodology is not just a side-concern or external construction, but rather crucial for understanding both Levinas's own work and the possibilities of extending his insights. Now, as with the claim in *Totality and Infinity*, Levinas's embrace of the method for all philosophy entails a fundamental overturning. 'Psychic contents,' that propensity of philosophy to render what presents itself in representation-to-self, are subverted by the fundamental *firstness* of the object of intentionality in the ante- and anti-experience of transcendence we find in obsession and desire. So, for example, Levinas writes in *Otherwise Than Being*:

> Intentionality, the noesis which the philosophy of consciousness distinguished in sensing, and which it wanted, in a regressive movement, to take hold of again as the origin of the sense ascribed, the sensible intuition, *is already in the mode of apprehension and obsession, assailed by the sensed . . . a non-thematizable alterity.*[8]

The structure of obsession dominates so much of *Otherwise Than Being*. Rightly so. With the notion of obsession, Levinas is able to articulate in urgent terms the spatial and temporal dimensions of the breakup of intentionality. The *affect* of obsession is already spatially dis- and delocated; my feeling of obsession with another already places the dynamics of my inner life in the hands of the

Other, whether that be an obsession with guilt, culpability, responsibility, love, or even just mystery. Obsession in *Otherwise Than Being* inverts, in many ways, the structure of metaphysical desire in *Totality and Infinity* – which, Levinas writes, 'does not long to return'[9] and 'does not rest upon any prior kinship'[10] – but with one and the same lesson: we are oriented toward *and* oriented by the Other of the intentional relation. Method gets us into the structures of that orientation 'toward' and 'by.' How we *respond* to that obsession is another matter altogether, but the lived experiences of obsession and desire draw out the consequences of describing subjectivity as intentionally structured and assailed by the sensed. *Sensibility is singularity, which produces obsession and desire without closure.* What is outside the subject comes *first*. Obsession and desire spatialize this firstness in the affective life of being in another's hands, taken in by another to the point of losing the center of one's self – what Levinas elsewhere calls denucleation.

And there is also the structure of diachronic temporality. The spatial character of Levinas's descriptions – namely, the figure of 'the outside' – is of course never wholly spatial. Rather, the space between the intending subject and its Other, between sensibility and sense, or between the obsession and the obsessed-about is measured as a temporal distance. This is one of Levinas's strangest and most important innovations as a thinker. Diachrony names distance measured by time, locating the famous 'time of the Other' both inside subjectivity and outside its measure and grasp. Temporal distance allows Levinas to work in creative and complicated ways with borders. The border between subjectivity and the Other, what he simply calls 'separation' in *Totality and Infinity*, is both the condition of responsibility and the inevitability of failure. Proximity seals both. I am responsible for the Other and cannot fulfill that responsibility, something that the border of diachronic time establishes in irreducible terms. The border between the I and the Other is crossed in the accusative, enacted in proximity, but never in a way that leaves the Other – that alterity who seizes upon relationality in the making of subjectivity – in memory. Rather, there is the immemorial as epistemological and ontological enigma. And interruption of identity. So, Levinas writes of diachronic time that

> [i]t is the impossibility of the dispersion of time to assemble itself in the present, the insurmountable diachrony of time, a beyond the said. It is diachrony that determines the immemorial; a weakness of memory does not constitute diachrony.[11]

Diachrony does not and indeed cannot assemble itself into language, but there is still expression, relation, and sense. Desiring the Other or being obsessed by the Other – there is no language to capture such transcendence, and yet there is the affect of desire and obsession, an intervention of the Other's time into the time of the subject. Whatever is thematized *inside subjectivity* is already outside the subject. The relation to alterity is therefore manifest in the *ruining* or decomposition of what would seek to represent, catch sight of, and know the Other.

In the witness to ruin and decomposition, we have our theme: *intentionality disrupted by the reversal of intentionality*, the method of Levinasian thinking.

EMBODIMENT AS VULNERABILITY

Levinas's reconfiguration of intentionality, locating the constitutive agency of relation in the Other of that relation, yields a peculiar but absolutely fecund sense of method. It is a method that begins with subjectivity; we cannot but begin with the affective life of subjectivity. Levinas's work has always been about the life of subjectivity, even as his reputation is so tied to the idea of the Other. But that life is always thematized in order to identify our alienation from the flow of time and meaning. If interruption begins the ethical life of the subject, constituting the sense of moral consciousness from the outside *first*, then subjectivity is always outside of itself at one and the same moment that it lives its egoism. Indeed, interruption is only possible in this ambivalent space.

From Husserl, Levinas takes the insight into intentionality as irreducible. If we take Levinas's statements in both *Totality and Infinity* and *Otherwise Than Being* as indicative of the importance of this insight, then part of the task of appreciating his philosophical work lies in seeing the structure of intentionality in notions of time, space, place, perception, and so on. There is also the abiding influence of Martin Heidegger – a sense of influence too complex for our focused concerns here. But Heidegger's own transformation of Husserl's phenomenology is critical for at least one aspect of Levinas's conception of method, viz., the problem of formalization and deformalization. Heidegger's account of the existential analytic in *Being and Time* draws out a tension between the formal analysis of the structure of *Dasein* – outlining the modifications of notions of space, time, language, and so on – and how one catches sight of those structures in the deformalized descriptions of being-in-the-world. Deformalized descriptions are not literary indulgences or personal testimony. Rather, deformalization is Heidegger's attempt, through a critical practice of phenomenology, to document the ambiguous origins of what is rendered in formal analysis. So too with Levinas; the principle of concretion permeates his work, not only as a philosophical principle, but as a mode of description. What is analyzed formally as a reversal of intentionality *must* be seen as it is lived concretely in the affective life of the subject.

The formal analysis of spatiality and temporality is made concrete in Levinas's anchoring of intentionality in sensibility. *We live intentionality as sensual creatures.* This has been a central insight in Levinas's work since the beginning. Indeed, sensibility has been crucial for Levinas's work from the emphasis on axiological relation and life in *Theory of Intuition* onward, but it is arguably only in *Otherwise Than Being* that affective life is given a genuinely radical treatment. In *Totality and Infinity*, one could argue, the affective life of the subject is drawn across the vicissitudes of desire and enjoyment, such that sensibility is merely one occasion for critique among others. However, the austerity of *Otherwise Than Being*, where the readings of language, time, and so on sketch a sense of subjectivity devastated by the encounter with the Other and itself (for there is no difference, in that difference, for the later Levinas), places sensibility at the center of the analysis. Sensibility is the crossing of my presence to the world with the possibility of giving, which in turn becomes the pain of obligation lived in sensible presence. Sensibility is not pleasure and enjoyment, those dominant motifs of *Totality and Infinity*. Instead, in *Otherwise Than Being*, my sensible presence to the world marks usurpation and possession. This marks the possibility of my giving, to be sure, but also, at the same time, the very persistence of violence. Levinas writes:

> To give, to-be-for-another, despite oneself, but in interrupting the for-oneself, is to take the bread out of one's own mouth, to nourish the hunger of another with one's own fasting . . . For sensibility does not enact the play of essence, does not play any game, and is the very seriousness that interrupts the pleasure and complacency of games.[12]

Sensibility is saturated with the sincerity of relation. For Levinas, this means that the sensual enjoyment of the world is already interrupted, already opened to and opened by the ethical relation. Levinas's example of fasting is particularly interesting, and even a bit surprising. In fasting, I retract my place in the world and give to the Other, enacting ethical work in my sensible relation to the Other – a kind of embodied prayer. The pain of my retraction is the sublimated pleasure of the ethical relation lived in the body. Suffering for the Other, we might say, is subjectivity made sensible. And so, in the turn to sensibility in *Otherwise Than Being*, Levinas recasts his work on the body in order to rediscover ethical incarnation as the ambivalent site of obligation.

This recast is in some ways a retrieval, with decisive modifications, of Levinas's own work on the body in the 1930s and 1940s. In his earliest work, Levinas treats the theme of the body with a most peculiar vocabulary. Even before Merleau-Ponty published his groundbreaking studies of the lived body, Levinas had begun theorizing the body as a sheer materiality whose difference from, yet entwinement with, consciousness weights the body in being. In fact, in the early long essay entitled 'On Evasion,' Levinas describes the body as our enchainment to being. We are enchained to being because the body cannot escape or evade its materiality. Subjectivity's embodied character is irreducible, which in this context means that the body marks my place in the world and my place in being; no reflection or retreat to consciousness can neutralize the body or render it secondary. In the context of his concerns in the 1930s, informed as it is by the Heideggerian critique of dualism, this is tantamount to Levinas claiming that it is the body that seals Heidegger's critique of Husserl. Like Heidegger, Levinas is critical of Husserl's turn to the phenomenological and transcendental reduction as the condition of philosophy and philosophizing itself. The task of phenomenology, for both Heidegger and Levinas, lies in returning subjectivity to being. For Heidegger, this happens by way of the rather abstract – save for the central role of language – notion of the existential analytic. The existential analytic is an attempt to deformalize the formal account of *Dasein*'s being-in-the-world, but when incarnation moves to the center of Levinas's analysis, an important break from Heidegger is made. To be in the world is not firstly a relation of thrownness and projection. Rather, we are in the world because we are embodied; the enchainment to being anchors us in being without the possibility of evasion. What are we to make of this prominence of the body? How does the body return us to being?

We do not find much of an answer in the intervening years. Indeed, Levinas's philosophical work through the 1940s and 1950s turns more and more toward the structure of intentionality and the various modifications of conscious life enacted through experiences like insomnia, vigilance, desire, and so on. Descriptions of such experiences offer leading clues to what is more methodologically documented in the late 1950s as the ruin of representation. Ruining representation, through a strange and compelling reading of the logic of *Sinngebung* as sense-bestowal from the outside, surely has elements of materiality, but the abstraction of that materiality, as well as the tendency to think material life as exteriority, keeps the body at some distance from key analyses. So, in *Totality and Infinity*, the text toward which these various modifications and ruinations lead and in which they are fulfilled, the body is largely marginalized as problems of expression and the constitution of sense move to the center. To be sure, there are elements of embodied life scattered throughout the text, especially in the figure of the hands (the caress, how I meet the Other with full hands, put in question by the Other's fragility), the feminine, and in the short but suggestive exploration of sensual life in the final sections on fecundity. But no one can seriously claim that *Totality and Infinity* is a book about incarnation as a particularly ethical phenomenon or site of analysis. There is labor, enjoyment, and elemental life, so materiality plays an important role in the deformalization of transcendence, which is only then overturned in the reversal of intentionality in the face-to-face. My embodied presence to the world remains an occasional mention in the ethical, largely as a metaphor or evocative case of the full hands of welcoming and hospitality.

Otherwise Than Being sounds a very different note. In that text, materiality in general is a far more important motif, starting with the slow, careful unfolding of the diachronic structure of language in the relation of the Saying and the Said and culminating in problems of the trace, divinity, and the witness. At the center of the problem of materiality is the body. There is no subjectivity without sensibility in *Otherwise Than Being*, and there is no ethics in the sensible without the exposed, vulnerable body.

In its fully developed form, the body appears in *Otherwise Than Being* as a way of thinking responsibility as beyond evasion – revisiting the first essays on embodiment from the 1930s. Responsibility, which is described in *Otherwise Than Being* as the register of the affect of obligation in the experience of fractured subjectivity, makes me *uncomfortable in my skin*. I am accused in my skin and I also anxiously bear that responsibility as a fleshy being. In my skin, I become a subject: which is to say, I become creaturely as incarnate.

The skin therefore functions as a sort of interstitial conceptual site, set as it is between the workings of consciousness/conscience and the Other who has already departed the scene. My sensibility is split, generating discomfort. Having come to consciousness, I have the compulsion to flee responsibility; this is part of how being is violence. It is all just too much, too infinite, too devastating of my speech and action. And yet it is the fact of my embodiment that makes it impossible to escape this moment of responsibility. If I were just a consciousness or abstract *idea* of a person, then perhaps I could imagine myself interchangeable in the moment of having been obligated by the Other. Perhaps I could pass responsibility on to another, ask that another or an institution or a tradition take my place in the world. For, are we all not the same?

> Incarnation [Levinas writes] is not a transcendental operation of a subject that is situated in the midst of the world it represents to itself; the sensible experience of the body is already and from the start incarnate. The sensible – maternity, vulnerability, apprehension – binds the node of incarnation into a plot larger than the apperception of self. In this plot I am bound to others before being tied to my body.[13]

Just as with his conception of subjectivity as such, Levinas's account of embodiment places the question of origin in what is elsewhere of the ego or the I. We are not all the same. We *are* singular – no we at all. That is, I come to my body as accused and in the accusative; I am first a *me* (*moi*) and under a relation of obligation. Thereafter, in the plane of being, action, and politics, the freedom characterized as the *I* or *ego* (*je*) comes to the fore and is embodied at a secondary level. This secondary level, as late to the scene and now uncomfortable in its skin, bears an unredeemed (and unredeemable) debt, for I am not an I without the first position of the Other. Even in embodiment, *je est une autre.*

If I *is* an Other, then the very meaning of my being begins with the Other. This is the insight Levinas brings to intentionality, which is now brought to the thematic of incarnation. And so Levinas's discussion of the body is marked by a fundamental ambivalence: in the relation of responsibility, subjectivity is at once *expelled from being* and *contracted too tightly in my own being.* Levinas expresses this ambivalence in the unexpected, but enormously suggestive language of *exile* and *refuge.* Embodiment is the site of this ambivalence. He writes:

> The exile or refuge in itself is without conditions or support, far from the abundant covers and excuses which the essence exhibited in the said offers. In responsibility as one assigned or elected from the outside, assigned as irreplaceable, *the subject is accused in its skin, too tight for its skin.*[14]

The temporality of the accusative exiles the subject from itself, but always without the promise of return. In the drama of Levinasian subjectivity, there is never homecoming; Levinas, in his own peculiar way, is a thinker of diaspora, but it is here written as a metaphor of the life of incarnate ethical subjectivity. I am I because, as Paul Celan puts it, I am *you*, which at this moment in Levinas's analysis means the I is creaturely: created, given life by the Other's accusation. An I who becomes-subject, capable of thought, action, and practice, after being-me. And yet there is also the skin that makes it impossible to flee the scene of responsibility – *because the scene is the flesh of the me-become-I.* Creatureliness means I am I only *after* the Other. I am not I because of a pre-existing essence or core human something. I am *generated* in the interstitial space of sensibility. Levinas refers to this genesis as the original sense of *psyche.*

Levinas's well-known rejection of humanism in the name of an-archic responsibility is here blended with the fact of embodiment. I am accused *in this body.* The body takes up space in the world, a sort of material border that is pushed further and further into the world through my action and enjoyment and even desire, accumulating more as I expand the scope of my usurpation. This is the economy of action. But the embodied subject is also locked into that place in the world. Usurpation generates obligation. And in that moment of accusation, accused as I am in my own body, there is no question that *I am the one called to responsibility.* The body makes me singular in my election by the Other. Singular, not in the sense of some set of unique features or even geometric location, but in the sense of being made into the subject-for-the-Other *in this body.* Responsibility is thereby made irrecusable. I am uncomfortable in my skin because what is asked of me is too much, and the body in which I am accused makes me the singular elect. 'The body,' Levinas writes, 'is not only an image or figure here; it is the distinctive in-oneself of the contraction of ipseity and its breakup.'[15]

If responsibility is irrecusable and the body enchains me, not to being, but to the Other's accusation and election, then the body is fundamentally vulnerable and exposed. That is, the force of election is established firstly on the basis of an impossibility of evasion. This means that we have to think subjectivity against humanism – beyond essence, of course – without losing the humanity of the Other and of myself in the position of responsibility. The analysis and restructuring of intentionality already accomplishes a good bit of this, locating the first position (the quasi-originary condition) of relation in the Other who is not measured by the I or a third term. But the key to this non-evasion is my anchor in the world, that part of subjectivity that makes it impossible to evade the accusing face, which means the impossibility of being re-rendered a subject *in the accusative*. Incarnation is *passive* or, in Levinas's hyperbole, is more passive than any passivity. That modality of passivity means responsibility and the for-the-Other relation is not my choosing; I am elected. And we know this from experiences of dread, guilt, and other moral affects that, for Levinas, are not the ethical itself, but rather signifiers of relations of pre-history that then, as they sediment and work their way into the I of subjectivity, later trigger after-affects of prior obligation(s). The Other surprises me, against my will. Such is the nature of surprise. Surprise, as interruption of egoic life, exposes me to the Other *because* I am embodied and cannot flee that incarnate presence to the world. Levinas writes:

> The ego is not in itself like matter which, perfectly espoused by its form, is what it is; it is in itself like one is in one's skin, that is, already tight, ill at ease in one's own skin. It is as though the identity of matter resting in itself concealed a dimension in which a retreat to the hither side of immediate coincidence were possible, concealed a materiality more material than all matter – a materiality such that irritability, susceptibility or exposedness to wounds and outrage characterizes its passivity, more passive still than the passivity of effects. Maternity in the complete being 'for the other' which characterizes it, which is the very signifyingness of signification, is the ultimate sense of this vulnerability.[16]

This passage demonstrates the important distinction between the passivity beyond all passivity and the passivity of effects, a nuance that is important for many of the following reflections. But it is important to take note here of the intimate, if not nearly synonymous, relationship between materiality, exposure, vulnerability, and maternity. There is much to be said about the gender normativity and politics in Levinas's figure of the feminine, which is both problematic and even a bit silly, but the intention of the allusion is to describe the passive body as both giving to the world and something made into what it is – mother, subject, for-the-Other – by that which draws from it. Just as one could say that for Levinas every Other is a Jew, his account of incarnate vulnerability and exposure suggests that every body is a mother. The maternal body that *is* subjectivity cannot escape the sensual relation to the world. In that inescapability, the body is the condition of radical responsibility. Obligation is uprooted from the will, choice. I am in so far as I am elected, chosen *in this maternal(-ized) body*. Every ethical subject is a Jewish mother.

Consider, then, how Levinas rewrites the caress in *Otherwise Than Being*. In *Totality and Infinity*, the caress plays an interesting role in the economy of embodiment. Though Levinas is clearly suspicious, as always, of the caress as an expression of need or crass, paganized desire, he also understands the caress as linked to metaphysical desire. As a kind of desire, the caress solicits the infinite in the Other, working as a kind of palpation of the Other's skin in search of the infinity it cannot touch, but which nevertheless animates the desire to caress. Levinas writes:

> In every vision contact is announced: sight and hearing caress the visible and the audible. Contact is not an openness upon being, but an exposure of being. In this caress, proximity signifies as proximity, and not as an experience of proximity.[17]

Now, it is true that, as Levinas puts it in a short footnote to *Otherwise Than Being*, 'a caress can reenter the teleological order of the said and become a symbol or word,'[18] but exposure establishes an irreparable fracture in the order of being. This irreparable fracture, this exposure of being, keeps sensibility open to the Other, not as a disposition or generosity of the I, but as the accusing formation of the subject from the outside. Sensibility means sensitivity, a susceptibility to the Other that discloses the future-past temporality of the caress, contact, and any sensibility whatsoever: *I will have been obligated.*

The exposed and vulnerable body seals obligation in singularity. In the accusative, I am first *me*: the direct object of a speaking of responsibility. Exposed and vulnerable, this is a genesis and relation of election. Only I can answer, late to my responsibility. Only the singular Other issues this responsibility, this claim on me, and so only the singular Other makes me a moral consciousness. 'The Other calls upon that sensibility with a vocation that wounds,' Levinas writes, 'calls upon an irrevocable responsibility, and thus *the very identity of a subject. Signification is witness. . .'.*[19] Witness to the vulnerable, witnessing as my vulnerability. Embodiment, ever intentional, is always precarious.

INCARNATE HISTORIOGRAPHY AS DECOLONIZATION

How could it be that signification functions as witness? To what does signification witness? What are the boundaries on the pre-history that forms the historical genesis of the responsible subject? And how can those boundaries be transgressed by decolonized historical experience?

The vulnerability of the body in exposure opens Levinasian thinking to the Other in a manner that cedes priority absolutely. Openness is not a disposition of subjectivity. Rather, openness is an experience of will or even a discovery of condition that is late to the scene. *Something has already happened to subjectivity*. The 'I' of subjectivity, that assumption of the position of agent and actor, is opened up by a prior relation. That is, there is a *genetic* moment in the formation of ethical subjectivity that precedes – perhaps we could say it *pre-dates* – the coming to self that registers the feeling and compulsive action of responsibility. The response-ability of the subject comes from what cannot be subject: the Other.

In the *Phenomenology of Perception*, Maurice Merleau-Ponty makes a peculiar and provocative claim that the body has a *history*. Levinas takes up this notion in *Otherwise Than Being* in order to deepen the genetic problematic of subjectivity. The body has a history, Levinas claims, but there is an important difference from Merleau-Ponty's articulation of the same intuition. Whereas for Merleau-Ponty the body carries the history of the subject through gesture, expression, and general comportment, Levinas's body as vulnerability and exposure bears history as a wound. The pain of possession in *Otherwise Than Being* tells us part of that story of history as a wound, for at the moment the Other catches me with bread in my hands or in my mouth, the history of usurpation and my assertion of being – an incarnation of *conatus essendi* and duration, perhaps – is exposed not *because of* my body, but *as embodiment itself*.

And so Levinas's appeal to history is saturated with the immemorial. It is therefore crucial for Levinas to underscore the break the body's history has with conventional notions of memory and narrative. This is no easy break, for the grandest models of history and memory in Levinas's philosophical vocabulary – Hegel's movement of *Geist*, Husserl's elaborate account of retention, the history of Being in Heidegger – all conceive becoming on the model of totality, seeing folds of immanent transcendencies in movement and transition. The immemorial refuses this folding, transcends the immanence in transcendence, and thus marks a moment of loss and temporal dephasing in historical remembrance. In a certain sense, then, the body as exposure and vulnerability cannot be a matter of history. In *Otherwise Than Being*, Levinas writes:

> Beings remain always assembled, present, in a present that is extended, by memory and history, to the totality determined like matter, a present without fissures or surprises, from which becoming is expelled, a present largely made up of re-presentations, due to memory and history. Nothing is gratuitous.[20]

The gratuitous character of the Other changes everything, performing a ciphering function in relation to the presence of the self to itself. Memory and history are reduced to nothing, even less than nothing, not because of the violence done to the past, but because appeals to the past do violence to the singularity of the ethical. For Levinas, I am singular in my responsibility and my responsibility is to the singular Other. The Other addresses me from outside the world, otherwise than being and beyond essence, and in so doing divests me from, prior to my investments in, the worldliness of my being. Memory and history belong to the world. The ethical is outside the world, a kind of transcendental, even as the encounter that gives rise to diachrony, the Saying, vulnerability, and exposure makes its quirky detour through the empirical.

Now, the relation between the empirical and the transcendental has occasioned a decent bit of reflection in the secondary literature, and the story has a dominant thread. Against the privileging of one or the other, Levinas thinks the empirical and the transcendental at one and the same time, in one and the same site, and so as constitutive, in a sort of zigzag movement, of the meaning of the face-to-face. We can see this especially clearly in *Totality and Infinity*, where Levinas famously declares in the Preface that '[t]his "beyond" the totality and objective experience is, however, not to be described in a purely negative fashion,' but is instead 'reflected *within* the totality and history, *within* experience.'[21] The empirical-transcendental problematic of *Totality and Infinity* might declare the ethical to be between the worldly and the otherwise than being, but *Otherwise Than Being*, even as it emphasizes the unsettling function of sensibility, is significantly less concerned with the empirical event of the ethical. *Totality and Infinity* is a book about excess, a book about the surplus of sense and signification that pushes us out of the world, making both my presence in the world and the Other's demand on me too much for an analysis of worldliness to handle. *Otherwise Than Being* is a book about absence, written in a language and with a conceptual apparatus that is so austere that – and perhaps this is the point – one can barely catch sight of anything meaningful or present passing through the world. The later work is about denucleation, dephasing, and the utter devastation of anything that comes to presence in the world. And so the crossing of the empirical and the transcendental that defines the space of encounter in *Totality and Infinity*, producing so much excess, becomes the abstract, desert landscape of diachronic time and the hollowing out of language. But in both cases, and this is utterly crucial, the fate of the empirical is always to be pulled apart, from within the very heart of its identity, by a transcendental condition that could never sustain empirical life.

Excessive or austere, Levinas's account of the encounter with the Other always leaves the world. The only real difference is the conceptual ground on which such a departure is negotiated. And this is not simply a question of rhetoric or conceptual strategy. We see the consequences of this commitment to what lies outside the world and, from that outside, dismantles the force or aspiration of the worldly, in Levinas's articulation of the ethical. In particular, I am thinking of a now famous remark in an interview with Philippe Nemo. Nemo asks Levinas to walk through the terms of the ethical: what does it mean to say responsibility? Why is that responsibility infinite? Who am I in the relation of moral consciousness? And who is the Other? Levinas catches this last query in its formulation: it is not a question of *who* the Other is, but, instead, of *how* the Other in me is registered in my *conscience*. Regarding the Other, Levinas writes that we should not even notice the color of the Other's eyes or the particular shape or appearance of the specific face. The Other is *not of the worldly*, so thinking of the Other in worldly terms misses the point. Levinas remarks:

> The best way (*meilleure manière*) to encounter the Other is to not even take notice of the color of his eyes. When one observes the color of the eyes, one is not in the social relation with the Other. The relation with the face can certainly be dominated by perception, but what is meant *specifically* by the face cannot be reduced to the perceptual.[22]

This is what it means to think the otherwise than being and beyond essence as forming the very grounds-which-are-not-grounds of the ethical. To *notice* the Other in its specificity is to replace the outside-the-worldliness of the singular with the worldliness of visual characteristics. Ethics is an optics, to be sure, as Levinas says in *Totality and Infinity*; the Other comes to me in the field of vision as a material face, asking something of me in fragility, weakness, and height. But the ethical as such – the condition of ethics and response – is never optical in the sense of simple perceptual features. The Other as *l'autrui* signifies *kath auto* – a self-signification that refers only to itself, never to something outside by way of comparison, identification, or classification. So too is the Levinasian Other: singular, without comparison, without identity, and so nothing to which I might attach worldly predicates or values. *There is an Other.*

This departure from the perceptual ought to raise critical questions, however. Namely, we should begin by asking about the conditions under which such a detour from being and worldliness is possible. Levinas's proclamation regarding the color of eyes is, after all, in the normative register. This is the *best* way, the way one *should* encounter the Other. Is this subjectivity described as *only* otherwise than being, an encounter beyond essence from outside the subject, a kind of privilege? Does that account of the encounter conceal elements of embodied life – and so our vulnerable presence to the world – without which embodiment is impossible to conceive? Is Levinas's sense of embodiment sufficiently material?

One of the signature events in Levinas scholarship is Derrida's rigorous and provocative critique of *Totality and Infinity* in 'Violence and Metaphysics,' a tour de force book review that pushes the boundaries of thinking radical difference. Derrida's criticisms are multiple, but a thread throughout all of those criticisms is the persistence of the worldly. Ontology cannot be simply swept away by the hyperbolic rhetoric of height and separation. Language cannot be critiqued by a few evocative words about excessive expression alone. Rather, being and language haunt Levinas's every attempt to think difference without identity, alterity without sameness, and so singularity without comparison. Perhaps with that criticism in mind, Levinas's work undergoes significant critical revision in *Otherwise Than Being*. And yet the problem remains the same: materiality must, for Levinas, be wrested away from the being, language, culture, and politics of the worldly. What I want to propose here, at this moment and across the project, shares with Derrida the suspicion that such enormous distance from the worldly, as a total suspension of history, is impossible, but with an important tweak. Rather than the language of being or language as such, I want to ask if the body itself, thought in its vulnerability and exposure, is not already saturated with history and all of that attendant responsibility. I want to ask if the body does not signify this history, this responsibility, in the very moment of accusation. Perhaps the color of the Other and the color of the vulnerable body signify the specificity – and thus not singularity – of obligation, designating terms of responsibility that bear historical violence, memory, and pain into the upsurging moment of encounter. My appeal here is not ideological, but simply phenomenological. Do we not experience, in the sense of *Erlebnis*, the affect of responsibility precisely as the weight of history bearing upon the moment? Is there not this other diachrony in the embodied encounter that splits the time of *my* present not just from the time of the Other, but also the time of history and its pain as the time of other Others? If history and pain inform the event of the ethical, deepening (rather than distracting from) our sense of the obligation, then history is written into the body itself. Perhaps, even, I am vulnerable and exposed *on the basis of* this history and its incarnation.

Incarnate historiography. Even as Levinas points us to the claim that the body has a history, he pauses before so many the implications of Merleau-Ponty's account of embodiment. Merleau-Ponty, after all, is concerned with the existential signification of the body and how phenomenology might account for the cultural habits of embodiment that give comportment character and, in a provisional and open sense, a kind of objectivity in the intersubjective world. That is, for Merleau-Ponty, the historicity of the body helps us understand how gesture and movement take on social significance; his interest, at least in the *Phenomenology of Perception,* is primarily with the body as a cognitive and communicative site. Levinas's advance on (or at least modification of) Merleau-Ponty's account is to see the body's sense of obligation as bearing a history to which it could not have been witness. Exposure is revealed as the body suspended in diachronic time. Obligation comes from the Other: which is to say, from a time not my own. I register that time as other than my time *and at the same time bearing upon me as responsibility* in the embodied sensation, then affect, of being vulnerable and exposed to the Other's claim upon me. In that sense, could we not say that the body is both being and otherwise than being – a vulnerability 'reflected *within* the totality and history, *within* experience'? This means returning the decidedly non-worldly analysis of *Otherwise Than Being* to the crossing of the transcendental and empirical in *Totality and Infinity*, but there are plenty of legitimate motivations for such a return. As exposed, I am substantial. I commit violence on account of my being alone. My presence in the world is the usurpation of another's place, and so, from the moment of responsibility's occasion, I am irredeemably *in* being. But, as vulnerable to the Other, I also belong to a time – perhaps even times – that is otherwise than being. The denucleation of subjectivity is registered in embodiment; I feel my presence to the Other as *already having taken place*. I am late to myself, but my Self, my sense of 'I,' is constituted in part, perhaps firstly, by that Other, and therefore across that gap of temporal separation Levinas calls diachrony.

Does it make sense to call this moment of relation to self, which is a relation to the Other already late to the Other's formative constitution of my subjectivity, *only* singular, *so* austere, and *so* without context? For all of the theoretical sophistication of *Otherwise Than Being* – and it is a significantly more complicated book than *Totality and Infinity*, no doubt – I prefer the earlier work for much the same reason Derrida seems to prefer it. *Totality and Infinity* is so much more honest about the empirical moment of the ethical; the Other crosses the worldly, exposing himself or herself to violence while at the same time making that radical claim upon my life. There is also a crucial, even (as Levinas often says of Husserl's work) 'unsuspected' horizon when we return exposure and vulnerability to the transcendental and empirical chiasm: crossing the worldly opens up the question of history in a very different context. To be sure, it can prompt us to revisit Merleau-Ponty if our interest is in epistemology or in how gestures come to be perceived as ethical. But, most fundamentally, this strange chiasm puts the ethical suddenly in contact with history *concretely*. The Other comes to me, not just as a singular face who signifies without context, but as an embodied being whose appearance to me is irreducibly saturated with historical meaning. The traffic of the world is neither a betrayal nor a compromise of the Other's otherness; nor does the trace of worldliness drawn into the face-to-face detour obligation into those structures of the world that have so often vitiated responsibility. Rather, when we *notice* the color of the Other, so to speak, our responsibility takes on particular, specific characteristics that, without that worldliness, might have remained simply empty – even if profound – senses of ethical obligation. What would it mean to take notice of the Other's particularity, seeing the body of the Other a specific lived history, rather than a face from elsewhere? What if the elsewhere of the face was the immediacy of history and the world? And what would it mean to be seen by the Other – the optics of the ethical revisited – in my own particularity?

In a sense, this is a misplaced question. Levinas's account is always an attempt to draw us into the strange and unfamiliar sphere of the ethical, the face-to-face, and so a world, whether excessive or austere, that can never resemble the world. Levinas wants us to catch sight of that moment of disturbance in which our relation to self, world, and Other is transformed and transported into the relation of singularities. At the same time, if we hold Levinas to a phenomenological principle of evidence, then we are surely warranted in asking if the evidence of such non-worldly signification is sufficient for his claims. I would propose, quite straightforwardly, that this is where Levinas's work needs a significant and transformative rethinking – one inspired methodologically by both phenomenology (the question of evidence derived from the *Erlebnis* of responsibility) and the recovery of historical experience in embodied life – that site in which the empirical and the transcendental have the most peculiar and most productive intersection. One might say that this is simply a return to perception, but the saturation of the perceptual with history, violence, and pain – saturation to the point of the unbearable and themes such as Fanon's inferiority complex, Spivak's description of ciphering, and so on – tells us that perception is *also* a mode of carrying history into the encounter on the vulnerable and exposed body of Same and Other. Sure, there is the risk for forgetting singularity in perception. There is also the risk of forgetting historical responsibility and the transformation of ideas of difference in the emphatic concern with the singular. Embodiment is always precarious. Incarnate historiography widens and destabilizes the foundations of centered subjectivity even further. The real question, then, is how the language of alterity and our senses of obligation are transformed by the writing of history into the body, and so into the fleshiness of encounter. As a matter of method, posing this question – and thus letting it function as a frame of sorts for thinking through radical difference – is an imperative for Levinasian thinking.

And so, as a larger claim built on the preceding reflections, we can begin to see how returning Levinas to the historical dynamics of embodied life begins a decolonization of his thought. Incarnate historiography, or the erasure of it in the emphasis on singularity alone, shows the insistence on the context-neutral life of the face-to-face to be an expression of a certain privilege of thinking in the European context alone. The differences conceived in the European context play on notions of tradition, where Levinas can identify the Greek and the Judaic as forces at tension, yet also constitutive of a unity of the West and Western-ness. This *Western-ness* is perhaps the most important enigma here, an operative concept whose near-invisibility helps make sense of Levinas's normative claims about a *proper* encounter with the Other. The familiar stranger is the stranger in the singular. That familiarity conceals the historical weight of the encounter. Even the Western context is incarnate historiography, after all, for a common history is what makes the solely singular possible. If we occupy the same place, the same tradition, and so, at some level, the same *project*, then our obligations have the kind of sheer materiality we find in the language of singularity. Levinas's account of this singularity *might* resonate clearly, but it also might sound quite odd. If the project and identity of the West, from monotheism to liberal ideas of the political to certain philosophical rhetorics, are trafficked across borders, then surely those projects and identities take on new resonance, producing new obligations and new languages of difference. Historical experience suddenly becomes fraught. *Who* is the Same? *Who* is the Other? These companion questions, asked in the context of a reversed intentionality and incarnate historiography, thereby emerge as decisive for thinking about alterity. The question of decolonization places such questions at the center of thinking about difference and responsibility. Decolonization means taking that historical experience seriously and allowing it a disturbing, interruptive register – exposing unsuspected comforts with tradition and language, delimitations of the relation between perception, knowledge, and justice, and thus placing the Other and other Others at the heart of Levinasian thinking. A thinking without borders, perhaps. A Levinasian thinking thought otherwise, without question.

OPENING OF METHOD, OPENING TO THE OTHER

Incarnate historiography is opened by and opens to the Other. This opening is not simply a matter of methodological preference, but an imperative borne by the body itself. The motif of decolonization broadens the scope of the historical trail of responsibility without reassembling the memory and history of violence in narrative form. There is instead only the fracturing of the body's presence to the world in the vulnerability and exposure of the body to the wound of the Other's accusation. An accusation that, after breaking with the Eurocentrism of incarnate historiography, is now opened by and open to what crosses borders. Vulnerable and exposed to that crossing. Made an object by that gaze, in the accusative, such that the power of constitution and hegemony over meaning and identity is put in question, however precariously.

How, then, are we to think? How are we to form a relationship to this claim on the body and the implication of Levinasian thinking in a wider sense of responsibility? How does one work as an intellectual, especially an intellectual (like Levinas) concerned with the meaning of radical difference?

Those questions can only be answered in context, with particular analyses in view. Our studies of subalternity, hybridity, creolization, and rhizomatics in the following chapters begin answering those transitional questions – though they are questions one cannot cease asking, even after such studies. Still, a few words can be said about the imperative to radicalize Levinas's putatively radical notion of difference. For it is worth pausing for a moment to consider the obvious Levinasian question: why push the boundaries of singularity? Why thematize the problem of borders and postcolonial experience? Incarnate historiography breaks up the provincialism of the Levinasian text, but the transitional questions are methodological, tasking theory with a whole new collage of literacy and analysis. Why read these thinkers with Levinas? Why shift analysis toward historical experience and the worldly character of race and nation?

In these transitional questions, we can identify some of the relevance of Derrida's later work on reason and reasonableness. In particular, we might consider the meditation on Husserl's account of reason, history, and responsibility in the second essay of *Rogues*. Derrida's work in that text, like so much of his writing in the late 1980s and after, is saturated with Levinasian insights and sensibilities. In Derrida's distinction between three forms of reason – the traditional totalizing conception, the Husserlian recast of reason as teleological, and the reason of the unconditional – we begin to see the relation of reason and reasonableness to the Other, not as something to be seized upon, but as a recurrent interruption and self-interruption. Part of what makes *Rogues* such an interesting text is how Derrida rethinks reason, not simply as the target of deconstructive practice (though it is certainly that), but also that which seeks out interruption in its infinite task. Husserl's articulation of the infinite task of reason becomes, in Derrida's hands, deconstructive practice itself, where reason and reasonableness formulate and theorize *only* and *always* in order to be interrupted. Never in the interest of closure or domination. Reason is therefore a movement, ceaseless, toward the Other. An infinite task of *another* sort of reason. Perhaps, with our twist applied, this is the reason of Levinasian thinking motivated by incarnate historiography.

This is an interesting twist in Derrida's rethinking of reason for a simple reason: the problem of reason is immanent to the problem of method. The methodology of Levinasian thinking is less a matter of formal statement than a deformalization of orientation; opening to the Other is, in the first place, a sense of becoming subject in the being-opened-by-the-Other. At the same time, the insight into historiography and vulnerability reorients the question of orientation. The sedimentation of habits – that question of the unquestioned priority of Europe – still requires a certain Levinasian version of the phenomenological reduction: the tradition's prejudices and prerogatives must be put in brackets. This is no doubt part of the irony of our claims here, given that Levinas is such a profound critic of, yet also loyalist to, the European tradition – and yet in need of this further reduction of sorts. What is granted first value and priority as a matter of habit – the tradition's prerogative – is exposed to its Other, transnational historical experience, and is thereby revealed as insular and distorting in the reasonableness of *another* reduction. Whereas the phenomenological reduction in Husserl's hands neutralizes the gaze and cements a contemplative distance between the knowing ego and the horizon of the known and the knowable, the Levinasian reduction reverses the order of priority and activity, shifting from a participatory or even centered subjectivity toward the modalities of vulnerability and exposure as traces of an already passed trauma of ethical awakening. Reason, which on the Kantian and Husserlian model regulates the infinite adumbrations of the world, is reversed in Derrida's hands and given over to the horizon of the Other and the other Others for whom I find myself already responsible. The infinite task reverses, moving from the regulation of the infinite to the infinite's regulation of *us*. Reason, in the paradoxical formulation of *Rogues*, as the reasonableness of the unconditional – this reason seeks alterity rather than repelling or neutralizing it. For Husserl, this is the infinite striving of science. For Derrida, reversing the economy of regulation and moved by the Levinasian imperatives of the ethical, this is the infinite exposure to the Other and the other Others that stages, without cessation, the *mise en question* of sovereignty. Derrida writes:

> On both sides, then, whether it is a question of singularity or univer-sality, and each time both at once, *both* calculation *and* the incalcu-lable *are necessary*. This responsibility of reason, this experience that consists in keeping within reason, in being responsible for a reason of which we are the heirs, could be situated with only the greatest difficulty. Indeed I would situate it precisely within this greatest of difficulties or, rather, in truth, within the autoimmune aporia of this impossible transaction between the conditional and the uncon-ditional, calculation and the incalculable ... An always perilous transaction must thus invent, each time, in a singular situation, its own law and norm, that is, a maxim that welcomes each time the event to come.[23]

Reason, then, implicates itself in the most precarious project, but also, perhaps, the fine risk of justice. In this case, for the present study, this means a reason whose reasonableness and commitment to the unconditional – a sense of Other that does not impose conditions upon what *interrupts* (and so not what *appears*) as Other – takes the fine risk of transacting across borders. There is always beginning again or what Derrida here calls inventing a maxim that welcomes. And so with each movement against or across borders, Levinasian thinking is this very reasonableness or, simply, the unconditional: exposed, vulnerable, and yet also seeking what is *still* Other and puts in question *otherwise*. A reasonable relation, to be sure, for the reversal of intentionality is nothing if not an overturning of prior-ity and an incessant seeking of interruption. *Intentionality, by way of vulnerability and exposure, as the maxim that welcomes* – this is Levinasian thinking.

If it lies in the 'nature,' as it were, of reason dedicated to the Other to seek what is other than identity, and we couple that imperative and vitality to a decolonized sense of alterity, then the reflections in the following chapters should not be surprising. In fact, they are perhaps even necessary. The other of Levinasian thinking is the transnational. Indeed, the now long-standing developments of the language of difference in postcolonial theory *ought to* provoke us to think outside the boundaries prescribed by Levinas's conception of Europe. But more importantly, historical experience, borne as it is in and on the body, transmits affects of responsibility and justice that propel the body not only out of – then recurrent to – itself, but also across the second sense of diachrony in the historical experience of pain, fragility, and responsibility. To think this historical experience is both to engage Levinas's work directly, exploring the meaning of exposure and vulnerability, and at the same time to blow up the provincialism of his formulations. While this will require – and we have already seen a fair amount of that above – a significant bit of revision of Levinas's particular formulations and dictums, I want to claim here, in an appeal to the argument above, that such revision is authorized by Levinas's methodology. *The reason of the unconditional seeks the Other as a maxim of welcoming.* And so, in turning to Spivak, Bhabha, Glissant, and Marcos, what we will see is not so much an encounter between Levinas and a given thinker, but rather an engagement with Levinasian thinking about companion – perhaps at times agonistic and rival – languages of difference.

What does Levinas mean by difference? How does the problem of difference undercut the pretensions of epistemology, while at the same time offering not just negation, but also a certain positivity of resistance? With these questions in mind, let us turn to the problem of the Other and the subaltern.

Notes

1. For a full treatment of Levinas and Husserlian phenomenology, see John E. Drabinski, *Sensibility and Singularity: The Problem of Phenomenology in Levinas*. Albany: SUNY, 2001. In that work, I walk through the key phases of Levinas's work in order to show the constant presence of Husserl, intentionality, and the phenomenological method. In the present work, I rewrite what was in *Sensibility and Singularity* a story of differentiation as a story about opening and vulnerability, which, in turn, exposes Levinas's thinking to other senses of the outside. This was the orientation of Levinas's work from the outset, though he himself grew increasingly insular over the years.

2. Emmanuel Levinas, *Théorie de l'intuition dans la phénoménologie de Husserl*. Paris: Vrin, 2000, 215; *Theory of Intuition in Husserl's Phenomenology*, trans. André Orianne. Evanston: Northwestern University Press, 1995, 151.

3. Emmanuel Levinas, *Totalité et l'infini*. The Hague: Martinus Nijhoff, 1961, xvi; *Totality and Infinity*, trans. Alphonso Lingis. Pittsburgh: Duquesne University Press, 1969, 28.

4. See Drabinski, *Sensibility and Singularity*, Chapter 2, especially 67–81.

5. Levinas, *Totalité et l'infini*, 3/23.

6. Emmanuel Levinas, *Autrement qu'être ou au-delà de l'essence*. The Hague: Martinus Nijhoff, 1974, 230–1; *Otherwise Than Being or Beyond Essence*, trans. Alphonso Lingis. Dordrecht: Kluwer Academic, 1991, 183. Emphasis mine.

7. Ibid., 230/183.

8. Ibid., 96–7/76–7.
9. Levinas, *Totalité et l'infini*, 3/33.
10. Ibid., 4/34.
11. Levinas, *Autrement qu'être*, 48–9/38.
12. Ibid., 72/56.
13. Ibid., 96/76.
14. Ibid., 134/105–6.
15. Ibid., 138–9/109.
16. Ibid., 137/108.
17. Ibid., 101/80.
18. Ibid., 114n30/193n30.
19. Ibid., 98/77. Emphasis mine.
20. Ibid., 5/5.
21. Levinas, *Totalité et l'infini*, xii/23. Emphasis in the original.
22. Emmanuel Levinas, *Éthique et infini*. Paris: Fayard, 1982, 79–80; *Ethics and Infinity*, trans. Richard Cohen. Pittsburgh: Duquesne University Press, 1985, 85–6. Translation modified. Emphasis mine.
23. Jacques Derrida, *Rogues: Two Essays on Reason*, trans. Pascal-Anne Brault and Michael Naas. Stanford: Stanford University Press, 2005, 150–1.

CHAPTER 2

Epistemological Fracture

[T]he relationship with the other involves more than relationships with mystery.

Levinas, *Time and the Other*

It is the subaltern, the fisher and the grass-roots peasant, who
produces a constant interruption for the full *telos* of Reason
and capitalism, for those who have the patience to learn.

Spivak, 'Responsibility'

As we have seen, incarnate historiography names at one and the
same time the intimacy of the ethical and what extends the ethical
beyond the initial borders of encounter. Incarnation bears the history
of the encounter with the singular Other, but also bears the traces of
a long history of violence, pain, and grievance. This insight, generated from the horizon of Levinas's own thinking, requires a cluster
of important modifications to the letter of his thought. The intimacy
or closed infinity of for-the-Other subjectivity becomes, in a moment
of historical stretch, obligated beyond Levinas's own articulation
of the ethical. This is the consequence of taking the body seriously;
we are obligated in our bodies, in our skin, by an Other who speaks
embodied, even as the language of responsibility sends us into an
elsewhere of time and relation. Embodiment reminds us of the historical and political context of not just knowing and being, but the
encounters with obligation that explode any attempt to think obligation as a matter of principle, habit, or duty. What does it mean to
be a body, to be embodied? It means to inherit a history one did not
choose. Just as Levinas argues that I am chosen by the Other in the
relation of obligation, I am chosen by history and memory at the
moment I enter the world, in its asymmetry, as an embodied creature. Created twice: the accusing face of the Other *and* the accusing
faces of history. So it is to be and to know *after* responsibility. This
is the method, provisionally articulated, of a decolonized Levinasian

thinking – *decolonized* precisely because it begins a movement away from Europe as the center.

In theorizing the body, history, and political life more broadly, and then conceiving the same more deeply with the ethical appeal of alterity, Levinasian thinking begins a different kind of conversation about otherness and obligation that extends well beyond Levinas's own words. Up to this point, Levinas's work has for the most part been received, and not without justification, with a certain breathlessness about responsibility. 'The ethical' and 'the Other' function almost as mantras in much of the secondary literature; it pains me to write this observation because it would seem to trivialize what is most revolutionary and provocative about Levinasian thinking. And yet there is a kind of dogmatism in much of the literature on Levinas, especially as his work becomes more and more entrenched in contemporary theory and, as a result, communities of scholars rally to defend his work against critique. Even in Levinas's own texts, the utterance of the words would at times seem to carry the gravity of thinking.

The ethical is clearly Levinas's biggest and most important thought. His sense of obligation subverts the dominant ideas of ethics in the Western tradition, illuminating the unsuspected horizons of experience that operate *before* experience comes to consciousness. Work on Levinas tends to rotate around this axis, adding at times a dimension of politics or aesthetics, but always with the gravity of the ethical. The emphasis on the hyperbolic character of responsibility tends to occlude the other subversions of Levinasian thinking: anti- or ante-epistemology and a reconfiguration of subjectivity. Levinas is certainly concerned with retrieving what is left of responsibility after so much violence – not only in the twentieth century, but across the history of Europe. But he is also concerned with another, perhaps even larger, philosophical problem: what does it mean to think at the limits of knowledge? How can what is beyond the grasp of knowledge have an utterly transformative relation to the affective life of the subject?

The present chapter isolates this part of Levinasian thinking: the epistemic intervention and reconfiguration of knowledge claims. In that thinking, we see both what lies before and what works vigilantly against the economy of knowing. We see with Levinas how the desire to know, what Aristotle famously deemed our very nature, is an expression of an all-encompassing and deeply problematic ideology of conquest, control, and possession. Though Levinas does not employ the language of ideology, a fact that will occasion some hesitation below, the point of his critique of epistemology and the relation of knowing more broadly is that knowledge claims traffic in more than just a curiosity of mind. Rather, wider – indeed, even determinative – cultural and historical forces are at work, and thus we can see those forces reflected in how we conceive the logic and economy of knowledge. *If knowing is obsessed with totality, then we should see the reflection of totalitarianism as such in epistemology.* The Other breaks up this project with the signification of fragility and the imprint of a prior (pre-historic) passing through incarnate subjectivity. This means thinking difference in a way that fully breaks with the equivalence – so common across the putatively radical tradition – of sameness and transcendence, as well as eschewing *measure*, perhaps the subtlest instantiation of equivalence, as the core problem in conceiving difference. To put epistemology in question with the Other is to contest the reach of totalitarianism with the resistance of the ethical.

This characterization of the knowing gaze also puts Levinas's work into an unexpected, yet organic conversation with Gayatri Spivak's notion of the subaltern. For Spivak, as we will see, rendering the other as subaltern also creates a fracture in the economy of knowing. The idea of the subaltern fractures any number of epistemic structures and strategies that have sought to foreclose the possibility of radical difference; the subaltern's withdrawal from the gaze of the knowing subject contests measure at its source by disputing relationality itself. *If knowing is obsessed with totality, then we should see the reflection of imperialism as such in epistemology.* Yet, in the end, the subaltern is irreducibly deconstructive of and resistant to the imperial force of the desire to know. Whatever the immanent content claimed concerning the meaning of subaltern life and desire – by way of theories of the oppressed, native informants, and so on – there is not just an irreducible *moment* of transcendence, but a transcendence of the wholly Other. The desire to know and its aspiration to comprehend the other appears in Spivak's work not just as a matter of overstepped boundaries or overstated power, but also as an expression – both loud and quiet – of Western chauvinism and colonial exploitation. Even in so-called radical thinkers, she argues, we find this chauvinism and exploitation in the casual prescription of theoretical structures to lives outside of the historical and political *Lebenswelt* in which those structures are embedded. To put epistemology in question with the subaltern is to contest the reach of imperialism with the resistance of another kind of heterology.

So, some questions to begin.

The larger question here is simple: what is the Levinasian Other to Spivak's subaltern? Part of this difference concerning difference draws on the distinction between the totalitarian and the imperial – contesting internal violence and domination *or* the violence of empire. How does the ethical figure into this conversation? That is, given the fracture of the epistemic relation in both the Levinasian Other and the subaltern, what is the meaning of responsibility between the breaks? For knowledge is contested both as a resistance to and a withdrawal from the knowing gaze, and yet the moment of resistance and withdrawal is also the emergence of another kind of justice – or at least the call to another kind of response to the Other, her place in the scene of (non-)encounter, and so the meaning of the life of subjects. I want to argue toward this very claim, framed in terms of the structure of knowing and alterity as deconstructive resistance, concerning the entwining of epistemology and the ethical. We move toward this claim by tracking first how Spivak's subaltern exposes the Europeanness of Levinas's Other in moving the language of difference across borders. The postcolonial experience of alterity as resistance elevates the stakes; resistance contests and withdraws from knowledge in the context of empire, the violence of domination, and its long aftermath in the epistemic conditions of the postcolony. Shifting our attention to empire and its wake changes the terms of conceiving difference, seeing the vigilant work against empire's epistemic traces in the frame of another historical experience, another incarnate historiography. Yet such vigilant work, and this is the important second conceptual twist in this chapter, appeals, albeit obliquely, to something very much like the ethical. This conceptual conversation between Levinas and Spivak, however fraught and even forced, promises to generate an important chiasm of ethical power in fragility and the historically freighted moment of subaltern resistance. Another sort of incarnate historiography against totalitarianism and empire, locating resistance in the non-locatable, ever-fragile figure of the wholly Other.

PARRICIDAL SIGNIFICATIONS

From its first expressions of original analysis in the late 1930s and early 1940s, which sought to build on his early and somewhat derivative treatments of Husserl, Levinas's work is concerned with a perplexing epistemological problem. The problem is simple in terms of its aspiration, but, given the scope of Levinas's programmatic claim, the answer to the problem is immediately weighed down by the power of tradition and a cluster of aporias. Tradition dies hard. It dies hard, not because of ideology, but because the Western commitment to knowing and being as totality has long strategized against change, difference, and enigma – or what we could simply call *heterology*. That is, difference is not a new problem for the Occident. Quite the contrary, one can see through Levinas's writings (and, importantly, from many discourses written from the postcolonial margins) how the West in part, if not nearly in whole, defines itself in terms of the domination of alterity. Totality does not self-define; totality is only totality in the *conquest* of otherness, of difference, of what asserts *itself* (and so is not asserted) *as* unruly and anarchic. (Let us recall that it is this 'asserting itself,' so crucial for Levinas's conception of the Other, that promises a movement of Levinasian thinking across borders without the reiteration of colonial domination and usurpation.) The question, then, which will ultimately say more than Levinas intended: how are we to conceive otherness outside the model of the traditional Western account, where difference is simply an unresolved modality of identity? How is difference thinkable outside the measure of sameness? All, of course, in anticipation of how the subaltern disturbs this disturbing difference.

In his lectures from 1946 to 1947, published in revised form as *Time and the Other*, Levinas documents the terms of this language difference with particularly dramatic rhetorical force. *Time and the Other* is of course not the first Levinasian text to begin thinking about radical difference. Indeed, the series of short essays written during the Second World War, collected as *De l'existence à l'existant*, had already seized upon the deconstructive force of alterity, there in terms of the *il y a* and other haunting images at the margins of subjective life. We will return to those meditations in a bit, but for now it is important to see how *Time and the Other* marks the culmination of motifs, gathered immediately in the wake of Levinas's first writings on phenomenology, concerning the fate of difference. As at first a thought experiment and radicalization of philosophy's horizon, Levinas's early work studies various modalities of marginal experience in order to mark the boundary of the Western tradition. A boundary marked in order to set the terms of the excessive. What is thinkable within the tradition? And how can difference, as it appears in epistemology and ontology, exceed the reach of identification?

Levinas begins with the tradition: the great thinker, whose mastery is not so much manifest in the expression of transhistorical truths, but rather in the setting of a tradition's course. Who makes the tradition move in a particular direction? Given Levinas's penchant for broad (and largely accurate) claims about the Western philosophical tradition – namely, its commitment to totalization – isolating the great thinker is crucial. In that thinker, we find the boundary of thinking, and so also, albeit indirectly, the terms of thinking otherwise than the tradition and its operative concept of totality. Yet, in thinking against the submission of difference to identity, Levinas resists the easy critique of the West's two most prominent thinkers of identity: Plato and Descartes. Critiques of dualism and the compulsion toward disembodied, abstract conceptions of meaning were already familiar by the middle of the twentieth century. Those critiques, in many ways, define the long twentieth century in European philosophy. Whether one begins with the evocative existential critiques by Kierkegaard and Nietzsche or the phenomenological confrontations with the epistemological and ontological conundrums of the Western tradition in Husserl's and Heidegger's work, the long twentieth century is consistently a story of critique. The dualism of the ancients and moderns does not arise as simply the observation of the distance or play of interiority and exteriority – the kind of thing that led Adorno, despite his own objections to the tradition, to call the subject–object distinction 'real' (though also illusory).[1] Rather, the history of dualism expresses a compulsion, at the heart of Western thought, to expel what is excessive, ambiguous, and unassimilable. Plato's great innovation is this: a dualistic conception of the world that enables a self-justifying and vital hierarchy, marking the stable and unchanging with the title *true* and all other parts of experience with the title *illusion*. The compulsion to expel difference is invigorated by the introduction of hierarchy, an order of being and knowing that gives clear privilege to the knowable and dominates what lacks this privilege with the rights to truth against illusion. This compulsion is therefore complicit with – as the after-effect or a causal force, depending on one's assessment of the sociological dimension of philosophical thinking – various forms of political and cultural authoritarianism and manifests what Nietzsche calls the hatred of life. To wit: if philosophical thinking and life itself springs from a primordial chaos or anarchy, then the rendering of that chaos or anarchy as dualistic, hierarchical, and conceptually stable is fundamentally a negation of life. Philosophy, so the argument goes, must be reattuned to and disrupted by the primordiality of the human – a leap of faith, a dancing star, the living present, the transcendence of *Dasein* – in order to regain (or even claim for the first time) the intensity of perhaps unthinkable origins.

And yet this is not the direction Levinas takes. The path is well worn, to be sure, but Levinas's interest in the late 1930s and 1940s lies not in the problems of dualism in the Western tradition, but rather with the smothering monism that, he argues, functions as the ante-chamber of the sort of hatred of life Nietzsche and others so famously document. Part of Levinas's strategy turns on the fact that the already maligned Western tradition has important moments of interruption *from within*. Levinas makes the tradition more complex, which in his rereading means that the aspirations of that tradition are already exceeded, at key conceptual sites and moments of argumentation, by the texts themselves. Transcendence of tradition is immanent to tradition. Indeed, the standard-bearers for the authoritarian dualism problem – Plato and Descartes – actually interrupt the flow and privilege of transparency, distinctness, and presence to self with notions of the Good and the Infinite, two notions whose importance in *Republic* and *Meditations on First Philosophy* cannot be overstated. Immanent to tradition, indeed, but also immanent to the foundational arguments of foundational texts. So, for Levinas, these interruptions are not simply actings-out of long-repressed forces of transcendence. Rather, Plato and Descartes (to name two of the most visible examples) show how the unfathomable lies at the very foundation of the West's most desperate attempts to secure a closed system of thinking. And yet there is still the compulsion to dominate with what runs contrary to the Good and the Infinite. No matter the prominence of transcendence, the trajectory and animating spirit remain compelled to dominate difference with identity – witness Descartes's pained and rigorous descriptions of G-d's perfection. After the argument, infinity is no real threat to the systematicity of the system. In fact, in what is a strange and perplexing turn for Levinas, that which would seem to threaten the clarity and distinctness of the Cartesian system ends up securing the system at its foundation. Difference never gathers its full force. Closed systematicity always wins out. Whence this compulsion, and how can a critical intervention be made?

If Socrates, as per Nietzsche's reading, initiates the West's war on the body, then the inspiration for that war on difference and the anarchic may in fact lie in the pre-Socratic. The pre-Socratic thus becomes the arena for critical intervention against the totalitarianism

of Western epistemology, not in terms of particular concepts, but, for
Levinas, in terms of in-spirations and figures of thinking. In-spiration
is here understood in Levinas's sense: the breathing of spirit into subjectivity, which, in this case, is the production of a disposition toward
knowledge and knowledge claims from a spirit of thinking. *A way of
being that makes ways of knowing – never in uniformity, always in
the variety of tradition – possible.* Disposition frames what appears
as the condition of the knowable.

Time and the Other takes up this problem of disposition in two
polemical sites: the parricide of Parmenides and a critical intervention against the economy of light. Levinas's turn to Parmenides opens
up important complexity in his historical thinking. Levinas not only
attempts to address the in-spired foundations of what he sees as
problematic in Western philosophy, but also obliquely addresses the
Heideggerian problematic of fundamental ontology and the history
of Being. Both the trajectory of the West and Heidegger's reconfiguration of that trajectory turn on Parmenides' famous turn of phrase
in the poem's third fragment. Whatever the particulars of translation,
the Parmenidean claim is clear: thinking and being are the same.
There are many insights to be garnered from Parmenides' claim,
for what it says about the possession of both being by thinking (the
being of a thing or being itself is inseparable from the thinking of it)
and thinking by being (thinking is incapable of thinking change and
differentiation because it is being itself, which is an indivisible unity).

Against Parmenides, Levinas of course proposes the thought of
difference. It is not just that Levinas opposes Parmenides; he shares
that opposition with many seeking to escape the equivalence of
thought and being. Rather, by identifying the equivalence of thinking
and being as the dispositional trajectory of the West and the animating spirit that conceals the radicality of those ruptures and irruptions
in the history of philosophy (the Good, infinity, and so on), Levinas
isolates the widest sense of the West. And also the most precise and
focused. For the equivalence of thinking and being slackens the
demand on epistemology and ontology by displacing excess in one on
to the other, but always, in the end, reconciling difference with the
simple and simplifying thought of unity. Thinking and being are the
same, despite illusory appearances. *Time and the Other* attempts to
shift this metaphysics. Difference in *Time and the Other* is explicated
across theories of spatiality and time as a pluralism without unity,
which promises to fragment thinking *and* being without reconciliation. Without reconciliation, that is, in the sense of an anti-dialectical

theory of difference and alterity. Difference, for Levinas, produces a differentiation and fragmentation of thinking and being without a promise of return to a past or future unity. Pluralism *as such*. An Abrahamic pluralism. He writes:

> The dialectic these developments may contain is in any case not Hegelian. It is not a matter of traversing a series of contradictions, or of reconciling them while stopping History. On the contrary, it is toward a pluralism that does not merge into unity that I should like to make my way and, if this can be dared, break with Parmenides.[2]

Breaking with Parmenides aims at closing out Western philosophy's oldest family romance. This aim seeks to accomplish what the history of philosophy has failed to complete over two and a half millennia: a parricide of the West's father-philosopher. The father must be killed. Parricide is an imperative, not simply out of a polemical concern for marking new theoretical terrain, but because, at some very deep level, the paternal line has produced a murderous intellectual *and* political culture. Parmenides is the author of philosophy's history and its disposition. That history and disposition is a fully material practice in a political life that, left to itself, is always totalitarian. Without a doubt, Levinas's language of parricide has its rhetorical flourish. And there is also the urgency and gravity of rethinking the very terms of the West after two catastrophic wars and the genocide of Europe's Jewish population.

Now, though Levinas, in *Time and the Other*, will initially propose sexual difference as a counter to Parmenides' principle of identity, the primary site of resistance to the father of Western philosophy is subjectivity itself – a subject thought *as* transcendence. The question of the feminine is of course an enormously complex issue in Levinas's work; on my reading, which I can only here assert, the feminine figures subjectivity itself, with an enormously problematic trope, as pure transcendence. In thinking subjectivity *as* transcendence, and so not a subject who has occasional encounters with the Good and the Infinite, Levinas revisits the motif of his first forays into theorizing the subject in the early 1930s.[3] And this motif continues well into his later work. But this is also where theorizing gets complicated and is full of impossible aporias. Parmenides' refutation of absence and nothingness in his poem already locks the language of difference in tight conceptual quarters; to speak of transcendence would *seem* to make transcendence the *thought* of transcendence. Language draws the theme of speaking into the space of thought; to speak is to think, which functions in Parmenides' poem as the name of the Nothing that makes Nothing a Something – and so not nothingness. The name gathers what is Other and foreign, and thereby makes alterity thinkable, thus compatible with being. The *thought* of transcendence is therefore an immanent grasping of the *idea* or *unity* of the meaning of transcendence, rather than a transcendence that, in its fleeing of presence and the moment, would threaten to dismantle space, time, and the pretensions of subjectivity. The rhetorical seal on this claims lies in the evocation of two paths at the beginning of Parmenides' poem. The path of the true, of course, sidesteps such threats with the promise and power of the identification of thinking and being. The other path, the path of difference, change, and nothingness, is illusory – or, put more crudely, just plain bad thinking.

The task for Levinas is set out clearly by Parmenides' delimitation of the philosophical field. There can be no difference in thinking and being, and the attempt to think difference within the language of thinking and being is the path of illusion. On this point, Parmenides is irrefutable; Levinas does not dispute his claim. So long as discussion of difference is located in thought and being, the compulsion toward totality will eclipse whatever sense of alterity one proposes. For Levinas, although the subject *is* transcendence, we cannot locate transcendence *inside* the subject; Parmenides warns us against that path, so another approach is needed. 'To take up the existing in the existent,' Levinas writes, 'is to enclose it within unity and to let Parmenides escape every parricide his descendants would be temped to commit against him.'[4] Enclosure, unity, parricide – in that sequence of notions, Levinas outlines what it means to fracture epistemology. Knowledge sets everything in place or, depending on the order of priority, is already set in place by the oneness and unity of being. Against this setting in place, parricidal desire is tasked with thinking transcendence as dislocation, where the activity of dislocating implicates an ante- and anti-location. Subjectivity returns to itself; there is the moment of reflexivity, of lived experience, which means that returning to self must be structured *before the return* as an irreducible difference. Otherwise, dialectical thinking takes hold and we are sent back to the equivalence of thinking and being. *Parricide is pure heterology without the recurrence of the logos.*[5] To be a subject is to be in the site of transcendence *before* existence takes up a particular location, and therefore *to be* in a manner quite emphatically *against* locality. *Toward a pluralism that does not merge into unity* – there is no location in a pure heterology. No unity. Just the plurality of difference without reconciliation, yet still with subjectivity – an identity against identity, fractured and broken apart. There is still a name – 'subjectivity' – even where there is no location. Already in 1946–7, Levinas has a theory of identity before consciousness, a dephasing of space and time that comes to full fruition in *Otherwise Than Being*.

As a crucial item to vanquish, the parricide of Parmenides carries with it one of the West's signature figures in the theory knowledge: light. Light is not simply a literary flourish in philosophical discourse. Knowledge illuminates being and being illuminates knowledge. The figure of light makes equivalence possible without the concealing of one by the other, for concealing is only possible without the economy of light (in which case, thinking dominates being or vice versa). Or perhaps concealment is always just a variation of light; what is concealed is only concealed because sufficient and even expected illumination does not obtain. But perhaps it can obtain with patience and vigilance. Thinking can fail to conceive being or to see it as a whole, but perhaps that is simply a postponement or privation of light. In this sense, light determines the meaning of concealment and unknowing even (perhaps especially) in its negation. It is revealing, then, that in a simple turn of phrase, so much of the Western tradition is revealed in its commitment to complete visibility. In its luminosity, bringing to visibility everything that might hide from knowing's gaze, light collapses or dialectically resolves what is simply an initial and largely illusory spatial distinction between self and world, consciousness and the other, and the psyche and the material world. The otherness or difference of the world is drenched in light, and this illumination makes difference the problem to be overcome, rather than the irreducible condition of subjectivity. In *Time and the Other*, Levinas writes that

> [t]he interval of space given by light is instantaneously absorbed by light. Light is that through which something is other than myself, but already as if it came from me. The illuminated object is something one encounters, but from the very fact that it is illuminated one encounters it as if it came from us. It does not have a fundamental strangeness. Its transcendence is wrapped in immanence.[6]

As if it came from me. With the figure of light and its location, Levinas sees the anchoring of epistemology in the knowing subject. The knowing subject is not just subject to light, but, in the illuminated relation to otherness or difference, the subject comes to see itself as the source of all meaning. *An anchor*. With that anchor, the knowing subject couples light to the Parmenidean prerogative. If knowing and being are the same for Parmenides, then securing knowing as light and being as illuminated in the subject who knows keeps transcendence under control. The wildness of being, as Merleau-Ponty will call it just a decade or so after *Time and the Other*, is tamed by subjectivity-as-knowing-consciousness. The very meaning of the being of difference (externality, materiality, and so on) is brought to light and is therefore dependent upon the source of that light: consciousness, the human.

Light, then, is more than simply a figure of total knowledge, comprehension, and insight. Light, we might say, is the *mood* of the Western tradition. If we take Heidegger's long meditation on *Befindlichkeit* in *Being and Time* seriously, then we can see how light determines the meaning of what appears as possible and necessary. It is how we find ourselves, already and without choice or will or distance from being-in-mood. Relationality is impossible without *Befindlichkeit*. In that sense, with all due caveats, we can say that mood *elects us*. For Heidegger, mood is how we find ourselves in the *world*, but with Levinas we can perhaps rewrite that claim and say that light is how we find ourselves *in tradition*. To take up the tradition is to say yes to filiations, to the paternal line, and thus to the figure of light that makes Parmenides' original claim work. Levinas's critique of light in the 1940s begins an important, indeed life-long, *counter-move* to Western philosophy's animating epistemological prerogative. Levinas enters into the tradition in order to critique it, thinking from within the economy of light and the scope and power of Parmenides' equivalence in order to posit a plurality outside unity. And this is a critique located in the dislocating power of the encounter with difference. In that sense, Levinas's criticisms in *Time and the Other* and after offer philosophy an elaborate counter-factual, an example or series of examples whose sheer affective force demands another account of the transmission of sense. As well, and this is probably the most provocative move in his work, Levinas sees the epistemological prerogative of the West as an expression of a prior and more expansive set of ideas whose cultural and political force drags across history with eliminationist violence. This cultural and political force is one of the signatures of Europe, so the stakes of contesting light and committing parricide against Parmenides could not be higher.

Whatever the innovations of *Time and the Other,* the motivating insights of that text only receive their full expression (and therefore their full revolutionary energy) with the 1961 publication of *Totality and Infinity*.

The explosive event of *Totality and Infinity* is the face-to-face. The event, this peculiar encounter and reconfiguration of relationality, knowing, and being, brings the thought of plurality without unity to the problem of signification. The turn to signification is utterly crucial. Positing plurality as an abstraction is hardly sufficient; Levinas's method is from the outset concerned with concretion and deformalization. Yet, running a theory of plurality through concrete, lived experience has its own risks; experience would *seem* to locate the event in the existent – the very location, that enclosed unity, against which Levinas warns in *Time and the Other*. The face, however, placed in embodied relation to the subject in the face-to-face, signifies *without enclosure,* and so keeps open the possibility of a plurality that comes to presence without being located in thought and illuminated by the knowing gaze or being. So, what does Levinas mean by the face? How does the face signify? And, perhaps most crucially, how does the veracity of that signification draw on the critical distance Levinas has taken from Parmenides and the epistemo-ideology of light?

With the notion of face, Levinas is presented with a profound enigma. The enigma lies in the difficult, if not impossible, task of wresting a sense of the Other away from dominant models of describing the encounter with otherness; though Levinas's signature idea is 'the Other,' French philosophy had already been interrogating the idea with great rigor since Sartre's early writing on the gaze, if not well before. Levinas's innovation in *Totality and Infinity* is his effort to cleave the signification of the Other from subjectivity without slipping back into the Cartesianism of a Sartre or monism of a Merleau-Ponty, while at the same time keeping that otherness internal to the meaning of subjectivity. Themes of interruption, surprise, elemental life, desire, and other forms of affective life dominate *Totality and Infinity* as sort of preparatory studies and *mise en scène* for the face, but that preparation or staging is intended to draw our attention to what cannot be in any sense *seen* or *known*. The stage brings to presence only in order to underscore the difference between what is sustained or made sense of by the staging and what signifies as difference without identification. Staging, after all, folds the meaning of what sustains signification into what is signified, the very sort of reconciliation of difference that reiterates the Parmenidean claim and reintroduces light to the economy of meaning. The parricidal project, rewritten in *Totality and Infinity* under the rubric of signification, is, to put it plainly, a matter of elaborating the structure of what Levinas calls 'signification without context.'[7] Signification – the *without context* in this simple phrasing already says everything. The Other as radically other is uprooted from the sorts of conceptual and comparative schemata that typically underpin notions of human alterity. Therefore, signification cannot appeal outside of itself, whether that 'outside' be a social or historical habit, political construction, or, most importantly, an epistemological apparatus. Against these interpretations and (often) constructions of otherness, Levinas proposes the affective life of the decentered, then interrupted subject of elemental, then ethical life.

Signification and the face cross complex conceptual boundaries. Ostensibly, the face, as the face of the *Other*, is a straightforward difference; I cannot know the interior life of another person. At the same time, the face has force and meaning only in so far as the interiority of *my* subjectivity is transformed by the ethical encounter. Thus, the double meaning of the face is to be both *located outside* the subject and affectively *relocated inside* subjectivity in moral consciousness. The delinking of the Other from schemata of knowing and being is simultaneous with the relinking of subjectivity in the affective life of obligation, which underscores Levinas's concern with the singularity of signification and its register. Shifting from context to signification without context reminds us of Levinas's primary foil: Husserl's famous treatment of the alter ego in the fifth of his *Cartesian Meditations*. Husserl's late work is important for Levinas's development for a couple of reasons. First, the *Cartesian Meditations* are based on a series of lectures Husserl gave at the Sorbonne in 1931, attended by Levinas and other important French intellectuals. Developing from those lectures, Husserl's subsequently drafted *Cartesian Meditations* was then translated from the German by Levinas and his collaborator Gabrielle Peiffer. But the importance of those lectures, and later Husserl's short book of five meditations, is not merely an occasion for new vocabulary or straightforward influence. Rather, and more deeply, Levinas's account of the face has to stake out its distance from the structure of encounter in Husserl's description precisely because Husserl sets out the terms of describing the Other so clearly. This distance is in many ways a reiteration of the parricidal wish in *Time and the Other*, re-rendered in the twentieth century as a confrontation with Husserl.

Husserl's problematic is fairly uncomplicated. In pursuit of an

account of human alterity (emphasis here on *human*), Husserl asks
a simple question: how can we account for the otherness of the
other subject while at the same time establishing sufficient symmetry
for the intersubjective constitution of objectivity and the objective,
shared world? That is, Husserl sets himself the task of describing the alterity of the Other *and* a sense of sameness. The *human*
of human alterity is the critical, operative term here, for, with the
Other-as-another-human, Husserl can assert the commonality of
the epistemic orientation. We are both *knowers*, and that knowing
disposition comprises not only the being of the subject, but also, in
a fine Parmenidean twist, the being of the world, being as such. At
the same time, the Other and the I are not the same. The Other withdraws in a unique manner from presence, showing itself while also
concealing something essential, not accidental. The intersubjective
field of relations is comprised of a peculiar intertwining of identity
and difference. The body proves decisive in Husserl's analysis of this
intertwining. The Other's body serves as an important epistemological limit in terms of both kind and space. I cannot see the interiority
of the Other, something that hides behind the flesh while at the same
time animating movement, gesture, and expression. In terms of *kind*,
the otherness of the Other – that distinctive *subjective* character of
the Other – is inaccessible to perception, and so does not offer itself
as a presentation to be later re-presented to consciousness. As well,
the body marks a spatial gap between subjectivities – I am *here*, the
Other is *there*. Spatial distance sets limits to knowledge; representation, the rendering of what is exterior as immanent to consciousness,
is impossible. The gap between subjects, whether that is the ego–
body distinction or the occupation of space, changes the character of
knowing the Other.

And yet the body is a *lived* body (*Leib*). The *animated* body
tempers the absolute epistemological gap first suggested by the
spatial separation of the I and the Other. In gesture and expression,
the Other, for Husserl, demonstrates an interest and knowing relation to the world. The Other moves, manipulates, declares, and in
so doing occupies a fundamentally *human* space with me. *With me.*
The relation to the Other in the *V. Cartesian Meditation* is therefore
not a relation of singularities. Rather, it is a relation between mobile,
seeking bodies whose gestures and language(s) describe – and therefore constitute – one and the same world. Being and knowing are
the same, not because in knowing I access the being of the world
or in being I am a knower, but because the intersubjective project

of knowledge as such constitutes the meaning (*Sinn*) of the being of the world. This is Husserl's decisive, if subtle, phenomenological nuance. In that nuance, intersubjectivity reiterates the Parmenidean prerogative within the immanence of lived experience.

So, when Levinas rewrites the encounter with the Other in the name of singularities against intersubjectivity, he revisits parricide in the phenomenological field. I am already in relation with the Other – this is the enduring insight of intentionality. What does incarnate historiography tell us about this intentionality? What horizons of relationality exceed the Husserlian account of intersubjectivity?

Or, to put it more directly, perhaps, how is a relation to the Other possible that does not traffic in the conventions of epistemology? Is it possible to know the Other *otherwise*? Levinas's response to Husserl is perhaps best glimpsed in the context of the discussion of expression in *Totality and Infinity*. In that discussion, Levinas is able to account for what Husserl finds so compelling and convincing about the experience of alterity: the unicity of embodied expression and the absence that saturates the presence of the lived body. For, in that unicity and saturation, Husserl is already flirting with radical difference. The limit point in Husserl's analysis lies of course in his commitment to objectivity as the endgame of the encounter with alterity. Levinas shows us how the ethical changes the terms of this encounter by eschewing objectivity and pursuing the language of singularity with rigor and without compromise. Signification in the ethical register – the face-to-face – withdraws the signified from the sign *without return*. In fact, not only *without return,* but without ever having been in the sign to begin with, even as the sign is sent in the face to face. Levinas writes:

> The signifier, he who gives a sign, is not signified. It is necessary to have already been in the society of signifiers for the sign to be able to appear as a sign. Hence the signifier must present himself before every sign, by himself – present a face.[8]

The Other signifies, but with parricidal effects on subjectivity. At the close of Section II of *Totality and Infinity*, Levinas makes it clear how the preceding meditations on signification and alterity alter the status and function of the sign of the Other, *then* the sign of the Other in me. The sign in me, my coming to consciousness as a moral creature, locates the meaning of that relation to signification in the outside. In that location, which properly speaking is really a dislocation, the constitution of the sense of otherness is irreversibly altered. We therefore ought to hear the echo of Husserl when Levinas writes in *Totality and Infinity*:

> To return to exterior being, to being in the univocal sense, the sense that hides no other sense, is to enter into the straightforwardness of the face to face. This is not a play of mirrors but my responsibility, that is, an existence already obligation. *It places at the center of gravitation of a being outside of that being.* The surpassing of phenomenal or inward existence does not consist of receiving the recognition of the Other, but in offering him one's being. To be in oneself is to express oneself, that is, already to serve the Other. The ground of expression is goodness. To be *kath auto* is to be good.[9]

Being is disrupted in the very same horizon in which Husserl sees the securing of being in intersubjectivity. Expression and gesture are placed in the horizon of goodness, which here instantiates the ethical relation of separation. Separation, a Husserlian theme in its spatial articulation through and through, is reconfigured in the appeal to a *center of gravitation*. Gravitation accomplishes two things. First, it locates the center in the absolute margin; Levinas will write that 'my existence' has its origins in 'the presence in me of the idea of Infinity.'[10] Second, it pulls apart any pretension to unity *as a matter of constitutive force and meaning*. The outside makes being possible, but does not enter into being. If the face-to-face accomplishes this, then the parricide of Parmenides is accomplished. And knowing – *ethical knowing* – takes the place of the gaze of the totalitarian subject, giving way to a subject thought in the accusative, liberating the Other from being and knowing in one gravitational strike against totality. Expression of the Other, Levinas writes, 'is of itself presence of a face, and hence appeal and teaching, *entry into relation* with me – the ethical relation.'[11]

The ethical as relation without knowing, an informing of obligation without the occluding power of being. Another kind of epistemology, perhaps. A parricidal signification.

But how radical is this notion of difference? To be sure, Levinas makes an important intervention against the Parmenidean eclipse of alterity by identifying an excessive horizon in the face-to-face relation, an intervention made so much more potent in the gravitational claim on presence to self. *The Other draws subjectivity outside being.* This drawing outside being is enacted in the expressive function of the sign as both the signature of the Other and the registration of that signature in the subject addressed in the face-to-face. Levinas's insistence is always on that excessive saying – later, the actual technical term *Saying* (*le Dire*) – that unravels what is gathered to the sign. '[I]t belongs to the very essence of language,' Levinas writes, '. . . in unsaying the said, in attempting to restate without ceremonies what has already been ill understood in the inevitable ceremonial in which the said delights.'[12] But the insight into incarnate historiography ought to raise a bit of suspicion. In particular, Levinas's contestation of light with parricidal signification understands what comes before the sign in a neutral phenomenological field; singularity is absolute. As we have seen in the reflections above on nation and identity, this particular and specific delineation of the phenomenological field presupposes a sense of alterity uninformed by, even prior to, questions of nation and race. What if the nation and transnational context were to inform signification and the absence that unravels the sign? How would the peculiar alternative epistemology of the Levinasian Other, fractured as a form of knowing oneself as interrupted and in relation to the unknowable, be transformed by this shift in context? Is it possible that nation and race inform the *mise en scène* of the face, such that Levinas is able to imagine a pure singularity? If so, then what happens to this anti- and ante-economy when a different difference initiates the face-to-face encounter? What if the gap Levinas notes between the signifier and signification is doubled in its refusal to come to presence by a refusal to signify even the desire for expression? Herein lies the important nuance of difference in Spivak's notion of the subaltern.

THE OTHER, THE OTHER OTHER, AND THE SUBALTERN

Among so many other things, Spivak's famous essay 'Can the Subaltern Speak?' functions as a deconstructive critique of putatively radical European theory, giving a systematic and still provocative account of how epistemologies of difference – those ways of claiming to organize, economize, and deploy alterity against systems of oppression – run up against their limit in the notion of the subaltern. In the horizon of Levinas's parricide of Parmenides in the critique of light, it is worth asking to what extent something of a European provincialism survives that parricidal act. This is not simply to reiterate Derrida's critique of Levinas, which turned (not unexpectedly, for those familiar with Derridean strategies) on the dependence of Levinas's text on the generalizing economy of the sign in the language of alterity. Rather, this rerouting attends to a very similar, very

Derridean question of language and the worldly, but transformed by Spivak through problems of national difference under and after colonialism. Levinas's account of the identifying gaze disrupted by radical difference is at once a mimic of the colonial gaze that formulates difference in relation to identity and a blanched version of the same. *Blanched* in the sense that something about the texture of race and nation in the identifying gaze is lost in Levinas's suspension of the worldly character of encounter: the literal and figurative loss of color. But that just gets the gaze wrong and we can begin this transition to Spivak with an assertion: Levinas's account of difference is only possible with the operative concept of Europe in place. Such provincialism, in addition to eclipsing the implication of Europe in a wider sense of moral and political identity, compromises the radicality of Levinasian thinking about difference by putting historical experience in brackets – while still functioning within the historical experience of Europe as an internal structural item. The historical experience of colonialism and its moment *after* (the postcolonial) therefore *must* transform much of how we understand signification, encounter, and the withdrawal from presence. Given that such an understanding is Levinas's prerogative *as such*, rather than as a specific case (Levinas is giving us a generalized theory of difference, not a regional phenomenology of a particular experience), Spivak's account of the subaltern withdrawal from presence poses an immanent problem for Levinasian thinking. The nuance of nation in Spivak, which alters the historical experience that generates incarnate historiography, repeats Levinas's parricidal work with a suspicion toward both theories of light, knowing, and being *and* the critical interventions against those theories in the name of difference. It is this second strategy in Spivak's work that poses so many questions to Levinas's account: *does a theory of difference have to attempt a parricide of the Levinasian text?*

'Can the Subaltern Speak?' and its many companion pieces, including the reformulation of so many of those themes in *Critique of Postcolonial Reason*, document the phases of Spivak's deconstruction of the language and epistemology of difference with a view toward the final, and indeed total, break with signification. In that break, which in her hands is absolute, Spivak arrives at a certain threshold between Levinas's notion of trace and the radical absence of the subaltern. With radical difference as the shared philosophical problematic, a series of questions arise. How does the transnational context of Spivak's account of alterity shift the language of otherness? Does that shift mark a deepening of the Levinasian account of the epistemological fracture? Or does the introduction of cultural difference, colonial history, and all of the attendant forms of violence open up a new sense of otherness – the *other* other – that opens new wounds of vulnerability and exposure? In short, what if we think radical difference against epistemologies of sameness *without* blanching the otherness of the Other?

The key conceptual question, then: what is the meaning and significance of Spivak's notion of the subaltern?

In a short retrospective piece, Spivak remarks that 'Can the Subaltern Speak?' seems to have been a new beginning in her work that parallels, as a readerly-theorist companion, 'a turning of Derrida toward politics' and that this beginning, alongside Derrida's turn, looks 'homeward' in order to 'make a change.'[13] The parallel with Derrida is especially interesting in our context here, for in his turn toward politics, Derrida returns to so much of the force of Levinas's account of the ethical. Whatever his early hesitations about Levinas's work, the later Derrida is able to retrieve the ethical as an anarchic, but fundamentally *just*, effort against the epistemological, aesthetic, and political reach of logocentrism. I am thinking in particular of the function of justice in relation to law, where the groundless, infinitely demanding, or even *voiceless* call of the Other denucleates law's pretension to universality. The singular interrupts the universal, to put it rather plainly and blandly, and yet the universal constantly intervenes against the singular as a sort of irreducible violence – the assertion of the universal is an (unavoidable) repetition of the conditions for interruption. In Derrida's work, this produces a variety of deconstructive political articulations: hauntology, friendship, reason, and so on. Throughout all of these articulations, the ethical and political pull of what is the other of language and meaning plays the crucial critical role of marking the limits to conceptual schemata. The Other functions as the limit site of any knowing or being or acting.

For Spivak, the function of the conceptual scheme goes by another name: *essentialism*. Now, to be sure, essentialism is itself a fraught term in Spivak's work, much as the universal is conflicted in the work of the later Derrida. On the face of it, one cannot speak without essentializing, without making claims about identity, so essentialism might be said to be an unavoidable violence. This is one of the crucial and formative insights Spivak garners from Derrida's work on language and the sign, and it underwrites much of what she calls her 'deconstructive critical practice,' which works within this unavoidable violence, yet refuses the totalizing *threat* of violence such an insight might suggest. To speak is to transgress singularity or otherness with the very meaning of speaking; language overlays the signified with an apparatus of signifier, enacting a kind of irreducible violence. Critique proceeds from the space of this intervention, such that every critique is a kind of counter-intervention or insurgency. Spivak notes this in an interview:

> In deconstructive critical practice, you have to be aware that you are going to essentialize anyway. So then strategically you can look at essentialisms, not as descriptions of the way things are, but as something that one must adopt to produce a critique of anything.[14]

We can see how this situates Spivak's work in the same formal, conceptual space as that of Levinas; the sign is necessary for Levinas, but only as an occasion for excess and the counter-violence of exceeding the given. This is the enigma of expression – the peculiar logic of withdrawal *and* relation – and the precise sense in which Levinas's philosophical language is always a fine risk. For Spivak, too, the necessity of essentialism, its perhaps terrifying irreducibility, makes critical work, by definition, a fraught practice. Spivak's remark suggests a number of paths for that practice, but what is key for us here is how she draws the epistemological distance between essentializing claims and what those claims might hope to decide. This is not merely an observation of the difference between the sign and the signified – a difference so easily overcome in the dialectical work of sense or meaning. Against dialectic, the undecidable functions, in its refusal to function, outside the economy of sign and signified. The undecidable only enters the sign–signified economy in order to disturb or haunt it by an absolute resistance (is Spivak's description of *sati* not ultimately haunting?), and thus never to *give* or *express* what has yet to come to expression. That is, and this is crucial for understanding her claim, Spivak does not mark epistemological distance in order to posit a reality outside language that would somehow take up special privileges in an ontological economy or metaphysics. Rather, instead, she marks epistemological distance in order to see the precarious, violent character of any claim whatsoever. In Spivak's words, she wants to avoid translating 'all of the elements within [a] larger structure into a kind of continuous configuration which the knowing subject can control.'[15] The control of or by the knowing subject is the persistent and confounding danger of any theoretical approach that anchors itself in an authorial subject.

Spivak's critique of the knowing subject is itself radical. Epistemological distance begins at home – in every sense. Indeed, as Spivak notes elsewhere, one cannot fully grasp even one's own sense of space or place. The ungraspable has a history, and so calls for a critical analysis and deconstructive practice, and yet the ungraspable is not defined by its aspiration to be grasped. There is no economy of light in Spivak's notion of difference; as in Levinas, the radical character of difference lies in its being uprooted from all of our habits of conceiving difference in relation to the measure of identity – *difference and the ungraspable as the privation of identity and the knowable.* Thus, it is not a question of properly clearing the conceptual or linguistic field in order to hear the Other's voice. The Other is not silenced by an improperly calibrated relation of knowing or being – the knowing subject – to what *might be* or *ought to be* known. Difference is absolute, first. And wholly intimate. The epistemological gap is part of the very meaning of home. She notes:

> No one can quite articulate the space she herself inhabits. My attempt has been to describe this relatively ungraspable space in terms of what might be its history. I'm always uneasy if I'm asked to speak for my space – it's the thing that seems to be most problematic, and something that one really only learns from other people ... If one has to define oneself irreducible, it must be in minimal terms.[16]

The problem of difference is intimate to one's own sense of space in the world; we learn space, not from reflection, but from the encounter. The effect and affect of otherness is therefore located in the very meaning of space and place, neither of which is authored by a subject, but which instead are entwined with history in such a way that the entwinement cannot be explicated by the author, the subject, or the conceptual apparatus brought to bear from elsewhere in explanation. The intrigue of the interhuman is here transformed by Spivak through the encounter with history.

The break with authorial authority is taken one step further. Spivak's critical deconstruction of space and place *might* suggest something akin to a strategy of counter-narration, the sort of storytelling that disrupts the continuity of the state, regimes of knowledge, and so on. That is, we might think of the intrigue of the interhuman as a revolutionary and agonistic space in which we document the struggle for authorship over dominant discourses or cultural-national narratives. But Spivak is careful to make the important distinction between the resistance of the Other produced on the margins of discourse (always internal, always center) and the Other whose alterity is determined from the outset by a lack of contact with narrative (her sense of subalternity). The nuance lies in how agonism over narrative – the logic of counter-narrative as a form of resistance – is itself a meta-narrative. To demand speaking, to insist that there is and will be a communicative practice in agonistic cultural and political space, is already to place storytelling and the author at the heart of the interhuman. And yet, if difference is thought radically, without recourse to shared spaces and common (or common *enough*) languages for narrative and counter-narrative, then we have to consider the possibility of a wholly accomplished withdrawal from presence *without narrative*. This would begin to mark some distance from Levinas from within one and the same epistemological gap. In 'Practical Politics of the Open End,' an interview conducted just after the publication 'Can the Subaltern Speak?,' Spivak makes this distinction and its consequences clear. She writes:

> If in that context and in de-colonized space, one looks at the genuinely disenfranchised who never had access to these grand narratives anyway, as a teacher one thinks of a pedagogy on a very generally post-structuralist model: without destroying these narratives, making all of their structures one's own structures, nevertheless, one takes a distance from them and shows what incredible and necessary crimes are attendant upon them: not just aberrations but necessary supplements. One does not, then, produce some kind of legitimizing counter-narrative of nativist continuity. And within this frame, the one most consistently exiled from episteme is the disenfranchised woman, the figure I have called the 'gendered subaltern.' Her continuing heterogeneity, her continuing subalternization and loneliness, have defined the subaltern subject for me.[17]

Continuing – with that qualifier, Spivak sets the question of difference outside the recuperable by assigning difference a future. Not a future in which a promised and somehow radically heterogeneous community comes to resolve the various gaps in presence, but instead a future in which the subaltern is thought in the sense of becoming. The gendered subaltern becomes subaltern; subalternization defines the subaltern as subaltern. Such a definition already poses a critical problem for the Levinasian claim to think difference radically, in so far as, for Levinas, difference is manifest in the excessiveness of signification *kath auto*, whereas Spivak's subaltern is already outside the conflicted work of signification.

As well, Spivak's evocation of post-structuralism here is instructive and, as expected, there is important complexity to her use of the term. To be sure, the insistence upon difference is what links her interest in the subaltern to various post-structuralist versions of the (putatively) same. At the same time, part of what makes the 'Can the Subaltern Speak?' essay so compelling is the conceptually subtle, yet rhetorically sharp-tongued difference in Spivak's notion of difference. From this particular passage above, though, we catch sight of the motifs of that make difference different – here, largely by way of negation. It is not a matter of nativism, which would aspire to ground the idea of counter-narration. It is not simply a matter of offering another story of cultural and political life. It is not a strategic political question. It is rather difference as difference, outside the economy of struggle, counter-narrative, and action. That is, it is an epistemological question: how does the loneliness of the subaltern, her *continuing heterogeneity*, upend, not just one approach to knowing, but the very idea of knowledge itself? Nativist continuity *would* promise difference in the form of resistance to dominant cultural and political narratives, but, and this is crucial, such difference turns on the claim to a prior identity. How radical is this nativist continuity, in terms of generating a language of difference? Deconstructive critique, in Spivak's practice of it, raises suspicions precisely because, as noted above, every story of continuity is, as a *necessary supplement*, a form of violence. Necessary crimes. The assertion of a retrieved identity as the basis of a sense of alterity mixes the radical with the conservative (for every retrieval is conservation), which, in turn, commits the very kind of violence the language of difference wants to contest. A necessary violence – that supplement which is always a crime against difference. Continuing heterogeneity must be thought otherwise.

The question, then: how does Spivak legitimate such a radical claim? The claim is lodged within the matter of postcolony life, the matter of how one is to understand the epistemology, politics, and aesthetics of life after colonialism. And with her refusal to appeal to a suppressed or repressed native identity as the foundation of a counter-narrative, Spivak proceeds without the security or comfort of atavism. Were we to rewrite the face-to-face at this moment in the analysis, we already have a very different formal proposal: the Other who faces me does not, in some sense, face me. There is no signification, no delight of the said or communication that is subsequently unraveled (or seen to have been already unraveled). There is instead a cipher *as such*, a less than zero in the narrative and conceptual schema, that we cannot hear – expression and its unraveling are already an undoing. The historical experience of colonialism and its aftermath registers here as an epistemological problem. In the approach, in the very gesture of knowledge, the knowing subject is implicated in a history of violence *even as the subject seeks to understand the Other as Other*. It is not enough to be interested in difference. In fact, interest is perhaps what is most problematic.

In much the same register as Levinas, then, though initially without the language of the ethical, Spivak works against the universalizing language of self-styled radical French philosophy with the notion of subalternity. The subaltern is, of course, originally a military term that designates relations of power and subordination. For Antonio Gramsci, from whom Spivak draws the term, the subaltern functions as a stand-in of sorts for proletariat. (He most likely used the term under censorship, masking the Marxist vocabulary of his prison writings.) If heterogeneity and historical experience are paramount, then we should not be surprised that Spivak is drawn to Gramsci's methodological remarks on the study of subaltern classes in his *Prison Notebooks*. 'The subaltern classes,' Gramsci writes, 'by definition, are not unified and cannot unite until they are able to become a 'State': their history, therefore, is intertwined with that of civil society, and thereby with the history of States and groups of States.'[18] The entwinement of subaltern classes with the history of the State – which is to say, the history of domination – makes the silence of the subaltern an issue of critical, urgent importance. Gramsci's long meditations on the organic intellectual, corporative class, and hegemony rotate around the imperative for the subaltern to speak, to mobilize, and so to intervene in history. This has been the primary aim of European theory after Gramsci when conceiving difference: the problem is the speaking and non-speaking of the margin. Revolution cures this ill.

Levinas's work is different in that sense, given his emphasis on the deconstructive (and so not mobilizing) power of the face and the absence of an account of collective will or revolutionary political vision. Such deconstructive power is not the subaltern in the Gramsci's sense. In Spivak's hands, informed as they are by a very similar deconstructive practice, the subaltern becomes something quite different, while at the same time retaining the relation of subalternity to the history of the (colonial) state. Alongside projects and practices of political and institutional domination, the colonial state is also an epistemic project, informing what it means to know, to express, and so to speak. In that sense, the Gramscian notion of subalternity is well suited to thinking through the effect and after-effect of colonialism; the entwinement with the history of the State, coupled with the problematic of granting subaltern autonomy within previously exploitative and exclusionary frameworks (postcolonial anxiety *par excellence*), makes Gramsci's idea fecund even as it is transformed by another context and historical experience. In fact, and to this very point, Spivak remarks that she prefers the term subaltern to other names for difference because '[i]t is truly situational.'[19] Gramsci's articulation sets the concept free, rather than constraining it against other histories of other others. By situational, Spivak means simply that the subaltern is not a subordinate concept in a wider diagnosis, implicating a host of other critical structures, but rather functions, perhaps in a nomadic conceptual space, *against* the very theories that would hope to contain it within conventional conceptual, political, and cultural schemata.

The situational character of the subaltern is disclosed in Spivak's hesitation before Gramsci's account of the political urgency and future of subaltern classes. For Gramsci, the crucial question with the subaltern classes – and this is what marks him as a very particular kind of revolutionary, wedded to the notion of organicity from the intellectual to hegemonic action – is how those classes transform the social whole at the moment of integration. Integration means transgression, probably through revolutionary action, across the class boundaries that define the anxieties of political life. Even as Gramsci will famously describe the history of subaltern classes as 'necessarily fragmented and episodic,'[20] integration and transgression still operate within the logics of speaking–silence, representation–exclusion, and so narrative–counter-narrative. Fragmentation is overcome in hegemonic action. The imperialist project of colonialism and its reiterative aftermath changes something central to these agonistic binaries, locating a different sort of absence outside the play of presence–absence in those logics. A different difference. Spivak writes:

> Gramsci considers the movement of historical-political economy in Italy within what can be seen as an allegory of reading taken from or prefiguring an international division of labor. Yet an account of the phased development of the subaltern is thrown out of joint when his cultural macrology is operated, however remotely, by the epistemic interference with legal and disciplinary definitions accompanying the imperialist project.[21]

This moment of interference produces a different sort of dynamic than Gramsci's account. The 'subaltern's cultural and political movement into the hegemony,' Spivak writes, 'determine[s] the production of history as narrative (of truth).'[22] Colonialism's reach, however, is detected in the observation of how colonial structures themselves formulate the preconditions of any discourse whatsoever, such that even the subaltern, in Gramsci's sense, speaks within (and as) the ideological forms of imperialism. What happens when we think from – and so not against or in a dialectical address to – the interference with what Spivak calls the 'legal and disciplinary definitions' that bear the preconditions of the colonial project? Such a thinking-from-interference must proceed without the atavism of nativist continuity. Spivak does not offer a precolonial organic intellectual report.

To the extent that such matters can be settled, the moment of interference allows Spivak to begin answering her two leading questions in 'Can the Subaltern Speak?' First, there is her subtle but also uncompromising 'critique of . . . how the third-world subject is represented within Western discourse.'[23] How is it that Western discourses of difference, written in the name of the subaltern, fail to render what they seek to represent? In what sense are languages of revolutionary difference fundamentally languages of conservation and hegemony? Deleuze and Foucault come under Spivak's critical scrutiny here and the conclusion is a straightforward rejection of their pretensions to thinking difference. Whatever their aspirations, Deleuze and Foucault reiterate the same sorts of provincial, if even neo-imperial, theorizing about the Other they might profess to critique. Second, and this is Spivak's ultimate end in 'Can the Subaltern Speak?,' there is the question of how to draw together, then radically apart, the 'discourses of the West and the possibility of speaking of (or for) the subaltern woman.'[24] This is a difficult and subtle point in her essay. At the limit of Western theories of difference, which is the best promise of the colonial gaze that suspends questions of nation and race, there is the other Other. The other Other, that is, as *continuing heterogeneity* – this sense of radical alterity begins to *not* show itself, and so disturbs discourse about the Other in the failure of the still colonized approach. The heterogeneity of the gendered subaltern emerges for Spivak, not *as such* in a transformative signification, but as the cipher who ciphers every theorization of her place. Difference in the most difficult, and indeed most radical, sense emerges in this liminal space of *fantasied*, but always *non*-encounter. The effect of these two guiding problematics is what she calls, in a programmatic characterization, 'a still more radical decentering of the subject [than] is, in fact, implicit in both Marx and Derrida.'[25] The subaltern accomplishes the decentering of the subject in the act of ciphering – quite literally, making into a zero – of knowing and being; epistemology and ontology, in the approach that cannot grasp or understand, become an empty set incapable of asserting itself.

The enactment of ciphering in Spivak's work is deconstructive. That is, she suspends concern with 'the voice' and other variations of counter-narrativity in order to seize upon how the heterological seizes up the act of knowing. The subaltern is therefore not simply another name for the oppressed or the marginal; the oppressed and marginal, as we can already see in Gramsci's interpretation of the meaning and problematic of subaltern history, are still lodged within the economy of speaking, expression, and, after sufficient intellectual work, hegemony. The example of *sati* in 'Can the Subaltern Speak?' takes us in a different direction, one that is surely maddening to those in search of a straightforward political or cultural programme. Spivak's example undermines an epistemic project that gives deep roots to conscious and subconscious expressions of the colonization of people, places, and ideas. This undermining operates by way of an appeal to a very particular sense of *singularity* and its devastating effects on language. For some critics, such as Peter Hallward in *Absolutely Postcolonial*, this kind of linguistic and epistemological critique forgets Kamau Brathwaite's dictum in *History of the Voice*: people, not language, make revolution.[26] As well, the insistence on the problem of singularity – the ciphering work of the subaltern that offers nothing in place of the empty set – might seem to suggest a divorce from the material and historical processes, undermining what Hallward calls the 'aspiration to specificity' or 'the particularity of discrete sequences.'[27] And yet it is precisely the specificity of the specific colonial situation in Spivak's example of *sati* that generates the continuing heterogeneity of the wholly singular, always incomparable, subaltern; the saturation of all forms of knowing and being by the colonial gaze – which includes most prominently the universalizing gaze of liberatory projects – specifies in order to catch sight of the ciphering effect of the singular. Perhaps, with Levinas, we can also catch sight of the ethical moment in this ciphering. But that means confronting the ethical with its own ghosts, in order to radicalize the problem of heterogeneity.

European critical theory is not enough, precisely because that theory does not interrogate the specific conditions under which it formulates strategies of resistance, liberation, and heterology. Indeed, part of Spivak's project lies in decolonizing critical theory in the name of a more original (radical) sense of difference. This strikes me as a wholly worthy project (postcolonial struggle is not only crassly political, it is also intellectual, cultural, and bookish) and one that raises again the ethical question. This struggle and these questions arise from a sense of resistance rooted in a critique of the West *without recourse to the atavistic space of nativism*. Once this distance is drawn between the discourses of the West and the continuing heterogeneity of the gendered subaltern, we can see how the epistemology of this relation entails a rejection of dialectical thinking. Spivak's example of *sati*, in its final articulation, could be characterized as a kind of phenomenology of the limit; Spivak's theorizing does not say what it cannot say and allows itself, in language often unfairly described as obscure, to be ciphered by what cannot be said. The relationality of *sati* is exemplary of this ciphering. Only in the act of self-immolation does the 'category,' if we can use such a word here, of subaltern arise, which means that the life of the category is death. Ciphering is thereby located in each site of relation. The subaltern ciphers in the act of self-immolation – a wholly different, though surely companion, signification *kath auto* – and, in that immolation, there is the ciphering of the subject who wants to know and wants to say. The language of the subaltern and the language of the subject vanish, and, in that vanishing, fracture epistemology. Comprehensive decentering accomplished, in prose and the writing of theory.

Now of course we could argue that such a construction of a critically deconstructive (anti-)relation simply stands in need of an intermediary term, concept, or some such item in the transmission of knowledge. That is, there is still the problem of dialectical thinking. When relationality fails and vanishes, the dynamic structure of dialectics reopens the question. For, whatever the moment of incomprehension, there is surely another (last) return to the project of knowing *after ciphering* with the tools of mediation. Persisting heterogeneity promises that there can be no resolution of the gap or distance between the sender and receiver, and so no mediating term that might translate the different into, if not a certain sameness, at least a negotiable communicative medium. The subaltern is not a minim, but a self-immolating concept. In Spivak's essay, we see the specter of the dialectic most plainly in her account of the so-called 'native informant.' The native informant is both a political and cultural operative *and* an epistemological intervention deployed to vitiate the deconstructive effect of subaltern difference. If the undecidable is neutralized and overcome by dialectic (the interpretative or translation act of the native informant), then the decision can be made *for* knowledge and, as it were, halt the self-immolation of the concept in *sati*. Or, put another way, if the native informant is capable of *translating* the meaning of the subaltern for the one who is different (and for whom the subaltern is different), then the dismantling force of subalternity, the generative act of the undecidable, is neutralized by a third term. Is there a translation manual for the informant? Or is the informant himself capable of functioning as a translation manual, given his proximity to the cultural forms 'embodied' in the subaltern? Indeed, it is a matter here of whether or not the concept can be embodied, as self-immolation, if it immolates the concept *as the very manner in which the concept comes into being*, contests the very idea of the persistence of the body. How could we conceive such a translation manual, and what is at stake in the very idea?

Spivak's critique of this dialectical strategy, in which the native informant can be seen to create, then sustain the dynamism of dialectical epistemology, is both straightforward and profound. The theoretical conclusion is not surprising, of course: there is no possibility of translation. Difference is intractable. But the claim is not rooted here in an unrooted or generalized theory of difference. Rather, her case proceeds from the ideological formation of perception under colonialism – the specificity in her language of singularity. Perception, as the visual field of incarnate historiography, names a movement that informs both s/he who wants to know and, if considerably more obliquely, s/he who attends to that wanting to know in the act of translation. Intractable difference thus lies in the nature of relation (which is a non-relation or relation of ciphering to the self-immolating concept) and in the perceptual *doxa* of the knower. The subaltern stalls relation and perception. So, with a turn of phrase from Lyotard's work in hand, Spivak's discussion of feminism, law, and the moral crime posits the *différend* at the heart of the British translation of the act of *sati*. Spivak writes:

> What Jean-François Lyotard has termed the '*différend*,' the inaccessibility of, or untranslatability from, one mode of discourse in a dispute to another is vividly illustrated here. As the discourse of what the British perceive as heathen ritual is sublated (but not, Lyotard would argue, translated) into what the British perceive as a crime, one diagnosis of female free will is substituted for another.[28]

The distinction here between sublation and translation is crucial. Dialectical thinking, which is accomplished in the moment of sublation (*Aufheben*), turns in this case on the relation between the act of *sati* and the normative valuation of it as either heathen ritual or moral crime. This is an epistemic act: naming *sati* in even the barest normative terms produces and reproduces knowledge. The act becomes knowable *as* a crime, but that knowability turns on a sublation. Whence the *différend* that would seize up this dialectical movement?

Sublation, of course, only arises as a possibility – or at least a seductive strategy – on the basis of a mediating term. The epistemological gap opened up by Spivak is the space between the intellectual and the object of study; in this case, colonial historiography (even in its moralizing register) and the Other (or other Other) documented by that history. How, the epistemic and political question goes, is it possible for the voice of the Other to be heard, registered, and then written by the writer of history? This is a question of translation and its dialectic. The epistemological gap between writer and object requires a structural item that lifts the unheard voice into the aural and cognitive medium. Spivak refers to this structural item, which drives the hopeful dialectic of the historiographer, as the native informant – the Indian elite. And yet there is difference in the difference mediated by the native informant that situates the *différend*. Spivak writes:

> Certain varieties of the Indian elite are at best native informants for first-world intellectuals interested in the voice of the Other. But one must nevertheless insist that the colonized subaltern *subject* is irretrievably heterogeneous.[29]

This doubling of the sense of heterogeneity, marking the difference between an alterity as concealed narrative (disclosed by the native informant) and an alterity that self-immolates in coming to being, seals difference as difference, radicalizing what could be gathered, through difference, by recognition, cognition, and historical documentation. Dialectical thinking is therefore stalled by the informant himself, whose status as the transmitter of knowledge presupposes narrative (perhaps counter-narrative, perhaps simply atavistic, nativist narrative). The signification of *sati* functions otherwise than storytelling; the native informant, were he to intervene, is akin to a category mistake. A misapplication of categories thus proceeds with the mediating work of dialectic on false grounds.

If the doubling of heterogeneity brings another kind of difference into (non-)view, then a sense of epistemological fracture is clear. The reach of the knowing gaze is not innocent; as in Levinas, knowing or the desire to know enacts violence. Aristotle names, not the nature of the human, but the imperialism of the West to come. Spivak's identification of violence in the act of knowing or desire to know opens up a horizon of justice – always risky, always precarious – in subaltern difference. Epistemological fracture is supplemented, decisively, by the resistance of alterity, and that resistance to normalization interrupts the flow of normative social, cultural, and political life with something akin to Levinas's call of the Other. But it is a call that, in its failure to speak, poses a very different set of problems than Levinas's excessively verbal Other. How do we think *after* radical difference? Spivak writes in *Critique of Postcolonial Reason* that

> [t]he excavation, retrieval, and celebration of the historical individual, the effort of bringing her within accessibility, is written within that double find at which we begin. But a just world must entail normalization; the promise of justice must attend not only to the seduction of power, but also to the anguish that knowledge must suppress difference as well as differance, that a fully just world is impossible, forever deferred and different from our projections, the undecidable in the face of which we must risk the decision that we can hear the other.[30]

Spivak begins, in this passage, to take account of the relation between difference, knowledge, and the undecidable. The language is most obviously indebted to or in dialogue with Derrida's variations on the problem of democracy and law, but it also raises the difficult – if not impossible – problem of how to think *after* heteronomy moves away from the margin and outside the reach of dialectics. What if we think the ethical back into the self-immolating concept? Is it possible to think knowledge after the fracturing of epistemology? For, as Levinas makes clear and as Spivak indicates here, to act is already to make a passage and enter the plane of knowing and being. What are we to make of this impossible passage?

CIPHER AND SPEECH

In *Monolingualism of the Other*, Derrida takes up the compelling and largely under-explored problem of multiple languages in a singular site. For Derrida, and here he takes his cue from Édouard Glissant's work on creolizing cultural and linguistic forms, the problem of difference or the Other is limited by the sedimented, unreflective commitment in theorizing alterity to a single language.

Something very much like what Derrida brings into focus in his reflection on monolingualism is nuanced by Spivak's work by the absoluteness of difference in the transnational context of colonialism in India. For Derrida, the commitment to a single language conceals what in Glissant's work becomes so radical: the mixture of languages, the mixture of memory and history carried by those languages, and so a decentered subject called to the Other and the other Other as a condition of its being. The mixture of languages, for Glissant, produces a sense of entanglement with the Other, which, in turn, complicates the meaning of my address to the Other. How can I address the Other from the non-space of subjectivity? Who and what am I to the subaltern who cannot speak, after the ciphering work of that subaltern? Spivak's account of the epistemological fracture between Same and Other is not itself a theory of entanglement; as we will see below in Chapter 4, the rhizomatic identity-which-is-not-one articulated in the Caribbean context labors without roots. While Spivak's account eschews nativism and nostalgia for the precolonial past, the example of *sati* and the critique of the native informant proceed, for lack of a better way of putting it, from a kind of radical empiricism – a distinct and incomparable location in memory and history. The particularities and specificities of historical experience inform her rendering of difference. Thus, Spivak generates a language of singularity, not a language of rhizome. But this rewritten subaltern, as it emerges as a ciphering concept across the gap opened up by colonialism's linguistic and epistemic structure of domination, splits language in two. This splitting marks that difference with a version of radical diachrony that, while not rhizomatic, confronts the language of knowledge with the language of difference. A different mixed site, to be sure, but still a site and still multiple. Whereas Levinas's account of diachrony is ultimately an already transgressed fracture of time (the Other has spoken *in* me, unsaying my said from within signification), Spivak's subaltern splits the site of encounter with a form of epistemic resistance that is both temporal (the time gap is evident in the anti-historiographic claim) and spatial (self-immolation is both literal and figurative). There is no transgression. There is no crossing. And this is why her critique of the native informant is so important. The native informant promises the transgression across the diachronic structure, as well as (perhaps most importantly) exposing the latent colonialism of the gaze that wants to know, and so the critique of the native informant on epistemological grounds blocks the crossing of difference.

What are we to make of this different difference?

In the context of Levinas's critique of epistemology's dependence on economies of light and transparency, Spivak's subaltern (and so the colonial context more generally) underscores just how intimate the Levinasian Other is with monolingualism. There is one language, even as it is split by the ethical encounter. In *Totality and Infinity*, for example, Levinas describes the relation to the Other as separation. The spatial metaphor is furthered by the ethical language in which separation is a face-to-face relation – which is always, in some sense, *without* relation – of height; in a moral sense, the I looks up at the Other. Difference both decenters and obligates subjectivity from across this distance. In Levinas's analysis, this means that there must be a moment of transgression or passing across the interval between Same and Other. Though in some sense a relation *without* relation, this is also a relation that *gives the I to the Me from the Other* – relation *par excellence* in terms of the genesis of subjectivity. *Totality and Infinity* describes this event most concretely as signification or expression of the face. From the position of separation and height, the Other speaks the language of responsibility and initiates the constitution of moral consciousness through a radical *excess*. In *Otherwise Than Being*, Levinas shifts the language of separation away from the face-to-face in favor of the language of the pre-history of the I and the denucleation of a subjectivity always late to itself. The sign retains its central function in Levinas's work, plotted in the later work over the problem of difference as radical *absence*. The shift from signification and expression to the Saying and the Said, then, represents an immensely important shift in conceptual frame and sustaining structure, but Levinas's commitment to the monolingual nevertheless remains foundational, even vital to the analysis. That is, the Saying has its power to denucleate and devastate language, making the Said the trace that fails in its memorial function, in so far as the language-play of *dire-dit* derives its ethical purchase from its capacity to register, resonate, and fore-structure the exposed subject. The Saying only denucleates *if* it communicates (with all caveats in place regarding communication) a sense of responsibility. Such conditionality binds Levinas's analysis to the passage of language across the interval of spatial and temporal separation. The Other speaks itself into subjectivity and produces the for-the-Other subject. The monolingual holds this storyline together by allowing the Other – whether through expression or immemorial Saying – to transgress the spatial and temporal distance of difference. Incarnate historiography exposes the condition of exposure as, in Levinas's analysis, a continuity of bodies and their history. Such continuity, however nascent, makes the communicability of the sign possible. *I know that the Other accuses.* The discontinuity that comes to define notions of separation, interruption, and diachrony proceeds from a prior continuity of language disclosed in the monolingualism of communication. Spivak's hesitation before the subaltern's speaking, not to mention her hesitation before the compulsion even just to seek a voice, takes on another significance in this context.

We cannot of course take the monolingual too literally. It is not the case that Levinas presupposes the particularly *French* expression or Saying or that the simple fact of a mixture of languages somehow overturns the terms of the Levinasian ethical. Rather, my point here is that Levinas levels off the problem of signification by understanding the sign to be communicative of interruption and disruption. The Other's speech must communicate the call or having been called to responsibility; otherwise, the Other is otherwise than Other. Perhaps mere dance. Perhaps, for the worse, an enemy. So, no matter what Levinas's distance from dialogical thinking – and his critique of Martin Buber in these terms is both important and profound – there is a certain presupposition of symmetry at the level of the sign without which Levinas's work will not properly work. This symmetry of the sign is a sort of meta-monolingualism, a sameness of signification that makes responsibility possible. Expression and Saying must first register in subjectivity in order to show the after-effect and affect of irrecusable obligation. In his own way, Derrida noted this in 'Violence and Metaphysics' in terms of the worldliness *in general* of language, but the postcolonial moment sees another movement in the movement through the worldly. The worldly marked by nation and race, by the history of colonialism's fullest reaches and what Spivak calls the tradition of white men protecting brown women, breaks up the symmetry of the sign and exposes the monolingual as its own kind of violence. *Who speaks and the condition of that speaking, even when it disrupts epistemological pretensions, are already an assertion of exclusion and silencing and all attendant violence.* Contrary to the complaint that the ciphered and ciphering subaltern closes off any sense of politics, then, this crossing of Levinas and Spivak shows just how fraught the languages of responsibility and justice are, even when those languages proceed from a sense of radical difference and operate outside the epistemologies of identification, duty, virtue, and so on. A cultural politics, to be sure – or even a conceptual politics. Certainly a politics of the ethical. The articulation of the terms of difference is always transformative of how we imagine our lives together or alongside one another.

The subaltern changes the terms of this discussion in a single gesture of retreat from the monolingual. Rather than speaking back in another language, the subaltern, on Spivak's rendering, ciphers. Her return to the question of justice in *Critique of Postcolonial Reason* and other works is instructive. The subaltern does not generate a sense of responsible subjectivity – what Levinas calls the for-the-Other subject or just simply moral consciousness (*conscience*) – and so there are no immediate terms for an appeal to obligation. And yet, Spivak makes a restrained, careful, and almost confessional appeal to a return to the worldly when she reiterates the necessity of justice. It is worth recalling here the final words of 'Can the Subaltern Speak?,' where Spivak gives her answer to the essay's title-question and offers a maddeningly obscure vision of the consequences. She writes:

> The subaltern cannot speak. There is no virtue in global laundry lists with 'woman' as a pious item. Representation has not withered away. The female intellectual as intellectual has a circumscribed task which she must not disown with a flourish.[31]

Representation has not withered away – for all the devastation brought to language by the subaltern's distance from speaking, there is still the urgent and impossibly difficult task of speaking *after* this moment of the 'cannot speak.' There must be speaking for, even where such speaking is conceptually and ethically unimaginable. When we draw this closing passage from 'Can the Subaltern Speak?' forward to *Critique of Postcolonial Reason*, we catch sight of the wholly fraught character of this moment of speaking. The epistemology of relation is fractured. There is no commonality presupposed in the movement through the worldly; neither radical political theory nor nativism nor patient listening (every listening is a translation, so fundamentally monolingual) can save this moment or give it workable, actionable substance. Responsibility is therefore *impossible* in a manner that is, frankly, *more impossible* than in Levinas's work on justice and politics. In one of the subtler points of transnational difference, Spivak takes on the question of impossibility *without the excessive thought of the messianic*. That is, Spivak works in a conceptual space haunted by the cipher, the empty set, rather than, as with Levinas (and even Derrida, in many cases), the ghosts of the trace or the difficult, uncanny abundance of excess. So, when Spivak writes in a very Levinasian and Derridean register about 'the undecidable in the face of which we must risk the decision that we can hear the other,' we must keep in mind how such deciding and the catastrophic force of the undecidable proceeds without the promises made possible by the messianic. This is a very different difference, producing a very different justice.

Another kind of parricide, perhaps? To be sure, such parricidal thoughts, were we to cast them as such, begin the process of rethinking the language of alterity and the fracture of epistemology *after* the provincialism of the Levinasian text. Spivak's account of the subaltern, when put into conversation with Levinas's Other, decolonizes that sense of the Other by thinking, with him, outside of the economy of light, but also against him with the elimination of what little, *almost* nothing, can remain of the Levinasian Other. In that sense, the conceptual encounter with the subaltern is devastating for Levinas's formulation of the language of alterity. It exposes his work as anchored, both consciously (as we saw in the Introduction above) and subconsciously (as we see in the clandestine function of the monolingual), in provincial relations that do not survive, in terms of structure and key conceptual moments, the movement into the postcolonial context.

Yet, this is also a very Levinasian gesture – not only to reckon with interruption and the perpetual problem of beginning again, but also to seek out what is other in order to reconceive that beauty which still adorns the earth. As well, Spivak's turn toward the question of justice by way of the question of radical difference, lodged as it is within a variety of epistemological puzzles and resistance to the strategies for resolving those puzzles, reminds us that the question of the Other or other Other always has an ethical moment. Ciphering modulates, rather than eliminates, the accusative. Why does the Other matter? Why does the unraveling or ciphering – the work of Levinas, the work of Spivak – provoke our attention to matters of the good and the just? Levinas's face makes that case with a sort of anti-humanist humanism, which grounds obligation in the saintliness of the Other. Spivak's case is more difficult, and this is probably why the question of justice is given the largely Derridean characterization of *impossible*. If the subaltern is a cipher and ciphers, then the question of response is forever altered (and not altared). The ciphered subject who asks the subaltern to speak is not holy or saintly or mobilized to action. And yet, it must be said that ciphering institutes a profound humility in the knowing subject; broken apart, disassembled to the point of the empty set, there can be no pretensions. In that moment of humility, unredeemed and not supplemented by the fullness of the messianic, there is another sort of ethical call, a call to justice and what Spivak calls a 'legal instrument of social justice that can accommodate the subaltern.'[32] Legal instrumentation, like the institutions of the state in Levinas's work, can only be a shock to the austere epistemological space opened up after the subaltern's moment against knowing and being. It is a risk that is not only called for, but demanded – Spivak's moment of *rapprochement* with Levinas. For both the institutions of justice and the fragile lives put into relation with those institutions, this is an enormous risk – though surely, in the Levinasian phrase, *a fine risk*.

Notes

1. Theodor Adorno, 'Subject and Object,' in *The Essential Frankfurt School Reader*, ed Andrew Arato and Eike Gebhardt. New York: Continuum, 1997, 498.
2. Emmanuel Levinas, *Le Temps et l'autre*. Paris: Presses Universitaires de France, 2004, 20; *Time and the Other*, trans. Richard Cohen. Pittsburgh: Duquesne University Press, 1990, 42.
3. On the early work on transcendence in *The Theory of Intuition in Husserl's Phenomenology*, see John E. Drabinski, *Sensibility and Singularity* (Albany: SUNY, 2001), Chapter 1.
4. Levinas, *Le Temps et l'autre*, 22/43.
5. Levinas's argument for a pure heterology and the refusal of *logos*, coupled with the problem of parricide, is one of the foci of Derrida's famous 'Violence and Metaphysics,' where he argues that parricide is impossible within Levinas's particular formulations in *Time and the Other* and *Totality and Infinity*. On this issue, see John Protevi, 'Repeating the Parricide: Levinas and the Question of Closure,' *Journal of the British Society for Phenomenology*, vol. 23, no. 1 (January 1992): 21–32.
6. Levinas, *Le Temps et l'autre*, 47/64–5.
7. Emmanuel Levinas, *Éthique et infini*. Paris: Fayard, 1982, 80; *Ethics and Infinity*, trans. Richard Cohen. Pittsburgh: Duquesne University Press, 1985, 86.
8. Emmanuel Levinas, *Totalité et l'infini*. The Hague: Martinus Nijhoff, 1961, 157; *Totality and Infinity*, trans. Alphonso Lingis. Pittsburgh: Duquesne University Press, 1969, 182.

9. Ibid., 158/183. Emphasis mine.
10. Ibid., 154/179.
11. Ibid., 156–7/181.
12. Ibid., xviii/30.
13. Gayatri Spivak, 'In Response: Looking Backward, Looking Forward,' in *Can the Subaltern Speak? Reflections on the History of an Idea*, ed Rosalind C. Morris. New York: Columbia University Press, 2010, 227–8.
14. Gayatri Spivak, 'The Problem of Cultural Self-Representation,' in *The Post-Colonial Critic: Interviews, Strategies, Dialogues*, ed Sarah Harasym. New York: Routledge, 1990, 51.
15. Ibid., 52.
16. Gayatri Spivak, 'The Post-colonial Critic,' in *The Post-Colonial Critic*, 68.
17. Gayatri Spivak, 'Practical Politics of the Open End,' in *The Post-Colonial Critic*, 102–3.
18. Antonio Gramsci, *Selections from the Prison Notebooks*, ed and trans. Quintin Hoare and Geoffrey Nowell Smith. New York: International, 1971, 52.
19. Gayatri Spivak, 'Negotiating the Structures of Violence,' in *The Post-Colonial Critic*, 141.
20. Gramsci, *Selections from the Prison Notebooks*, 54–5.
21. Gayatri Spivak, 'Can the Subaltern Speak?,' in *Marxism and the Interpretation of Culture*, ed Cary Nelson and Lawrence Grossberg. Urbana: University of Illinois Press, 1988, 283.
22. Ibid., 283.
23. Ibid., 271.
24. Ibid.
25. Ibid.
26. Peter Hallward, *Absolutely Postcolonial: Writing Between the Singular and the Specific*. Manchester: Manchester University Press, 2001, 27.
27. Ibid., xv.
28. Spivak, 'Can the Subaltern Speak?,' 300.
29. Ibid., 284.
30. Gayatri Spivak, *Critique of Postcolonial Reason*. Cambridge, MA: Harvard University Press, 1999, 198–9.
31. Spivak, 'Can the Subaltern Speak?,' 308.
32. Spivak, 'In Response,' 236.

CHAPTER 3

The Ontology of Fracture

> Our existence today is marked by a tenebrous sense of sur-
> vival, living on the borderlines of the 'present,' for which there
> seems to be no proper name other than the current and contro-
> versial shiftiness of the prefix 'post'.
>
> Bhabha, 'Locations of Culture'

Reading Levinas and Spivak face to face reveals a cultural and historical complexity at the center of the language of absolute difference. Absolute difference, which locates absoluteness in a sense of
difference *without measure or contrast*, commits parricide against
the paternal line of the West, singling out, on our reading, the twin
prerogatives of Parmenides and of the economy of light.

With Parmenides and light as the lead figures, the problem of
difference could be easily read as another language for or dramatic
staging of the now familiar critique of the metaphysics of presence.
But both Levinas and Spivak understand the problem of difference
in the space of encounter, where the unraveling or self-immolation
of the concept happens at the point of contact. Embodiment in its
fullest and most vulnerable sense: the exposure to the world and the
materiality of the languages of address, response, and silence. This
irreducible *intentionality* or *relationality*, mixed with a certain sheer-
ness of materiality, means that the otherness of the Other is not just
an epistemic event of fracture, but also a moment of concern with
the ethical and justice. The transnational nuance introduced by the
historical experience of colonialism changes the terms of difference.
Spivak's nuance reroutes the problem of alterity, marking the space
of separation with a deeper sense of language as foundational difference and a more robust notion of historical experience as trauma.
Rather than the pre-history of the I, which dominates so much of
Levinas's work from *Totality and Infinity* on, there is, after the transnational moment, another history of the I's pre-history: the sense
of global entanglement that makes difference reconstitute in another

kind of diachrony. The epistemology of Otherness becomes subalternity when the spatiality and time-structure of relation are deformalized in and by historical experience. Two kinds of impossible justice with the problem of decolonization between them.

This leaves us with a question of *living after* the fracturing of epistemology. That is, the question of justice arises as an imperative at the very moment difference becomes absolute. Ethics and politics move to the center, but are always answerable to the absolute heterogeneity from which they arise. We will pause on that particular problematic here, rejoining the question in the final chapter below. But that sense of ethics and politics can only begin after we have sorted out the transition from what lies outside being to the plane of being-as-practice. In other words, we have to understand what it means *to be* after the fracture of epistemology. If we cannot know, and indeed the very project of knowing commits us to a primary violence, then how is it possible to think the being of the subject otherwise? What is subjectivity as absolute difference? How do historical experience and the transnational context alter the Levinasian account of the ethical subject?

In what follows, I would like to rewrite the problem of originary fracture, shifting from the question of epistemology to the problem of *being-after*. This latter problematic is not quite yet the problem of action; rather, *being-after* underwrites the problem of practice (ethics, politics) with a conception of fractured subjectivity. Fractured subjectivity moves in the element of decision: ethics and politics. As we shall see in the final chapter below, an ontology of the subject is necessary in order to make ethics and politics work, not as the accomplishment of a particular vision of action, but as the strategic orientation toward knowing and being that minimizes violence. The *less* of violence springs, as a theoretical and strategic problem, from an account of the subject emergent from absolute difference. *From anti-knowing to ante-being and being.* How precisely we are to locate this subject is a matter for the following reflections, but we can say a few words here at the outset. Levinas's account of the genesis of the Me (the accusative), which then becomes, on the plane of being and acting, the I (the accomplished, active subject), culminates in the 'Substitution' chapter from *Otherwise Than Being*. In that chapter, Levinas argues that the subject is denucleated; the Other is *in* the subject, not as an overwhelming and excessive presence (the claim of *Totality and Infinity*), but as an absence that hollows out the subject's sense of itself. This later account of subjectivity is ghostly, haunted by the Other in every assertion of Self. A haunting, of course, that gives Levinas a new and considerably more complex notion of the ethical. Part of what sets his later work apart from, as well as marking an advance on, *Totality and Infinity* is the detailed account of subjectivity. However decentered it may be, however close to vanishing completely, Levinas conceives subjectivity in the boldest terms: embodied, exposed to the world, and comprised, from the interior, by what is outside the traditional borders or boundaries of subjectivity. No matter how fractured, *this is still a subject.*

Once we fracture subjectivity and still call it a subject, we can begin thinking *after* the fracture of epistemology. Something remains, however broken apart by the thought of difference, after the loss of the knowing subject. And so, in a very particular and complex sense, we can begin to rethink ontology. *What remains calls for another conception of being* – and on this, in the end, we have to revise some of the Levinasian rhetoric. In that rethinking of being and subjectivity, embedded as it is in ideas of embodiment and material presence to the world, we also (again) raise the question of the transnational as an immanent problematic. Levinas's geography of reason sustains and is sustained by a certain fantasy of Europe, a continent comprised of cultural and political (and so not physical) borders that constrain movement. The fracturing of the subject mimics exactly Levinas's imagination of Europe as 'the Bible and the Greeks,' a massive collective subjectivity constituted against itself by the contrary forces of persistence in being (the Greek) and the wandering of singularity (the Bible). This is Europe's story. This is also the story of an anxious European subject whose fantasied insularity cannot keep it safe from haunting others.

At the same time, and as a companion theory of difference, the theoretical narrative of originary fracture is also the story of migration. Migration names a history of movement across cultural and political borders that, far from conserving the root of what came before, reconfigures the meaning of the subject *without reassembling into a single identity.* That is, migration is not simply (or in any sense) location moved across geometric space; migration blends as it moves, disassembling and reassembling at the very same moment of deterritorialization and reterritorialization. Migration is an undecidable movement. In particular, I have in mind the work of Homi Bhabha, whose long meditations on the problem of hybridity, narration, and the insurgent power of migration in the nation comprise another account of an ontology of fracture. With hybridity, Bhabha is able to think about subjectivity – writ large as the story of the nation, written and rewritten from the resistance of counter-narratives – as both fractured and persistent. Something is broken apart, irretrievable even in nostalgia, and yet the irreparable trauma of location–dislocation–relocation makes a subjectivity whose life needs its own accounting outside the rhetoric of roots, fixity, and national narrative. The hybrid subject is a subject un-at-home in its home, yet formative in the very meaning of the future of home. Indeed, the anxiety and power of Bhabha's subject lie in its ability to put the Same in question as the cultural and political Other, while, at one and the same time, what emerges from this *mise en question* is subjectivity thought otherwise: fractured in its very being, hybrid, and open to an unanticipated future. Interruption, surprise, inde-terminacy as the infinite – between Levinas and Bhabha, this is the ontology of subjectivity as irreducibly fractured.

What does it mean that the fractured, yet persistent, subject lies at the center of Levinas's and Bhabha's work? What does that shared concern with split identities, which are always reconciled in the body and in languages of address and response, say about the place of the transnational in Levinas's work (what elements of diachrony and the like survive the critical juxtaposition) and of the ethical in Bhabha's conception of hybridity (does that conception require, or is it supplemented in important ways by, the ethical)?

This problematic allows us to return to one of the promissory notes from the Introduction above. If we put Bhabha's exploration of hybridity and subjectivity in contact with Levinas's denucleated, for-the-Other subject, then the legacy of Frantz Fanon's work takes on an interesting new register. In many ways, the meaning of Fanon's work is at stake in this discussion; his theorizing of the emptying effect of the colonial gaze, language, and historical experience denu-cleates the subject whose future remains, well, always just a *future*. Which is to say, Fanon's is a thought of the open *after* the devastat-ing encounter with otherness outside oneself, which is then rediscov-ered in the interior of psychic life. Wholly alienating, to be sure, in Fanon's case, but it also gives birth to a new subject. That subject is mixed in its history and sense of the present, and such conflicted openness opens Fanon's text and theoretical field to important inter-ventions. 'To read Fanon,' Bhabha writes in 'Interrogating Identity,' 'is to experience the sense of division that prefigures – and fissures – the emergence of a truly radical thought that never dawns without casting an uncertain dark.'[1] This thought, Bhabha notes, operates in a space of ambivalence for which there is no predetermined destination (the future is the future), but instead an orientation of hope set out from a fundamentally dislocated structure. How is this structure ethical? What obligates in this space? And how is otherness embedded within the subject such that the very being of the human is suspended without foundation or atavistic roots? Between Levinas and Bhabha, between denucleation and hybridity, there is the ambivalent future of the subject without center who none the less persists in being. In this without-center and persistence in being, there is the future of ethics and politics. High stakes indeed.

After Subject

Levinas's account of subjectivity in *Otherwise Than Being* deepens, and in many ways corrects, the analysis of moral consciousness in *Totality and Infinity*. The shift in theoretical terms and approaches between these two texts responds to a conceptual impasse at the center of *Totality and Infinity*. In that work, Levinas attempts to think otherness outside the Husserlian problematic of intentionality-as-correlation, that anchoring of meaning and sense in the non-worldly subject, by appealing the excess of phenomenality and the separation between the subject and the Other in metaphysical desire, enjoyment, and then the ethical. Levinas has not yet theorized passivity in *Totality and Infinity*; the subject is interrupted, jolted out of the activity of habitual egoism, but subjectivity is not yet passive beyond passivity. The Other comes to me by surprise, to be sure, so the implication of passivity is everywhere, and yet the analysis is always of the dynamism of encounter. There is always *so much* said to and by the Other. In *Totality and Infinity*, we see a portrait of the Other in the relation of height and all of the other kinds of surpluses of meaning such a relation implies. The Other is separate and, in the paradoxical relation without relation, imposes a sense of obligation upon me – something Levinas will describe as a *Sinngebung* from the outside.[2] The for-the-Other subject, to impose a later turn of phrase, is made *ethical* from the outside and is compelled, by what is outside, to give the bread from one's own mouth. I do not face the Other with empty hands. The bread, of course, is mine and perhaps even in my own mouth.

I am made ethical from the outside, created as moral consciousness by the call of the Other, but I am also and at the same time a presence to the world, *ab initio* egoistic in the sense of a will, body, and subjective comportment. Levinas's subject in *Totality and Infinity* is simultaneously inside and outside itself. Subjectivity then becomes the aporetic condition of *being* and *being put in question*. Derrida explores this aporetic condition in detail in *Adieu to Emmanuel Levinas*, which frames the paradox of the Levinasian subject in terms of welcoming, the host, and hospitality. And Derrida's reading is both devastating and productive: subjectivity is exposed as the condition of violence and exclusion, which grounds the possibility of subjectivity as goodness and welcome. In the conceptual and theoretical terms of *Totality and Infinity*, this simultaneity cannot be overcome. It is foundational and irreducible. The aporia, then, inheres in the fact that the only possibility for obligation is the necessity of having already taken a place in the world. To be ethical is to be first unethical. The ante-ethical is the anti-ethical. The very interruption that overturns the *conatus essendi* presupposes a persistence in being. Perhaps this is where Levinas offers his most profound meditation on the finitude of the human, where we find ourselves bound by the conditions of our being in the world in the very same moment that we are put into the non-worldly space of responsibility. Whatever the spectacle and even beauty of the face-to-face, Levinas's work always had an edge of melancholy. If there is no primacy of the ethical relation, except as the *most high* (and so most important) call, then we suffer not just for the Other, but also because of the Self we irreducibly are.

But this rendering of the ethical relation leaves too much of the subject intact. Indeed, it draws an ambiguous line between the gravity of obligation and the violence of egoism – why should the Other concern me? In what sense am I for-the-Other if I am, from the outset and as a matter of original condition, for-the-Same? I would not call this an impasse, but something more like a quandary. Levinas is clear that the ethical is the ultimate endgame of his work; everything leads to the relation with the Other. Still, there is the pesky problem of subjectivity. The subject remains, both before and after the encounter with the Other. How do we think about subjectivity without making violence simultaneous with goodness? Perhaps this is irreducible, even in the later work, but the problem of originary violence remains a bit too under-theorized in *Totality and Infinity*. And this clearly troubles Levinas.

So, we should not be surprised that by the time Levinas publishes *Otherwise Than Being*, thirteen years later, the ethical subject has taken on a very different character. One could argue, with a certain bit of support from Derrida's claims in 'Violence and Metaphysics,' that a fundamental naïveté lies at the heart of *Totality and Infinity*. While Levinas affirms, in the originary character of violence, the worldly aspect of the face-to-face, he does not grant the same to language, and so there is a kind of discontinuity built into the project of that text. Clearly, Levinas wants to set aside the worldly character of language *and* the ethical, re- or dis-locating ethical subjectivity in what he later calls the non-place of relation. *Totality and Infinity* cannot accomplish this task. In this sense, subjectivity suffers an identity crisis, taking up too much space at the very moment we are told it is obligated outside being. *That* subjectivity is still not sufficiently broken apart by alterity. And so, in place of excess and surplus, *Otherwise Than Being* offers the languages of persecution, substitution, and denucleation. This is its advance. Whereas the subject in the early work overflows with *both* obligation *and* the capacity to give, the later work conceives a subject already late to the scene, impoverished, unable to give, having already failed, and incapable of even a modest address to the moral crime of being in one's place in the sun. The exuberance of the face-to-face, and even the ecstatic solemnity of the relation of height, gives way to a deserted landscape. One has the distinct sense in *Totality and Infinity* of an abundant world, where the gift, welcoming, and hospitality are all possible when faced, literally or figuratively, with the widow, the orphan, and the stranger. Even as there is so much (albeit rhetorically suppressed) originary violence to subjectivity, there is a counter-measure of goodness that exceeds whatever violence I enact in the world. The figures of welcome – the home, the feminine, the host – make that goodness both material and economic. There is real ethical work to be done and the conditions for that work are plenty in place. *Otherwise Than Being* is altogether more austere. Perhaps not to the point of despair, but surely something close. Obsessions, recurrences, persecutions – the text is wholly haunted by both the Other who never appears and the devastation she leaves behind. That devastation is the subject. Subjectivity in *Otherwise Than Being* is broken apart, just like epistemology, before it gathers footing in the world.

Now, to be sure, the story of this subject in *Otherwise Than Being* resonates as familiar and is arguably a repetition of Levinas's central insight: *to be* moral consciousness is *to be* for-the-Other. I want to underscore the sense of being here, not because Levinas rekindles a relation to conventional ontology, but because the central issue in *Otherwise Than Being* concerns identity – a concern that, at some level, must be rearticulated under the rubric of a fractured ontology. An ontology which is not one, perhaps, but also an ontology in reconfigured terms. Levinas's question in *Otherwise Than Being* is an identity question that submits ontology to the structure of identity, but also one that remakes ontology after this traumatic breakup: what *is* the ethical subject? What does it mean to say ethical, which breaks up epistemology and ontology traditionally conceived, at the same time as saying subject, which locates the ethical in a singularity put under the relation of responsibility? Or, put with more theoretical detail: what does for-the-Other subjectivity look like in its temporal, spatial, and linguistic configurations? In the exploration of these questions in his later work, Levinas can be read as addressing the foundational quirk of *Totality and Infinity*: the aspiration to a radical notion of difference and the conservatism of its theoretical language. At its best and most precise theoretical moment, we see this unfold in Levinas's outline of the contours of the subject – an ontology of the fractured subject – with a cluster of concepts dedicated to the articulation of the *denucleation* of subjectivity.

The critical element of denucleation is the temporality proper to the ethical subject. In *Totality and Infinity*, Levinas's sense of temporality is largely informed by the excessive present; for that reason, time seems to play a secondary role to space and a sense of place. After *Totality and Infinity*, temporality moves to the center of the analysis and takes on a very different character. Time means everything in *Otherwise Than Being*, replacing, with enormous consequences, the language of excessive presence with diachrony. Diachrony, the splitting of time that also splits the subject, is deployed by Levinas in order to name the distance between the Me or I and the Other. Far from the prominent, even decisive role it played in the early work, separation is no longer the operative characterization of subjectivity-as-for-the-Other in Levinas's later writings, except in so far as separation takes on the language of time. Separation as time, and so not space or place, is located outside the play of empirical or worldly life in a very specific sense. Time is the *element* of genesis. Subjectivity *becomes* subject through time, which is then repeated, forgotten, or perverted in the play of space and place in worldly being. *Time is that before of subjectivity that is subjectivity itself.* Levinas writes:

> The knot tied in subjectivity, which when subjectivity becomes a consciousness of being is still attested to in questioning, signifies an allegiance of the same to the other, imposed before any exhibition of the other, preliminary to all consciousness – or a being affected by the other whom I do not know and who could not justify himself with any identity, who as other will not identify himself with anything.[3]

This passage nicely delineates the new conceptual space of *Otherwise Than Being*. 'Questioning,' which amounted to the founding event of the ethical in *Totality and Infinity*, is here rewritten as attestation. That is, the empirical or worldly event of being put in question *signals* a prior relation, rather than initiating the relation of disruption itself. With this gesture, Levinas is able to locate the question of genesis outside being, while at the same time taking account of how what is within being – the practice of everyday life, the commonplaceness of obligation and being surprised by responsibility – bears the marks and features of ethical subjectivity. Ethical subjectivity is not created in the moment of questioning. Rather, questioning tells us of another history of the subject, one that binds the subject to its Other at the very same moment the ethical subject came into being – into being, that is, from the otherwise than being. A subject beyond essence. The empirical events of ethical life are therefore remembrances of subjectivity's past, to be sure, but that past is itself always before or outside the machinations of memory.

The enigma this raises is clear. Levinas calls subjectivity a *knot*, by which he means, if I read him correctly, that a binding or intertwining of two distinct threads comprises the identity of the subject. The Me and the Other. One might be tempted to see in this expression a *rapprochement* of sorts with Merleau-Ponty's figure of the *chiasm*, except that, in Levinas's case, the knot is tied *in* subjectivity, a crucial nuance that locates the identity between Me and Other *prior to* my place or the Other's place in the world. Further, the subject *is* the knot. The crossing is not one of two distinct items put in knotted contact, both of which signal an independence and persistence in being before encounter. The Other is not exhibited *first*; nor am I firstly present to the world. Rather, the knot is tied in subjectivity before the subject is aware of itself as a subject. Even the accusative, that peculiar awareness Levinas describes as a being made, created, or brought into being by the Other's accusation, is late to itself. Subjectivity is therefore constituted in a time lapse. Diachrony explains this lapse and seals it as both different than and resistant to any rendering of split time as a theme in and for consciousness. That is, diachrony does not come to consciousness as a theme in reflection, but is instead signaled in various modes of affective life without ever making itself a representation of itself. Diachrony is the infinite in the finite, the sort of paradoxical or contradictory identity Levinas often describes in his earlier work with reference to Descartes. Still, this turn to the temporal dimension of subjectivity and its identity comes to sustain a significantly more radical language of alterity. In 'Diachrony and Representation,' an essay written a decade or so after the publication of *Otherwise Than Being*, Levinas writes:

> The anteriority of responsibility is not that of an a priori idea inter-preted on the basis of reminiscence – that is, referred to perception and the glimpsed intemporal presence based on the ideality of the idea or the eternity of a presence that does not pass, and whose dura-tion or dia-chrony of time would be only a dissimulation, decline, deformation, or privation, in finite human consciousness.[4]

The final bit of this passage underscores why it is so difficult to talk about diachrony, especially when we think diachrony in terms of the subject's identity. Whatever language we lend to the meaning of diachrony is a perversion and mundanization of the split time of identity. That is, to give finite expression to what lies before expres-sion's deepest resources (consciousness, memory, will) is to alter the form of diachrony and make what is otherwise than being wholly worldly. As well, if subjectivity is diachrony, the relation of temporal separation 'preliminary to all consciousness,' then we start down a path of repeating paradoxes that conventional conceptual tools can neither describe nor resolve. All of the paradoxes revolve around the foundational event of time, which, rather than dispersing itself into the world of interruptions, is itself fractured from the outset, split in two, and so disperses itself into the world as the peculiar mixture of identity and difference whose affective signals remind us of, without ever showing us, the generative event of diachrony. This peculiar mixture, *as a worldly event in its own right*, is the empirical event of encounter to which *Totality and Infinity* dedicates itself. A whole text, late to the scene. In turning to diachrony as the original scene of identity – a peculiar, fractured ontology of the subject – *Otherwise Than Being* takes place in a very different time.

With the problem of diachrony, and so of a subject generated before consciousness and the manifestation of the Other, Levinas gives shape and contour to his characterization of ethical subjectiv-ity as denucleated. On Levinas's description, the subject is carved out in its very center. The location of this carving-out at the center indicates how profoundly disruptive the thought of denucleation is for ontology. This is not for Levinas a matter of the subject inter-rupted or thrown off its center by a peculiar encounter or a tense relation between, say, the intentionality of language and its material-ity. Rather, before the subject can even call itself a subject, it lacks a center; that decentered conceptual site or space generates the subject as such. The Other, who names the non-center of genesis, is not merely a margin that, with proper attunement and attention, could be made a now-center, former-margin. The rhetoric of 'the outside' is in some ways misleading, even as it appears repeatedly in *Otherwise Than Being* and many essays published after. In terms of its founding 'moment' in diachrony, ethical subjectivity is not a relation to the outside; nor is it called to move outside of itself. The subject collapses into itself without a center, and is then expelled back out into the world, saturated with the affects of a founding loss and a lapsed temporality. A melancholic subject. In other words, Levinas is not describing a relocation of subjectivity to the exterior – something one *might* see in the accounts of welcoming and the host in *Totality and Infinity*, where the Other moves to the center and defines, in the living-presence of the home, the meaning of subjective life. The later Levinas gives no such abundance, reprieve, or positive vision of ethical work. That is part of the desert and deserted landscape Levinas describes in *Otherwise Than Being*. Subjectivity is just that barren and austere. More than a dangerous encounter, perhaps, the Other who denucleates the subject and introduces an irreconcilable diachrony to the heart of the Me is a devastating event or place of non-relation. There is no recovery. Levinas calls this devastating non-relation both the *locus* and the *null-site* of identity's breakup; which is to say, non-relation is at once the impossibility *and* persistence of the identity of the subject. He writes:

> The break up of identity, this changing of being into signification, that is, into substitution, is the subject's subjectivity, or its subjection to everything . . .
>
> Subjectivity, locus and null-site of this breakup, comes to pass as a passivity more passive than all passivity. To the diachronic past, which cannot be recuperated by representation effected by memory or history . . . corresponds or answers the unassumable passivity of the self. 'Se passer' – to come to pass – is for us a precious expression.[5]

Passivity does so much work in this passage, just as it does so much work in *Otherwise Than Being* and related texts in the later Levinas. Passivity seals identity against the will, egoism, and self-constitution by disassembling the borders of the subject with the passage of time – the 'to come to pass,' which Levinas often clarifies with the analogy of ageing. We are late to ourselves and find, in ourselves as the very identity of the subject, not the trace of the Other, but the trace of what has never been. Denucleation reworks and repeats the idea of the relation of height, except that here the temporal language of diachrony wholly removes the genesis of ethical subjectivity from the traffic of worldly life. Subjection to the Other, yes, but in *Otherwise Than Being* I was never myself to begin with; I begin, *as Me*, as already having been subjected, which is signaled (and so not manifested in an event) in the material experience of denucleation (vulnerability, exposure) and the affect of temporal lapse. Thus, again, Levinas nuances the notion of subjection, expressed in *Totality and Infinity* by the relations of separation and height, in order to establish the broken identity of subjectivity in a non-recuperable time.

What motivates this rethinking of time? Surely part of the motivation is internal to the problem of difference. *Totality and Infinity* accomplishes a lot, to be sure, but its primary accomplishment in this context is to set a program in motion. The analytical tools in that text are not nearly sufficient to the task of thinking identity, subjectivity, and fractured ontology, however, so it falls on later developments in the idea of time to sustain the programme of thinking difference radically. Crucial for thinking difference radically is the meaning of *absence*, for absence lies at the heart of the problem of subjectivity, the Other, and the identity that issues from the knotting of difference. Absence challenges ontology by withdrawing from being and beings – moving outside the economies of manifestation, showing, and phenomenality. But, for Levinas, the conceptually disturbing moment comes when that unrecoverable absence structures what comes to play in both presence and the exchanges of presence and absence.

In this sense, even if Levinas does not offer a citation or nod of approval in his direction, we can see how the denucleated for-the-Other of subjectivity draws close to Derrida's notion of supplementarity. The Other in *Otherwise Than Being* functions like the supplement: it is not part of the subject as an internal feature of the I, but the I is unthinkable without it. That is, the supplement makes what it supplements possible, while at the same time destabilizing any and every description of identities. A radical absence at the heart of presence and the play of presence and absence, *denucleating* what it supplements as a matter of *creating* the very being of the supplemented. We therefore have to understand the supplement in its dynamic work and effects, rather than seizing upon it itself; reading affects and after-effects catches sight of the *signaling* of the supplement – that wholly Other at the center of a decentered identity – in its works. In the concluding pages of *Of Grammatology*, Derrida writes:

> It is the strange essence of the supplement not to have essentiality: it may always not have taken place. Moreover, literally, it has never taken place: it is never present, here and now ... Less than nothing and yet, to judge by its effects, much more than nothing. The supplement is neither a presence nor an absence. No ontology can think its operation.[6]

Like Derrida's supplement – a conception of an addition to that which *pretends* to be self-sufficient, which then unravels self-sufficiency with a constitutive contingency – the Other in Levinas comes from the outside, from what is beyond and otherwise, and yet is shown, in the devastating force of the Saying of responsibility, to form or *create* the interiority of the subject. A peculiar reversal, indeed, this dangerous supplement of the Other makes the interiority of the subject from the outside, but this making – what Levinas calls, with real precision, the *creatureliness* of subjectivity – leaves the subject both carved out by its other *and* response-able. Denucleation is an introduction to being and decision and agency, even as that carving out of the subject makes the I always late to itself and the temporality of action.

The most complex elements of Levinasian thinking lie in this double movement: to be *creaturely* is at once to be *as* absolute passivity and *as* responsible to the Other. That is what identity means, after all, in the sense that to be identified as *this* subject is to speak a pre-history in one's affects and to make a way into the world as the effected and affected subject. To be sure, Levinas's work is committed to 'the ethical' and not 'ethics'; he is not concerned with producing a plan of responsible action. The ethical names the structural dynamic of the formation of a subject who, in the moment of recognizing a responsibility to the Other and feeling the disconcerting affects of infinite obligation, is never again at home with itself. This is not (yet) the plane of action, though it is arguably a rewriting of the being of the subject, even if that means abusing the language of ontology.

In that naming and creation, there is a kind of ontology of subjectivity at work in Levinas's thought. Despite his explicit claims to the contrary, the problematic of ontology recurs, here under a fractured rubric – does this not simply demand another language of ontology, rather than the eschewing of the very idea? Now, Levinas's distance from ontology, particularly the ontology of the subject, is clear and largely convincing. Against Heidegger's existential analytic, Levinas proposes the separated, then denucleated subject who, unlike *Dasein* in *Being and Time*, does not project into the world, but rather has the world created out of an encounter that is not first worldly. Otherwise than being and beyond essence, there is subjectivity. *Yet, there is still, always after, subjectivity.* A structure that becomes visible in the moment affects of persecution, obsession, and recurrence converge across diachronic time to *create* a responsible subject. And so the enigma of a Levinasian ontology of the subject in *Otherwise Than Being* lies in thinking *ontos* and creatureliness at the same time. Unlike the account of moral consciousness in *Totality and Infinity*, thinking *ontos* and creatureliness at the same time in the later work is not a matter of how the Other unravels the pretensions of the I. By the time Levinas gets to *Otherwise Than Being*, the story has become considerably more complex and the language of identity and origin, especially in the 'Substitution' chapter, moves to the forefront. Ontology is fractured, just like identity, for both speak the same philosophical language: subjectivity and its originary conditions of emergence, then worldly being. Before and after, there is fracture, but there is also a sense of being as the Me becomes the I.

The Me becomes the I. That formulation suggests so much.

What is curious about this story of subjectivity, however, is Levinas's lack of attention to the problem of *being-after* as this denucleated, then creaturely subject. The knot of subjectivity, that generative sense of entwinement, gives birth to another sort of being, identity, and so sense of place in the world. Is this not a description of a fundamental hybridity of the subject? Knotted, the hybrid subject confounds conventional ontology, yet still persists in being, living after: differently and differentially. That is, there is in Levinas a fractured ontology of the subject that suggests so much for understanding the element of mixed cultural, national, and racial life. Borders are disassembled – what, then, does it mean to live with fractured borders as a matter of ontology, not just occasional politics or geography? With that suggestiveness in mind, let us turn to Homi Bhabha's work on narration and subjectivity.

LOCATION AND DISLOCATION

When Fanon published *Black Skin, White Masks* in 1952, he brought the collective force of Sartrean existentialism, psychoanalysis, and the anti-colonial intellectual struggles of Negritude and Surrealism to bear on an analysis of postcolonial subjectivity. Fanon's postcolonial subject, glimpsed for the first time in the upsurge of independence struggles, is compelled by the violence of history and historical experience to configure itself anew, walking a fractured, fracturing, and even neurotic line between what alienates and what will come to sustain life after colonialism. Disassembled borders and the difficult question of thinking contradictory forces at once, in the same subject. This is Fanon's task. So, perhaps it would be more accurate to say that Fanon's work operates in the *becoming* postcolonial of subjectivity, situated as that work is between colonialism and the accomplishment of its overcoming.

Fanon's is an anxious subject. The anxiety of this subject is both straightforward and profound: the home in which the colonized subject finds himself – language – is always alienating. We need not look further than the function of the *métropole* to understand the basis for Fanon's anxious subject. The mother city is not just geographic; the *métropole* is as psychological as it is cultural, so the question of legitimacy and illegitimacy in relation to the mother city means everything for the colonized subject. For Fanon, the language of the *métropole* pulls the colonial gaze and its measure into both the interior and exterior of subjective life. To speak French is always to speak as a black French speaker, in Fanon's work, which condemns the speaker to a certain kind of irredeemable and unalterable subaltern status. Anti-black racism fixes expression in this economy. 'To speak a language,' Fanon writes in *Black Skin, White Masks*, 'is to appropriate its world and culture.'[7] This initially reads as a banal observation, one that simply notes how language and culture are intertwined in embodiment and voice, but of course moving the question of speaking, language, and world across borders and histories makes what is banal into a massive, transhistorical, collective existential crisis. Precisely because it is banal. Anxiety is powerful because it works in the everyday, without exceptional character or shock. When we speak a language, we tell the story of a nation – even as our telling is saturated with anxiety, never finding ourselves at home in the language or the story.

In response to this anxiety, Fanon proposes the enigmatic and, in the end, largely suggestive concept of a 'new humanism.' Fanon's elusive new humanism promises or seeks the possibility of being, culture, and politics in a field of difference without the violent imposition of the colonial measure. This lifting of measure would putatively allow subjectivity to emerge with the proper authenticity, generating a sense of meaning, self, world, and, ultimately, *language* that refers only to the intensity of expression, not a prior measure. '[U]niversality,' Fanon writes at the close of 'Racism and Culture,' 'resides in this decision to recognize and accept the reciprocal relativism of different cultures, once the colonial status is irreversibly excluded.'[8] Colonialism creates the anxiety of comparison, placing the colonized in a space where they will always lose and assume the subaltern position. Lifting that colonial relation makes an authentic, or perhaps just less violent, relation to language possible. Perhaps just a bit of home. There is of course so much more to be said about this moment in Fanon's work, but what is important here is how Fanon's Sartreanism commits him to a conception of the future beyond Caribbean historicity. We can glimpse a small sense of the future in the outline of the new humanism and its commitment to asking a *question* (rather than arriving as a predetermined answer), though, in the end, we see it even more clearly by way of the negative: Fanon's critical remarks on pidgin and creole. Pidgin and creole, Fanon claims in *Black Skin, White Masks*, cannot sustain a new humanism. The former is a degradation of French, the latter is incapable of literary and theoretical expression. This leaves Fanon to suggest a universality of difference-without-measure, presumably under the fractured umbrella of the French language. A fractured language fractures the story of a nation, which in turn opens new spaces for identity creation and formation. Fanon's new humanism, we can presume, begins in this fractured sense of language, world, culture, and home.

Fanon moves through an ambivalent space. A future regulated by the vision of a new humanism seeks (it is never accomplished in his work) another beginning and a break from what Fanon calls 'the prison of history.' His conception of anti-colonial struggle decides *against* history, not just as what continues from the past (revolutionary action always seeks to change history), but also against history as a bequeathing; Fanon does not seek to inherit the meaning of the past and its suffering, but to overcome it in theory and action. But that decision comes from a complicated space of contradiction and anxiety. Indeed, on Fanon's rendering of the relation of past–present–future, he could not decide otherwise. Fanon encounters the mixed space of colonial historicity – the historical experience of cultural destruction, then cultural adaptation under colonial rule – as abjection, which folds over into his account of how anti-black racism constructs an impossible situation for the black subjects of colonialism. This situation is impossible because it appears to offer a choice between mimicry fated to alienation and nothingness. (Fanon of course proceeds without the atavistic spirit of Negritude.) His way out of the impossible situation is to think outside the economy of mixture. Having rejected pidgin and creole – two hybrid forms of historical language and language appropriation – Fanon faces an open future in search of the elimination of measure. And one can hardly blame him for this formulation, really, given the severity of history and the intensity of psychological violence across centuries of colonial relation. What grounds *could* there be for possibility in the past? Mixture, for Fanon, is fated to the inferiority complex.

As perhaps his most important reader and subtlest critic, Bhabha's return to the anxious or even neurotic moment of mixture in Fanon's work changes so much. Bhabha's transformation of Fanon's work revisits this ambivalent space in order to retrieve a still potent and important sense of interstitial identity. In Fanon's formulation, interstitial identity is a suspended question, however much it might be suggested by the terms of analysis. Indeed, in Fanon's formulation we see how his vision of history transforms the possibility of the future with an ambiguous, yet still explosive, concept of the new. Still, Fanon's encounter with interstitiality is never fully developed as a *positive* position, functioning instead as at once a phenomenology of the postcolonial moment and a witness to history's greatest violence. In order to make a claim to positivity in the interstitial, moving outside and beyond the suspended moment, mixture must be rethought without abjection. Or better: we must catch sight of the experience of mixture as generative of new forms of meaning and subjectivity, not just as the repetition of pain and sadness. The historical experience of movement, dislocation, relocation, and dislocation again – that story of migration's constant renewal – mixes cultures, dismantles and reconstructs subjectivities, and so is always at once mournful and new.

And so to this end, and in order to begin again with Fanon, Bhabha sees something different in the moment of history's crossing in culture and subjectivity. Mixture is not abject, even as it is saturated with anxiety. Bhabha makes this shift in affect (for it is largely a question of affectivity) in part because he writes after anti-colonial struggle has accumulated both practical and theoretical history, but also, just as much, because he writes from (and about) the perspective of a different kind of migration. (One wonders how informed Fanon's work is by the very particular violence of the Middle Passage, which drowns the possibility of any substantial atavism – and about which he says nearly nothing.) Migration, on Bhabha's account, has all the anxieties of Fanon's postcolonial moment, but with a decisive re-interrogation of mixture that recasts the foundations of being. Identity is put in question, there is the violence to language, and so there is also the uncanny as the foundational experience of the new. And yet in that uncanniness, Bhabha finds the 'uncanny fluency of another's language,' a formulation that, in the context of Fanon's remarks on language, ought to resonate as a deeper claim about connection to place. Migration is defined by loss, to be sure, and sometimes that loss is profound and nearly unredeemable. But migration is also uncanny fluency, that strange experience of finding oneself in another place, culture, and world, and, with all sorts of transformative moments comprising it, making that *new* into a sense of home. Or, at the very least, contesting the comforts of what *was* a home place by the counter-narrative of *merely being present*. Uncanniness, after all, flows both ways.

This is all to say that Bhabha's very different postcolonial moment begins a long story about the possibilities of a decentered subject whose center is cored out by the onto-cultural labor of movement. Such stories are of course often told in the memoir or testimonial genre, but such stories also contest philosophical conventions regarding subjectivity. Let us consider, then, the rightly famous opening remarks to his essay 'DissemiNation.' Bhabha writes in a personal voice, to be sure, but his remarks blend the testimonial with a certain kind of phenomenology of the fracturing of subjectivity. The fracture happens in the *halving* of life and language – the defining characteristics of subjectivity. As well, and perhaps most importantly, these remarks underscore the problematic of hybridity that lies at the center of both 'DissemiNation' and the larger trajectory of Bhabha's thinking. In the edges, boundaries, and borders of a culture, things fall apart. When they fall apart, subjectivity is gathered again in the horizon of the new. The reflections in 'DissemiNation,' he writes, owe

> something more to my own experience of migration. I have lived that moment of the scattering of the people that in other times and other places, in the nations of others, becomes a time of gathering. Gatherings of exiles and *émigrés* and refugees; gathering on the edge of 'foreign' cultures; gathering at the frontiers; gatherings in the ghettos or cafés of city centres; *gathering in the half-life, half-light of foreign tongues, or in the uncanny fluency of another's language.*[9]

Now, at first glance, this might simply read as a sketch of a definition of diaspora: the scattering of people, the reseeding in foreign places, and the memory of past places and meanings. And while Bhabha is surely saying that, he is also saying something more. Rather than formulate migration on the matrices of scattering-gathering, forgetting-memory, and so any variety of retention of identity, Bhabha sets out his problematic in terms of a series of halves and uncanny experiences. Both characterizations change the language of diaspora away from the problem of memory and identity, toward what we might call the *creatureliness of home*. Home is uncanny in this passage, in so far as home is formed, deformed, and reformed in the language of a place. None the less, no matter how uncanny, it is home.

The problem of home is also the problem of subjectivity, for the historical experience of migration blends home and migration as the defining movement across borders. So, his reflections quickly (and rightly) turn toward the complex relation between concepts of nation and the storytelling – what Bhabha calls simply *narration* – that makes nation-identity work. Identity is a *felt* relation, but also one whose affectivity is carried through language. Narration, the 'range of discourses' in which 'the concept of the "people" emerges,'[10] plays a double function in the constitution of nation and its identity. The double function makes identity fragile and unstable in its hybridity, rather than – through some sort of dialectical resolution – calcifying the mixture of narratives. On the one hand, narration opens and closes the identity of nation from the very heart of collective identity; to speak a language is not only to adopt a culture, but also to reproduce it across time. In that sense, narration plays a role very similar to Althusser's conception of ideology, but without the social theory adherence to state apparatuses. Bhabha's twist, if we can simply assert the commonality here, is to delink identity from social institutions and their stability-instability and deepen the problematic with the materiality of language. On the other hand, language proves to be vulnerable to migration in unique and important ways. Movement across borders changes not only inflection and the like – something assimilation addresses with some ease – but also the kinds of experiences that underpin and sustain the narration of the nation. 'From the place of the "meanwhile," ' Bhabha writes, 'where cultural homogeneity and democratic anonymity articulate the national community, there emerges a more instantaneous and subaltern voice of the people, minority discourses that speak betwixt and between times and places.'[11] That is, migration changes the experiences and stories that arise from being in a place precisely because the migrant – not unlike Fanon's becoming-postcolonial subject – speaks from and as interstitial space. When those experiences and stories change and alter the received story of national community, the meta-function of narrative is exposed as ever precarious, vulnerable to the counter-narration arising in those unexpected stories from an outside that is nevertheless inside. The migrant is precisely this outside who is inside, what Bhabha describes as 'wandering peoples who will not be contained within the *Heim* of the national culture . . . but are themselves the marks of a shifting boundary that alienates the frontiers of the modern nation.'[12] Thus, we quickly discover that the story about how stories make identity begins before narration performs its work in the massive project of producing, then re-producing, a nation. That beginning before is as unstable as it is fragile. Wandering peoples expose this instability.

Indeed, this ante-space of ambivalence, indecision, and even undecidability functions very much like the condition for the possibility of the nation's narration and the subsequent precarious formations of identity. The ante-space is not a pre-established identity lost in the nation's narration, contested when the migrant's insurgent counter-narrative is spoken. Rather, the ground of narration is a sense of difference that is also a shared, fractured boundary captured in Bhabha's casual – though enormously important – use of the word 'gathering.' *Gathering.* This is such a crucial item in a turn of phrase, for with a characterization of difference, movement, and displacement as a *gathering* (and so not dispersion, fragmentation, or ciphering) Bhabha is able to posit, then explore, the historical experience of hybridity as fecund. That is, unlike Fanon's speaking from interstitial and hybrid space, which produces pure loss, alienation, and the inferiority complex, Bhabha sees a notion of identity emergent in and from the liminal spaces of migration. Hybridity is not simply loss and the memory of pain. Rather, and this is something Bhabha tries to recover from Fanon's work, hybridity opens up a new conception of being: interstitial subjectivity. Fractured, yes, by the migration – forced or otherwise – and yet always still an identity. Just as the storytelling of the migrant disrupts cultural homogeneity by exposing the fragile fabrication of narration, the migrant too is transformed from atavistic to hybrid in the moment of contact with *his* outside: the nation. Literally and figuratively at the margins of the nation – interstitial, liminal, constituted and constituting the between of an insurgent counter-narrative – the nation of others, the gathering of exiles, and the others of nation form a subjectivity. The question is how to articulate that subjectivity and begin to take it seriously as a way of being *without an appeal to calcified identity*. And so Bhabha, as part of a brief discussion of Salman Rushdie's *The Satanic Verses*, writes that 'the radical alterity of the national culture will create new forms of living and writing.'[13] Bhabha's appeal here to living and writing, which we could call (as with Levinas) a very different kind of ontology of the subject, must be framed and constantly informed by the anti-logic of fracture. Everything is broken apart; liminality promises no closure, no recuperation of the center, and so no resolution of the conflict, but rather the precarious, fractured integration of conflicting elements into subjectivity. Hybridity as subjectivity after interruption, but subjectivity also after the location of being in the interstitial. *Originary fracture.*

How does Bhabha understand the conditions of fracture? How does fracture turn into hybridity, and therefore surmount what initially seems to be the intractability of trauma and loss? And how does hybridity name an identity in precarious relation to any narration whatsoever?

The problem of postmodernity frames Bhabha's exploration of these questions. From the postmodern, Bhabha draws on both the contestation of the meta-narrative – in an implicit rewriting of Jean-François Lyotard's famous formulation of postmodernity in *The Postmodern Condition* – and the instability of the sign – a direct conversation with Derrida's work. In the remarks immediately above, we can see exactly how the exilic, migratory moment is already a lived postmodern. The counter-narrative of migration is at once posed against and lodged within the narration of national identity as a sort of political *différance*, insurgent, disrupting and destabilizing without taking power. The power of migration, which is perhaps better described as *force*, lies in resistance and transformation. Both resistance and transformation are enabled by the exposure of narration's (and so the nation's) fragility in its founding moment. Homogeneity is entrusted to a meta-narrative, and yet stories are entrusted to time, written from particular spaces, and the gathering of migrants reminds the nation (and the subjectivities it produces) that its narrative is itself temporal and spatial. Narrative, as meta-narrative, of course fantasizes otherwise, locating identity in a timeless place. The uncanniness of home complicates, if not outright overturns, the purity of identity, denucleating identity before it turns (and so not re-turns) to itself.

In this sense, migration is not revolutionary. It is, rather, insurgent at the moment before politics and the struggle over cultural forms. Migration as gathering names an interstitial subjectivity that recalls the nation's narrative back to its originary ante-chamber: the agonistic and ambivalent telling of stories of movement across and in the between borders. Nor is migration simply the lateral production of difference we expect in discourses of multiculturalism. The terms of identity as meta-narrative are put in question, rather than proliferated laterally as multiple forms of nostalgic atavism or rooted and centered identity claims. Migration, then, marks its force and significance in a mixture of the incommensurable, creating anxious spaces and subjects and schemata of identification. On this model, otherness collapses the colonial construction of center-margin, though always without recourse to a dialectic of liberation. Bhabha will talk about subjectivity in the margins of the nation, of course, which might suggest that he thinks marginality as such, but the margin always functions deconstructively; the margin contaminates the center, the center contaminates the margin, and so there is never a resolution of the conflicting conceptual space. Hybridity and its undecidable character therefore function as deconstructive or, perhaps more broadly, postmodern transcendentals – conditions for the possibility *and* impossibility of narrative, nation, and subjectivity. Claims for certain formulations of subjectivity and claims against the very idea of subjectivity are put under the same critique; hybridity is both decentered and subjectivity. Unlike Fanon's alienated subject, Bhabha attaches to the subjectivity of the subject at the very moment we lose sight of its core and center. Not unlike Levinas's for-the-Other of subjectivity, Bhabha's subject carves out the center of identification and then refuses to recenter the symbolic domain. In 'The Postcolonial and the Postmodern,' he writes:

> Postcolonial critical discourses require forms of dialectical thinking that do not disavow or sublate the otherness (alterity) that constitutes the symbolic domain of psychic and social identifications. The incommensurability of cultural values and priorities that the postcolonial critic represents cannot be accommodated within theories of cultural relativism or pluralism.[14]

Dialectical thinking without sublation is of course not dialectics at all. It is, rather, a way of thinking, which Bhabha here identifies as the signature of the postmodern, that is Heraclitean through and through. Strife or unrelieved tension constitutes the meaning of identity, rather than identity resolving conflicting forces through the hegemony of the homogeneous or the sublating work of assimilationist dialectics. *An always uneasy, anxious identity.* Relativism and pluralism are not sufficient because, in each, narrative – and so subjectivity – would remain undisturbed by difference. Hybridity disturbs by being at once an identity and a non-identity.

The postmodern, having eschewed meta-narrative and dialectics, opens up the horizon of thinking the between. Or, perhaps we should be more modest: the postmodern underscores the impossibility of thinking the between on conventional models of analysis and understanding by refusing the very idea of reconciling difference. However, in Bhabha's work, the context shifts just a bit and alters the terms of discussion. In place of, or maybe just alongside, the epistemological and ontological enigmas inherent in thinking difference radically, Bhabha locates disturbance and non-reconciling difference in the relation of cultures across and crossing borders. Difference is lived in narrative identities, rather than solely in, say, the infrastructure of the sign. This is an impossible identity, a broader and historically informed denucleation of the subject that is nevertheless generative of a certain subjectivity. In this sense, modernity is confronted in its cultural formations. Such confrontation exposes the strange and fantasied foundations of modernity's concern with uniformity. The postmodern motifs of difference and resistance lend depth and important strategic resources for such a confrontation. Thus, we could say that Bhabha's engagement with the postmodern helps begin the administration of the conceptual work of what he calls 'contramodernity.' He writes:

> Culture becomes as much an uncomfortable, disturbing practice of survival and supplementarity – between art and politics, past and present, the public and the private – as its resplendent being is a moment of pleasure, enlightenment or liberation. It is from such narrative positions that the postcolonial prerogative seeks to affirm and extend a new collaborative dimension, both within the margins of a nation-space and across boundaries between nations and peoples.[15]

This passage makes careful distinction between difference and collaboration, a distinction that is utterly crucial for maintaining a sense of difference that does not bear a nascent dialectic within it. That is, collaboration *could* surmount difference with an emerging or teleological identity. But such a surmounting is only possible if we understand difference as mere juxtaposition. Bhabha here alters that sense of difference with the evocation of Derrida's notion of supplementarity. If migration and movement place contesting and agonistic stories on the margins of the nation, then we have to read that marginality in terms of the logic of the supplement. And so, if the supplement, as per Derrida's articulation, is that Other who constitutes the meaning of the Same by way of a radical absence withdrawn *before* presence, then we can see how Bhabha's conception of collaboration across boundaries proceeds from a prior dismantling of the terms of juxtaposition. Again, the interstitial is a space *before* narrative, and so is a space that contests narrative's veracity in its very foundation: the ante-chamber of narration as cultural difference without resolution. In this precise sense, Bhabha asserts the first position of hybridity.

As well, Bhabha's evocation of the supplement, functioning here as the exilic between *and* the transnational more broadly, raises the question of the full and most radical significance of the name 'difference.' That is, it raises this question about the relation of the postmodern to the postcolonial: to what sort of difference is the postmodern directed, especially as postmodernity's deconstruction of and resistance to metanarrative appeal to the sorts of movements, mixtures, and emerging identity-which-is-not-one characteristic of the postcolonial situation? Or, put more concisely, what does it mean to contest modernity with a fracturing of identity? There is a lot at stake in these questions, in particular with the question of the name of resistance, and thus the possibility of the new. And Bhabha's claim is straightforward: rename the postmodern as the postcolonial, thereby asserting postcolonial historical experience as a primary datum, rather than an object of study for an instrumentalized postmodernity. Like Fanon, Bhabha's task is to wrest the language of postcolonial difference free from the logic of comparison; instrumentalization of theory and rendering the postcolonial as merely an example would repeat colonization, here at the level of ideas.

Bhabha's particular use of poststructuralist theory emerges from what he calls 'postcolonial contramodernity,' a sense of the Other that marks the failure of logocentrism not just with a counter-theoretical gesture, but also with an insurgent subaltern history embedded in the margins of modernity – a sort of denucleation of modernity by way of language and migratory movement. Denucleation, if we may write the term over contramodernity, is perhaps best put in Bhabha's description of 'colonial non-sense,' that moment of internal disruption that exposes identity as fractured in its originary formulation.

In-between-ness is certainly called to expression and signification; this is the risk of any coming to presence in the world, even if from the (non-)position of the supplement. The postmodern helps Bhabha begin thinking through the problem of signification and difference in the baffling logic of contramodernity. In 'Articulating the Archaic,' he writes:

> In-between culture, at the point of its articulation of identity or dis-tinctiveness, comes the question of signification. This is not simply a matter of language; it is the question of culture's representation of difference . . . inscribed *without* a transcendent subject that knows, outside of a mimetic social memory, and across the – ouboum – kernal of non-sense. What becomes of cultural identity, the ability to put the right word in the right place at the right time, when it crosses the colonial non-sense?[16]

The answer to this final question is of course the undecidable. In-between culture, undecidability *par excellence*, splits signification such that expression of hybridity – this new twist on denucleated subjectivity, perhaps – is always fractured at the moment of assigning a name. This is no doubt a name which is not one. Such a paradoxi-cal formulation, Bhabha claims, is necessary, built as it is into the meaning of colonialism's ambivalent relation to difference. 'It is in the enunciatory act of splitting,' Bhabha writes, 'that the colonial signifier creates its strategies of differentiation that produce an unde-cidability between contraries or oppositions.'[17] We catch sight of undecidability as historical experience in the postcolonial moment, full of the anxiety Fanon describes, but also full of the positivity of resistance and counter-narration. This immanence of undecidability to historical experience allows Bhabha to 'rename the postmodern from the position of the postcolonial.'[18] *Renaming the postmodern condition itself.* The postmodern, in that moment of taking on a new name from the position of the postcolonial, is re-embedded in the historical experience of migration and the *différance* produced by the interstitial forms of life gathered in the margins. The postcolonial is already the story of postmodernity.

In his 'The Postcolonial and the Postmodern,' Bhabha gives further dimensionality to this renaming in the distinction he draws between the names Casablanca and Tangiers. The distinction is, in name, between the two Moroccan cities for the sake of illuminating the postcolonial revision of the postmodern. But most importantly the distinction is between two senses of time. For both Bhabha and

Levinas, and this is of ultimate significance, the time structure of subjectivity and language accounts for the senses of separation and fracture in both. Neither subjectivity nor language can be understood in terms of spatial distribution and differentiation; in this sense, 'the transnational' is as much a figure as it is a geography of historical experience. Movement is not itself the meaning of hybridity. Rather, the radicality of hybrid subjectivity and its cultural forms lies in the temporalization of spatialized difference and its constitutive disjuncts. With Tangiers, Bhabha makes geography figurative and temporal, seeing in the space or place of the Moroccan city the sort of incommensurability that makes hybridity denucleating and never dialectical. 'In Tangiers,' Bhabha writes, 'as time goes by, it produces an iterative temporality that erases the Occidental spaces of language' and 'opens up disjunctive, incommensurable relations of spacing and temporality *within* the sign.'[19] Further, this suggestive evocation of language, incommensurability, and time helps us retrieve the importance and enormity of Bhabha's short narration of diasporic life in 'DissemiNation' quoted above. The gathering of migrants is already a splitting of time and identity: the bearing of the nation on those communities and the nostalgic aesthetic of the gathering place. The repetition of *half* in that passage sets a limit on both ends of diasporic encounter. There is the first limit placed on the scope of the nation's claim on the migrant. Such communities are already sites of resistance because the stories told in those sites form the counter-narration *before and against* narrative's attachment to nation. As well, and this is only the counter-force of this first limit, there is the limit on the migrant's atavistic sensibility. Movement consigns the past to memory, and the language with which the migrant approaches memory is already itself hybrid, which in turn intervenes to split the time of memorialization. Atavism meets much the same fate as nation: vulnerable to time and mixture, it is exposed as a fantasy of a timeless, transcendent subject. Migration therefore produces a peculiar double. This is the doubling of denucleated, hybrid subjectivity Bhabha calls, in a certain abuse of the term, the postcolonial 'cosmopolitan.'

What is the cosmopolitan? And how does this cosmopolitan subject describe the denucleated, hybrid subject? The doubled subject, produced by migration and the work of the time of Tangiers on language and being, recalls Bhabha's repeated invocation of Derrida's notion of the undecidable. Indeed, what could the migrant's condition be *except* undecidable? The undecidable, seen in the frame of Tangiers time and the deconstruction of the sign, is precisely the cosmopolitan in the postcolonial context: to be in multiple places, never resolved into one place, and indeed disruptive of the very idea of a unified or universal place. For Bhabha, this occasions a rethinking of futurity (and so conceptions of the new) and what he calls the 'unsatisfied universal.' He writes:

> How do we conceive the 'object' of identification – the transnational or global differential – as the ground of a new cosmopolitanism, if cultural/social agency is positioned within the ethics of an unsatisfied 'universal'? Unsatisfied, not because it is mimetically in/non-adequate, but because 'unsatisfaction' is a sign of the movement or relocation of revision of the 'universal or the general, such that it is producing a process of unanticipated transformation' of what is local and what is global.[20]

From this notion of the unsatisfied universal – the irreducible hybridity produced by movement across borders – Bhabha establishes further grounds for his claim about the *uncanniness* of home. Hybridity is a home, after all, no matter how marginal and exilic, but it is always a home against itself. That is, there is only home at the same time that one is un-at-home with oneself and in a place. This is the double movement of subjectivity, which is the double movement that underpins the notion of a vernacular cosmopolitanism as 'an *uncanny* site/sign of the native, the indigenous.'[21] A cosmopolitan subject always to-come, thought in relation to a future without closure and the ontological effects (and affects) on a subjectivity subjected to that thought. The subject of Bhabha's postcolonial renaming of the postmodern is therefore a national subject – subjected to the nation, subjecting the nation to it. Time and narration keep this subjected and subjecting subject undecidable. Hybridity, forged in the to-come of the future, is in a certain sense no name at all, but rather a sign of becoming, process, and so constant interruption, localization, globalization, and detour. Rather than return, there is always another or the Other counter-movement. Counter-narration from what is begun as counter-modernity.

It is important to note the shift in emphasis here, as well. In 'The Other Question,' for example, Bhabha gives sustained attention to the construction of the Other, otherness, and how alterity forms the subject *within* colonial discourse. The colonial signifier is always ambivalent; ambivalence reflects the denucleating work of the Other who is constructed, yet does deconstructive work. In this thesis, Fanon's work, again, plays a crucial role. In fact, much of the essay is dedicated to rewriting and extending what Bhabha calls the 'two primal scenes' of Fanon's subject: encountering the racism of language in the gaze and the omnipresence of anti-black racism in children's fiction.[22] In colonial discourse, it would seem that otherness is installed in subjectivity as alienation alone; there is only loss and trauma and forgetting of origins, which Fanon works through in his critique of Negritude and assimilationist conceptions of the postcolonial subject. Race under colonialism, as Bhabha puts it, 'becomes the ineradicable sign of *negative difference*' for Fanon.[23] And yet there is also the *other* moment for the postcolonial, the moment documented by Bhabha first in terms of migration (which makes difference insurgent and narrative), second in terms of the *post* that defines contemporary life, and then, in its broadest sense, as the incarnate historiography of the cosmopolitan (everywhere and nowhere). This is not simply a case of agency, in which the formerly colonized speak back to colonial alienation. It is rather the speaking from interstitial, hybrid places that fracture the meaning of ontology and, yet, at the same time produce a sense of subjectivity. *An ontology of fracture, a fractured ontology.* Perhaps it is enough just to say that the desires of and desires for the *métropole* produce alienation. Fanon, perhaps, has not yet worked through those desires, so still suffers the same anxieties, however sublimated they may be. But that collage and clash of desires cannot fully account for thinking and being *after* colonialism, a sense of 'post' that, as we have seen, introduces a wholly different temporality. In this wholly different temporality, there is a wholly different subject. The other Other, being in time. *The postcolonial renaming of the denucleated subject.*

What are we to make of *this* renaming?

NEXT YEAR IN TANGIERS

Ontology cannot retain its traditional power and conventional connotations after the thought of difference, whether we negotiate that break with ontology by way of Levinas's or Bhabha's conception of a fractured subject. One of the consequences of operating under the deconstructive logic of the supplement is that nothing can be stabilized *as a matter of originary principle*. Dangerous supplements place the outside inside, which then makes any claim to being as persistence-of-the-same an act of violence against difference. To think difference first, however, is not yet enough, for even if subjectivity does not persist as *the same*, there is always subjectivity. Fractured, becoming, movement – the subject is renamed. In that renaming, a different relation between being and time. Subjectivity as denucleated and diachrony; subjectivity as hybrid and the time of Tangiers. The other – and other Other – ontology.

If we can put the meaning of ontology in a kind of brackets, retaining the force of naming the being of the subject while rejecting the neutralization of difference the term traditionally implies, then we can catch sight of a crossing of Levinas and Bhabha. This crossing has two important features. First, for both Levinas and Bhabha, subjectivity breaks with atavistic models of identity, whether that happens in the breakup induced by the interruptive force of the singular Other or the confounding mixture produced by border crossings and other transgressions. Levinas's frequent evocation of the Abrahamic sense of journey – evoking secondarily, perhaps, the Jewish diaspora – underscores the break with Greek models of homecoming and Christian-Hegelian notions of reconciliation. Hybridity interrupts the same sort of sense of return, in so far as the experience of marginality and its counter-narration produces undecidables where one might expect – or, in fits of nostalgia, just simply desire – stories of return. Bhabha thinks diaspora *as* diaspora, rather than assembling a story of return, persistence, and the full, pure presence of the past in acts of memorialization. That is, diasporic consciousness is for Bhabha always out of place with itself, cosmopolitan without satisfaction in a fixed or universal state. Indeed, this is what draws his work so close to that of Fanon: colonialism's work remaps subjectivity and its origins, and yet the Other produced by that remapping speaks, from the margins and in the center, against hegemony, the transcendent subject, and nation. The encounter and social experience, both thought as time and language, bring Levinas and Bhabha into an important kind of proximity. They meet in the peculiar temporality of being as fracture – the time of Tangiers.

What would it mean to imagine next year in Tangiers?

Next year in Tangiers, not next year in Jerusalem. In other words, what does it mean to place two thinkers in proximity without a common site of homecoming – even one envisioned, as with 'next year, in Jerusalem,' on the model of the messianic – and only a common site of the uncommon and non-iterable? The enigma here is of course thinking subjectivity without return, a sense of separation and division without final reconciliation. *Subjectivity lived without closure* – and yet, as Bhabha playfully puts it, such a subjectivity can

also be described as an agent without a cause. Bhabha's remarks on
Tangiers turn quickly to language and colonial discourse, and in
particular how hybridity comes to contest and undermine the fantasies of domination, but we can readily transpose the same on to the
question of subjectivity – for, subjectivity is precisely the subject of
language. That is, the theoretical stratum of time sustains the *agon*
of language and the difficult, even fractured subjectivity subjected to
postcolonial languages and histories. 'The temporality of Tangiers,'
Bhabha writes, 'is a lesson in reading the agency of the social text
as ambivalent and catachrestic.'[24] In so far as the temporality of
Tangiers sustains what Spivak, cited by Bhabha at this moment,
calls the '"negotiation" of the postcolonial position "in terms of
reversing, displacing and seizing the apparatus of value-coding,"'[25]
the turn toward Tangiers does not inscribe atavism into subjectivity. Hybridity moves in undecidable space. The time of this space is
chaotic and the spacing of this time, the sign brought to Tangiers, is
the catachrestic *deployment* of language. In time and language, in
the fractured and ambivalent spaces of migratory movement, there
is identity.

> The time-lag [Bhabha writes] opens up this negotiatory space
> between putting the question to the subject and the subject's repeti-
> tion 'around' the neither/nor of the third locus ... My contention,
> elaborated in my writings on postcolonial discourse in terms of
> mimicry, hybridity, sly civility, is that this liminal moment of iden-
> tification – eluding resemblance – produces a subversive strategy of
> subaltern agency that negotiates its own authority through a process
> of iterative 'unpicking' and incommensurable, insurgent relinking.[26]

Identity or identification is liminal, caught, as a sort of law of
hybridity, between the synchronic time and spacing in the language
of atavistic subjectivities and the roots of counter-narrative in the
experience of the colonized.

   In a certain sense, then, Bhabha repeats Fanon's anxiety about
the colonized as colonized; colonialism pretends totality, which
establishes the colonized as marginal, and so always in some sort of
relation to the center. The anxiety of the postcolonial moment lies in
just this configuration: how are the colonized to break with colonialism from a margin already determined in relation to the colonial
center? Catachresis begins that break with its insurgent character,
placing itself at the heart of language, but always with a decisive
swerve, detour, and generally deconstructive dynamic. Eluding

resemblance is critical for this insurgency as it seizes upon the character of the dangerous supplement. Counter-narratives produce hybridity – ambivalence gathered into a word – only in so far as the counter-storytelling maintains its incommensurability. Without commensuration, insurgency fundamentally changes the presence of the colonial identity. Nothing can remain the same. The counter-narrative changes – or, better put, *destabilizes* – that narration which makes a nation. Perhaps a broken and unsustainable nation. Perhaps a doubled and folded nation. Perhaps a nation only ironically. Or strategically. Certainly always an undecidable nation. This nation is the postcolonial subject writ large, those lives lived as migration, narrated in the opening paragraphs to 'DissemiNation.' Time and language make nation through narration. So too do we make subjects out of ourselves and others. After migration, hybridity – the ontology of the making of nation through narrative – is fractured by mixture and a new sense of being emerges *as* fracture, without reconciliation.

This is where philosophical language is particularly fraught. How can we *say* the subject is fractured without reinscribing that fracture into the conventional language of ontology? (This is always Derrida's question to the language of difference.) Next year in Tangiers, we begin to forge a language to come. In Tangiers, in that peculiar time, the problem of an ontology of subjectivity comes into its properly aporetic view and is left in that fractured state. That is, we catch sight of *something* in subjectivity, and yet the catching sight already unravels the economy of seeing, conceptualizing, and all the temporally neutralizing work that ontology threatens to bring to analysis. So, we might be tempted to see Bhabha's work on hybridity and interstitial identity as, like Levinas's words and proclamations, a project beyond or otherwise than being. Incommensurability, after all, is the crucial property of the otherwise than being in Levinas's work. Still, Bhabha's explicit concern is with identity, with how a person or a people *become* in diaspora, even as the colonial horizon of incarnate historiography moves against such becoming and articulation of identity, meaning, and – with all caveats in place – agency. This is not quite Levinas's subject, for he never conceives denucleation as hybridity. Indeed, diachronic time always signifies, for Levinas, outside the economy of combination or mixture, *even as there is a transgression across temporal separation.*

So, let us pause and ask the question: how is it that Levinas's radical rethinking of subjectivity as relationality – the for-the-Other subject created out of a denucleated I – comes short of a theory of hybridity or some other sort of configuration of mixture? Or, a bit more precisely, how does incarnate historiography lead other than to a theory of hybridity, especially given Levinas's own engagement with questions of diaspora in a Jewish context?

It is helpful here to return to Levinas's work on cultural difference and, especially, to consider how that work reveals the importance of his commitment to a certain idea of Europe. On the one hand, Levinas's remarks on cultural difference – one need only recall the characterization of everything non-European as 'dance' – seem to betray a lack of interest in, if not outright hostility toward the non-European expressions of meaning, culture, and politics. For all of his commitments to the Other, it is all too painfully true that Levinas privileges the comfort of home and common language over the encounter with the cultural, racial, and national Other. On the other hand, there is a lot to be learned from Levinas's less rhetorical, more theoretical treatments of cultural difference. In particular, his critique of Maurice Merleau-Ponty's account of difference in 'Sense and Signification' shows important sensitivity to the ontological and epistemological status of cultural diversity. Levinas begins with the fact of difference and the moral imperative of respect. The question is simply how that imperative of respect arises in cross-cultural encounter. For Merleau-Ponty, the inexhaustibility of Being or the Flesh as such levels off the question of diversity; the fact of diversity is derived from this inexhaustibility, and so every set of cultural formations, every 'people' and nation, is simply an interpretation of a fundamentally monistic, always untamable conception of being. Levinas does not contest the lateral relation of culture – expressed here in terms of language – but instead asks how this lateral relation comes to have moral resonance. It is not enough to turn the line of hierarchy ninety degrees. There must also be an ethical moment. In 'Signification and Sense,' Levinas writes:

> For there does exist the possibility of a Frenchman learning Chinese and passing from one culture into another, without the intermediary of an Esperanto that would falsify both tongues which it mediated. Yet what has not been taken into consideration in this case is that an *orientation* which leads the Frenchman to take up learning Chinese instead of declaring it to be barbarian (that is, bereft of the real virtues of language), to prefer speech to war, is needed.[27]

Levinas places difference at the center of his debate with Merleau-Ponty in order to overcome the limitations of the latter's rendering of cultural difference from within the question itself; Esperanto mediates, and so obliterates difference in the interests of instrumentalizing language and meaning. Language makes otherness possible across borders, proceeding, here, with the presupposition of distance. Merleau-Ponty's account of diversity acknowledges borders, but, in the end, derives that bordered difference from a third term. This is a sort of ontological Esperanto-figure, with the caveat that the third, mediating term is not transparent to difference, but rather an original ambiguity from which the refinements of culture derive.

It is not insignificant that Levinas makes language the bearer of culture, difference, and encounter. If language is how we inhabit a home and make our place in the world or Being, which is precisely the account of the word we find in Heidegger and even Merleau-Ponty, then configuring the relations language makes possible and impossible is the critical site for theorizing difference. How does language make diversity not just possible, but also a concern for moral consciousness? Is difference in language enough for obligation? Or does obligation require us to ask a more foundational question? For Levinas, of course, there is another question to ask. We are not merely caretakers of Being in cultural difference. The inexhaustibility of what lies prior to cultural difference is not sufficient for responsibility and affects of respect. Rather, it is the *uniqueness* of cultural sense that begins the intuitive chain, leading Levinas to the conclusion we might expect (and often do not see) from his ethics in contact with questions of culture: the Other obligates.

Even as he puts Merleau-Ponty's account of the lateral 'penetration' of cultures under his critical eye, Levinas produces very much the same account, with the primary – and indeed decisive – alteration of the cross-cultural encounter being the infusion of cultural questions with the question of the ethical. This infusion restages Levinas's theory of sense (*sens*) and signification. When Levinas asks, rhetorically, if cultural meanings 'take on meaning in a dialogue maintained with that which signifies *of itself* – with the other'[28] and then asks if 'meanings require a unique sense from which they derive their very signifyingness,'[29] the entire enterprise of cultural difference and exchange is reinscribed in the genealogy of ethical experience. That is, the *value of* and *respect for* cultural difference is traced back to how each cultural expression is ultimately grounded in signifyingness. That ground-which-is-not-one calls colonial discourse and its aftermath into question (Levinas makes that explicit), but only in the sense that cultural border-crossing is commanded to proceed with the ethical in view. *Sens unique* – this trope displaces the common root of Being or the Flesh and, in that displacement, renders comparison both epistemologically and ontologically misplaced, if not outright impossible. Without a common root, without Merleau-Ponty's (and maybe even Heidegger's) monist carryover, comparison has no grounds. Comparison is ungrounded by the *sens unique* and the signifyingness of cultural signification. For Levinas, and this seems to be an entirely convincing and even mundane observation, the lateral relation of cultures, left to itself, only reiterates the terms of colonial domination. 'One reasons,' Levinas writes of the lateral relation, 'as though the multiplicity of cultures from the beginning sunk its roots in the era of decolonization, as though incomprehension, war, and conquest did not derive just as naturally from the contiguity of multiple expressions of being.'[30] Diversity is no block against conquest and alienation. Rather, it is the precondition of violence – just as the alterity of the Other makes murder possible – and such terrifying history unfolds in a totalizing and totalitarian space that eclipses the *sens unique* of obligation. Unique sense, one-way traffic *into* and *as the orientation of* culture, resists the historical repetition of war and conquest.

Now, one might wonder how Levinas, with this account of cultural difference in view, is capable of baldly chauvinistic remarks about the non-European. Were we to take Levinas's claims seriously here, we could easily read Levinas against himself and ask why the *sens unique* of, say, the non-European's 'dance' garners such scorn and dismissal. And so on. That polemical orientation is plenty interesting and provocative, but what interests us here is how the lateral relation of cultures, infused as that relation is with the ethical, informs Levinas's conception of subjectivity *after* cross-cultural encounter. That is, we should ask how Levinas's work on cultural difference arrives at a lateral articulation difference, even as that difference is ultimately referred back to the unique sense of the ethical. Indeed, the crucial question here is how Levinas makes that reference to the *sens unique* possible. In attempting to 'fix with precision the conditions for such an orientation' of cross-cultural encounter and respect, Levinas turns to the familiar 'movement going outside of the identical, toward an other which is absolutely other.'[31] The language of the ethical intervenes, however, without carrying over the structure of denucleation or even the older language of *mise en question*. This is peculiar. After all, the ethical describes, always, a relation of height, fracturing, and the carving out of a (collective and singular?) subjectivity in relation to the Other as a precondition of that subjectivity in the first place.

Again, Levinas's conception of history is immanent to the question. In his work from the 1970s, Levinas juxtaposes what he terms the 'pre-history of the I' to the narrative (*récit*) conception of the subject. Surely, the distance Levinas wants to gain from narrative reminds us of Bhabha's commitment to storytelling, nation, and identity, as Levinas posits the pre-history of the I against collective identity. None the less, pre-history is still genesis; this turn to pre-history tells a story, but one without words. The ante- and anti-origins of subjectivity, structured by diachronic time, lie in this pre-history, embedded in affects and a non-relationality that generates the for-the-Other of subjectivity. Levinas's quasi-transcendental turn in the exploration of pre-history pushes aside the particularities of historical experience and narrative in favor of the idiosyncrasies of singularity, lived as sensibility. Even Levinas's claim that the body has a history – that peculiar and suggestive evocation of Merleau-Ponty's early work – makes a quasi-transcendental turn. So, when this is put forth in the context of culture and cultural difference, the stakes are suddenly elevated and the terms of discussion become perhaps unmanageably complex. These stakes engage colonialism's aftermath; despite his inattention to contemporary political events, and perhaps revealing the tepidness of his engagement in this case, Levinas in 'Signification and Sense' simply states the ethical objection to the vertical relation of cultures and subsequent colonial violence. That surely lowers the sense of stake. It is not all that radical to object to colonial violence, after all, and surely something altogether different to catch sight of the endurance of that violence across incarnate historiography. But he also finds the stakes elevated in the peculiar and under-explained relation between the *sens unique* – long opposed, at least in epistemic form, to political meaning and identity – and cultural signification. Levinas *asserts* that culture derives from the *sens unique*, and yet he appeals only to our intuitions about how cultural expression is both singular and collective. And that is where the complexity of the moment comes into view. Cultural identity has a narrative form for which the pre-history sense of history provides no model. And yet the urgency of responsibility, linked to the historical experience of violence and marginalization, depends upon a complex moment of the singularity of signifyingness and the historical embeddedness of the same. To wit: if culture's ethical command is rooted in the terrifying experience of colonization (that moment of vulnerability and suffering from which obligation first speaks), then we cannot think cultural formation outside the experience of history. And so too the experience of narration and counter-narration we find in Bhabha's work, where the interstitial must supplement the Levinasian conception of denucleation. As with all supplements, this one is dangerous for Levinas's unqualified commitment to the singular, but also absolutely crucial for understanding the scope and meaning of ethical life.

This is surely a difficult moment for both Levinas and Bhabha. Perhaps it forms a tentative, maybe precarious, chiasm in which the ethical and hybridity can be thought across the cultural subject. But that requires supplementing Levinas with Levinasian thinking about the incarnate historiography of the ethical, which moves denucleation back through the worldly life of the transnational. As well, it requires seeing the ethical moment more clearly in Bhabha's work – work that, in general, poses the identity question in the neutralized space of critique. What is the ethical moment in the fractured ontology of the worldly space of race, nation, and the Other?

The crux of this split between Levinas and Bhabha, we could say, lies in the question of the status of the social text. The pre-history of the I shifts the genesis of subjectivity away from the vicissitudes of history and social experience, which effectively erases the insurgent character of hybridity. Indeed, it is only on the basis of a certain kind of historical experience – the (fantasied) uniformity of European difference – that such a pre-history appears as not only possible, but also and firstly as the originary story of the originary movement of the subject. Incarnate historiography reveals itself here. Rather than being marked with movements across borders, forming and re-forming the social text through counter-narration, the Levinasian body is marked with the history of the singular Other and Me. I come to myself, exposed and vulnerable, because of the Other who speaks the first words of obligation. This is the only kind of history that registers in the formative movement of history – the *pre*-history, in so far as it precedes, ontologically and epistemologically (which is to say, *temporally*), the social text. Bhabha's claim moves in exactly the opposite direction, or at least in a contrary logic. The social text is first. Incarnate historiography is written not only on the body of racialized and nation-marked experience – that part of cultural difference Levinas leaves aside, given the priority of the *unique* in *sens unique* – but also in the embodiment of the word. Speaking, telling, writing, and the subsequent remaking of each transforms the totality of colonial hegemony with the undecidable transcendence of hybridity, sly civility, and so on. What is written is rewritten in the movement not of liberation, but of *disruption* and *reconfiguration* thought as liberatory *promise*. The social text becomes ethical at that very moment, that moment in which the center of itself is unlocatable within the language of the text, projected instead out of itself to the non-locatable margin whose supplementary position configures the subject in an always to-come future. This is a broken social text that is none the less still a social text, producing broken subjects who are none the less still subjects. Denucleated, hybrid.

We are here returned, again, to the problem of anxiety and identity in Fanon's work. Like Fanon's, Bhabha's work begins with the anxious situation of an identity formed without foundation; the reach of colonialism in Fanon's work, locating violence in language, world, and consciousness, provides a pointed and complex case of the transnational. Bhabha changes that context a bit with the example of exile and migration, which removes the terms of forced migration in the Middle Passage (a nascent, but potent force in Fanon's work), but keeps the question of mixed geography and being as the centerpiece to thinking about identity. There is also the ethical interval in Fanon's work that becomes visible when read across the Levinasian problem of denucleation. Bhabha sees this ethical moment in violence itself, writing of Fanon that '[t]he anxious struggle for the historical consciousness of freedom that eschews transcendence – or a higher unity – derives from violence an ethics that takes responsibility of the other in the transformation of the "thing." '[32] Violence is done in search of agency, but, Bhabha claims, this is an agency undertaken on the condition of being responsible for the Other whose life, under colonialism and in the immediate thereafter of anti-black racism, has been rendered a thing among other things. The existential reality of unrootedness is a loss of subjectivity – the phenomenon of being rendered a thing – and the loss of the sense of return to the lost subjectivity. Displacement devastates the center of subjectivity, so requires that, even in the search for another kind of agency, subjectivity be thought without center. On this moment, Bhabha is particularly interesting when he writes further that

> [t]he anxiety of displacement that troubles national rootedness transforms ethnicity or cultural difference into an ethical relation that serves as a subtle corrective to valiant attempts to achieve representativeness and moral equivalence in the matter of minorities. For too often these efforts result in hyphenated attempts to include all multiple subject positions – race, gender, class, geopolitical location,

generation – in an overburdened juggernaut that rides roughshod over the singularities and individuations of difference.[33]

Displacement *creates* anxiety. The ethical moment, on Bhabha's account here, lies not in a question of respect for difference – a chance reply to Levinas's 'Signification and Sense' – but in another reorientation toward difference and the structure of the subject. That is, displacement's anxiety must be dislodged from Bhabha's observation that '[a]nxiety is a culture's longing for place and its borderline existence,'[34] moving instead toward 'the taking up of a position, as Emmanuel Levinas would say, beyond the ontological consciousness of difference, in relation to the anxiety of a liberatory history whose object remains to be fulfilled.'[35]

The appearance of Levinas's name in this passage is more than a kind coincidence. Indeed, in this brief remark, Bhabha says so much of how we ought to think the ethical horizon of hybridity and, therefore, how we ought to think the ethical in the wake of Fanon's work. Levinas's work displaces the habits of displacement, moving from the consciousness of difference to difference as a condition of consciousness. In particular, Levinas's work allows us to see how subjectivity is thinkable even when the gravity of being is located outside the center of subjectivity – a fractured ontology of the subject. The location of that Other or outside, that decisive and dangerous supplement, brings the troubled term of relation between Levinas and Bhabha into relief: the future. If difference structures consciousness, that move from margin to dangerous supplement in denucleation and hybridity, then we have to ask about the moment *after* difference. Fanon's anxiety (and maybe our own), Bhabha notes, is perhaps still too rooted in the idea of roots, the idea that displacement points us to a past or a future in which the center is regained. Denucleation and hybridity point us elsewhere *in the register of infinite deferral*. The future, in other words, remains to be fulfilled – an unsatisfied universal. In this twist, Bhabha marks an important advance on Levinas's account of denucleation and difference, for, in Levinas's work, diachrony stalls the movement of subjectivity. Diachrony, left to itself, is altogether too arid. *There is also the future* – sure, Levinas says some words about this future in the idea of the messianic, but the messianic remains very separate from the incarnate historiography of the for-the-Other subject. The future is hybridized and denucleated, which allows us to break ontology free from atavism's long horizon of nostalgia and those related forms that attach anxiety to a future object. The objectless future, however, does not have to come, as it does for Levinas, without the worldly memory of race and nation. Quite the contrary, memory of race and nation reintegrates incarnate historiography and its diachronic time with the materiality of cultural life, a materiality that, in the end, reminds us that difference as such *and* cultural difference contest the very idea of the border with an alternative vision of being.

Being after, fractured ontology, persisting subjectivity.

Next year in Jerusalem? Perhaps this is Levinas's appeal. That messianic vision, no matter how deferred or how interruptive, appeals too readily to roots, return, and an object to soothe the anxiety of displacement. *Next year in Tangiers?* In Tangiers, difference finds a geographic site for displacement and a time that never settles, always defers. Perhaps this is the destiny of Levinasian thinking, the ethical and the transnational. *Indeed, next year in Tangiers.*

Notes

1. Homi Bhabha, 'Interrogating Identity: Frantz Fanon and the Postcolonial Prerogative,' in *The Location of Culture*. New York: Routledge, 1994, 40.

2. On the issue of *Sinngebung* in Levinas's work, see John E. Drabinski, 'Sense and Icon: The Problem of *Sinngebung* in Levinas and Marion,' in *Emmanuel Levinas: Levinas and the History of Philosophy*. New York: Routledge, 2005, 106–22.

3. Emmanuel Levinas, *Autrement qu'être ou au-delà de l'essence*. The Hague: Martinus Nijhoff, 1974, 32; *Otherwise than Being or Beyond Essence*, trans. Alphonso Lingis. Dordrecht: Kluwer Academic, 1991, 25.

4. Emmanuel Levinas, 'Diachronie et représentation,' in *Entre Nous*. Paris: Grasset, 1991, 189; 'Diachrony and Representation,' in *Entre Nous*, trans. Michael Smith. New York: Columbia University Press, 2000, 170.

5. Levinas, *Autrement qu'être*, 17–18/14.

6. Jacques Derrida, *De la grammatologie*. Paris: Minuit, 1967, 442; *Of Grammatology*, trans. Gayatri Spivak. Baltimore: Johns Hopkins University Press, 1997, 314.

7. Frantz Fanon, *Peau noire, masque blanc*. Paris: Points, 1990, 30; *Black Skin, White Masks*, trans. Richard Philcox. New York: Grove, 2008, 21.

8. Frantz Fanon, 'Racisme et culture,' in *Pour la révolution africaine*. Paris: Découverte, 2006, 52; 'Racism and Culture,' in *Toward the African Revolution*, trans. Haakon Chevalier. New York: Grove, 1967, 44.

9. Homi Bhabha, 'DissemiNation,' in *The Location of Culture*. New York: Routledge, 1994, 139. Emphasis mine.

10. Ibid., 145.

11. Ibid., 158.

12. Ibid., 164.

13. Ibid., 166.

14. Homi Bhabha, 'The Postcolonial and the Postmodern: The Question of Agency,' in *The Location of Culture*, 173.

15. Ibid., 175.

16. Homi Bhabha, 'Articulating the Archaic: Cultural Difference and Colonial Nonsense,' in *The Location of Culture*, 125.

17. Ibid., 128.

18. Bhabha, 'The Postcolonial and the Postmodern,' 175.

19. Ibid., 182.

20. Homi Bhabha, 'Unsatisfied: Notes on Vernacular Cosmopolitanism,' in *Text and Nation: Cross-Disciplinary Essays on Cultural and National Identities*. Columbia, SC: Camden House, 1996, 202.

21. Ibid., 202.

22. Homi Bhabha, 'The Other Question,' in *The Location of Culture*, 75–6.

23. Ibid., 75.

24. Bhabha, 'The Postcolonial and the Postmodern,' 183.

25. Ibid. Bhabha is here citing Gayatri Spivak's 'Poststructuralism, Marginality, Postcoloniality and Value,' in *Literary Theory Today*, ed Peter Collier and Helga Geyer-Ryan. London: Polity, 1990.

26. Bhabha, 'The Postcolonial and the Postmodern,' 184–5.

27. Emmanuel Levinas, 'Signification et sens,' in *Humanisme de l'autre homme*. Montpellier: Fata Morgana, 1972, 39; 'Meaning and Sense,' trans. Alphonso Lingis, in *Collected Philosophical Papers*. The Hague: Martinus Nijhoff, 1987, 88.

28. Ibid.

29. Ibid., 40/89.

30. Ibid., 39/88.

31. Ibid., 43/91.

32. Homi Bhabha, 'On the Irremovable Strangeness of Being Different,' *PMLA*, vol. 113, no. 1 (1998): 38.

33. Ibid., 34.

34. Ibid., 35.

35. Ibid., 38.

CHAPTER 4

Ethics of Entanglement

> It is a question of a nothingness distinct from the nothingness
> of anxiety: the nothingness of the future buried in the secrecy
> of the less than nothing.
>
> Levinas, Totality and Infinity

With the subaltern and the theory of hybridity, we begin to bring the
problem of incarnate historiography into clearer view. In particular, we see how the historical experience of colonialism challenges
the meaning of difference by moving both the sense of loss and the
reconfiguration of relation away from the margins and toward the
center of what it means to speak (or resist speech) and to conceive
place. In that movement, knowing and being are shifted away from
languages of totality and sameness, and thereby begin to engage with
the complex enigmas of radical difference. In that sense, the problems of race, nation, and other, framed by incarnate historiography,
cannot be seen as matters of autobiographical report or accidental
qualities of human experience. Rather, race and nation alter the
space or geography of epistemology and ontology; the Other makes
knowing possible and impossible, and breaks up the coherence of
being in specificity and in general. To the extent that Levinas's work
is concerned with radically overturned notions of knowing and being
– finding self-awareness and self-presence *after* the creative work of
the Other – the postcolonial revision of the terms of difference is an
immanent critical intervention. Levinasian thinking *must* revise itself
after the revision of its most intimate conceptual terms.

The sense of loss and how it reconfigures the relation to history,
knowledge, and being has hitherto been treated on the conquest-
occupation or migration model, where the epistemological gap of the
subaltern is conceived in terms of the withdrawal from a common
conceptual space and the fracturing of ontology is conceived in
the movement of the migrant. What we have not considered is the
meaning of loss, history, and its myriad consequences in a New

World context – that other site of colonial violence. In particular, I have in mind the Caribbean context, where the beginning of conceiving knowing, being, and the aesthetic forms of culture is initiated with a wholly unique sense of loss. The catastrophe of the Middle Passage determines the specificity of the meaning of loss; the figures for and structures of memory are cast in this moment. How do we conceive the past? What is the meaning of the present? And what is promised by the future? All of these crucial questions are transformed by the transnational experience of forced migration. That migration and the disastrous loss it entails call us to rethink some of the fundamental categories of philosophy, just as for so many European thinkers the experiences of the two world wars and the Shoah called for a revision of the meaning of theorizing subjectivity, culture, and so on. To put it simply, the Middle Passage alters the meaning of beginning by drowning the root in the past – what we will discuss below as the *abyss* of beginning – and marking the arrival, beginning proper, with a specific sense of trauma.

So, the wider question that concerns us here: how to begin again after catastrophe? When everything has been lost and what remain are ruins that only alienate, never edify, the question of beginning takes on a particularly urgent and melancholic character. After catastrophe, there is less than nothing in the past and present from which we might root a future; catastrophic loss suggests just such a cipher as the foundation. Conquest, occupation, and migration devastate roots and transform them with violence, without question. However, as we will see below, the sense of loss in the Middle Passage changes the meaning of roots, trauma, and mourning, replacing the attachment of memory to the hollowed out place of what was with the complete vanishing of the object. Instead of mourning, the relation to the past-with-no-object takes on the character of melancholia. If we take Freud's formulation of melancholia seriously, then write it larger across the historical experience of loss, then what is melancholic is addressed – perhaps even 'cured' – only by fiat. Perhaps, too, the future has its ultimate meaning in the surprise of fiat.

This is a question of historical experience, and so also how we understand philosophical thinking in the wake of catastrophe. How does philosophy theorize beginning after everything has been lost? In the European context, this is an old question. Massive historical shifts in meaning have always initiated a crisis in the meaning of commencing thought, both in terms of the anxious relation to tradition and the problem of forging a new and adequate theoretical language for the future of thought. As well, and in a global (or globally entangled) context, the enigma of beginning after catastrophe is especially central to the twentieth century and so many of its attendant anxieties. Whether it is the end of domination in postcolonial struggles, the closure of metaphysics and the old world of philosophy, or unprecedented internal and external violence, the just-ended century is in many ways one long witness to the anxiety of beginning again. Indeed, catastrophe is nearly synonymous with the long twentieth century. From the ecstasy of Frantz Fanon's imagination of life after revolution to the persistent call to renew the vocation of philosophy to projects of complex retrieval, beginning is made anxious by a loss that seems, at first glance, just so total.

Still, just as loss is surely devastation, there is also a tradition of seeing in loss fecundity and new possibility. Recall, for example, how in Martin Heidegger's long meditations on beginning, meditations that (among so many other things) sought to re-invest Husserl's project of perpetual beginning with historical sensibility, the problem of loss is prominent and decisive. Heidegger's famous remark on the Greek temple in 'The Origin of the Work of Art,' where he notes that we encounter only the having-lost the god and never the god's presence or presence in absence, locates the problem of philosophy's beginning in the experience of loss. The relation to the past has continuities, but also rifts and fractures that make a certain break with tradition total. What are we to make of that break with tradition? What does the tradition *want* to bequeath to our thinking? And what blocks that desire of tradition, challenging us to begin again with another vision (or lack thereof) of the future? Heidegger's loss is always a loss of a previous abundance, which is then eclipsed in the shifts and rifts of subsequent epochs. For Heidegger, the passage of time, marked in the failure of language to contain and carry meaning fully in its sedimentation, cracks open history's temporal flow. And so there is loss. There is not catastrophe. This is no small manifestation of Heidegger's all too familiar forgetting of the violence of Europe's twentieth century. At the same time, Heidegger's meditations – if we may evoke them just for this moment – propose an interesting and important interpretation of loss: after loss, there is mourning, but also retrieval of traces and the project of beginning again. Loss is not fixated on the past and its absence. Loss instead opens the horizon of thinking (thinking *Being*, for Heidegger) and a future attuned to a new and potent sense of abundance. Excess in the wake of loss – this is Heidegger's mourning and memory project.

If Heidegger's sense of beginning is informed by the double movement of loss and excess, as well as a seeming indifference to the disastrous violence of history, then what are we to make of Levinas's work as its own kind of production of historical experience? How do loss, excess, and violence figure as components of Levinas's sense of beginning? The two world wars, the Shoah, and the violence of colonialism all animate the period of Levinas's best and most important work. In some sense, then, whether by his own self-conscious articulation or our interpretative frame, Levinas is a thinker of beginning again after catastrophe. Levinas's philosophy tells a quirky and now familiar story about ethics, first philosophy, and the fate of every thinking that pre-dates the thought of *l'autrui*. Sure, there are plenty of blips along the way, with important figures finding their own work interrupted by the Good, the One, or the Infinite, though, in the end, excess is always defeated by the worst impulses of the Western tradition. Levinas's story about the history of philosophy-as-totalitarianism has been told many times. Sometimes with wild skepticism. Sometimes with uncritical adherence. What has rarely been told, however, is the story of beginning. How does Levinas's philosophy begin? That is, what is given to thinking from historical experience, that traumatized and traumatizing foundation of conceptual elaboration and creative extension? The tradition is totalitarian and we have seen its terrible consequences in catastrophic violence. How is beginning related to catastrophe? What is the future?

In what follows, I want to explore these questions through a rereading of the problem of futurity in *Totality and Infinity*. My claim here will be that, despite the absence of the particular word or phrasing, *Totality and Infinity* is fundamentally a book about beginning again, after catastrophe. But that is only part of my question here. I am also interested in how we might put Levinas into conversation with that other great Francophone thinker of beginnings: Édouard Glissant. Glissant also thinks disaster and beginning at one and the same time, conceiving the problem of theorizing the Americas as a moment of reckoning with the Middle Passage, the plantation, and colonialism. The postcolonial context, as we might expect, adds nuance to disaster and beginning, and this nuance, thought in proximity between Levinas and Glissant, will prove crucial for understanding what it means to begin. I want to put the two thinkers in proximity in order to accomplish two tasks. First, I hope to show how the problem of futurity is the critical issue for any thinking of beginning after catastrophe. Levinas's articulation of the terms and stakes of beginning again are indispensable for any project committed to imagining another possible world. Notions of fecundity, filiation, and an ethics beyond the entwinements of the moment, if broken from roots in the past by catastrophe, say so much about how to imagine the world after everything has been lost. When read with Glissant, whose ethical sensibility matches that of Levinas so well, a fuller sense of the project of an ethical metaphysics of the future emerges. For Glissant, however, this ethical metaphysics of the future is a globalizing and globally entangled imperative. Martinique, after all, *is* France, *is* the New World, and, in that crossing, *is* a specific kind of globalized space – a claim whose own futurity we will explore in a Levinasian register. Second, and perhaps most searchingly, I want to locate the particularly European tenor of Levinas's project and ask, in a critical voice, how that European tenor might limit our appreciation of the entangled responsibilities of moral life after modernity. That is, I do not simply want to charge Levinas with the rather common thought-failure of Eurocentrism (though that is not nothing). His strictly European interpretation of catastrophe, beginning, and futurity limits the scope of his claim and stalls the mobility of that theory. And yet there is still more to say with Levinas, after Glissant and his notion of entanglement. In particular, I want to contend here that Levinasian responsibility, when thought in the interval of catastrophe, beginning, and futurity, always exceeds his construal of the scope and character of our moral consciousness. To *be* responsible in historical experience – that is, to respond from the body's inheritance of history – is to engage, always, with the entanglements of local and global conscience.

METAPHYSICS OF THE FUTURE

How do we begin with Levinas and the problem of catastrophe?

In 'Signature,' Levinas offers an at times predictable, at other times engaging and surprising, account of his life in a sort of intellectual autobiography. I say 'sort of intellectual autobiography' because Levinas in many ways repeats old lists and common characterizations of his work – the sorts of comments we find well before the retrospective piece is published in 1970. The date of 'Signature' is of course well placed, situated as it is between the publication of his two major works and in the midst of the theoretical revolutions that culminate in *Otherwise Than Being*. In the essay, the remark that strikes me as most surprising and certainly most important for my remarks here is the claim Levinas makes about the Shoah. It is obvious that the Shoah was a transformative event for Levinas, as it was for every Jew and Roma, and indeed, though in different ways, for every other class of European. That is a personal speculation of sorts. What is less obvious is how that event functions in relation to Levinas's own writing, which is dedicated first and foremost to the infinity of obligation, to the singular other, and so to the non-racial or non-ethnic character of the human. This is of course not to say that the specificity of Judaism as a *tradition* and form of *wisdom* does not inform Levinas's thought, but just that the thinness of his sense of historical experience does not suggest the particularity of ethno-religious history. And yet here is Levinas, making a short remark about the centrality of the Shoah for his own thinking. What could he mean by this? Did the genocide of European Jews (and Roma, though Levinas does not note this – joining most theorists of the Shoah) impact Levinas's thinking? Or is it simply part of his biography, and his philosophy stands quite well apart, perhaps even independent? Though Levinas has written very little on the Shoah, the opening remarks in 'Signature' invite speculation and rereading. As a general characterization of the essay, he writes simply:

> This disparate inventory is a biography.
>   It is dominated by the presentiment and the memory of the Nazi horror.[1]

How are we to read this statement? What is the relation between biography, philosophical work, and presentiment? With this statement in view, the memory of the Nazi horror has been read by some as formative for Levinas's work, a reading nicely supplemented by the famous dedication of *Otherwise Than Being* to the memory of the dead. Such reading sets out an important claim. Were we to explore all of the consequences, thinking of Levinas's work as post-Holocaust theory would require a systematic rereading of that work as less a phenomenology of obligation than an elaborate exploration of traumatic memory. Perhaps Levinas's work has *always* been a response to Nazi terror and the Shoah, seeking an ethics after the catastrophe? Such a reading would frame Levinas's work as a memory project against history and narrative. A memory project, yes, but one that seeks to redeem humanity with the pure simplicity of the vulnerable face.

I have always been suspicious of this claim. Apart from the dedication of *Otherwise Than Being*, which is given over to the memory of the murdered in the death camps, the Shoah almost never appears in Levinas's philosophical work. Beyond predictable critiques of Husserlian and Heideggerian conceptions of remembrance and time, Levinas does not offer much to thinking the relation between history and memory (one of the signature concerns of post-Holocaust memory projects). If we consider other thinkers for whom the Shoah functions as the decisive event – especially Adorno and Horkheimer, as well as Arendt, Jaspers, and many others – then it becomes clear just how little Levinas engages with the central issues of post-Shoah theorizing: structures of modernity, bureaucracy, eliminationist culture, collective guilt, and so on. To be sure, Levinas's hyperbolic rhetoric equates ontology and certain epistemological orientations as 'totalitarian,' which can easily be inscribed in post-Shoah discourse, but that is hardly a sufficient engagement of the vast and deep cultural conditions of genocide. Glissant, for example, explicitly ties his linking of certain forms of thinking with totalitarian impulses to wider practices of violence, both in the Caribbean and in a global context. We just do not see this in Levinas's writings. Nor does Levinas explore with much (if any) depth the traumatic experience of loss, even as the language of trauma and persecution comes to dominate his work in the mid-1970s and after. If Levinas is a theorist of the Shoah, seeing a way to philosophize after the disaster, then why has that philosophizing never taken up the problem of trauma, memory, and history, such as we find in those companion thinkers *after* disaster, from Adorno to Blanchot to (at times) Derrida? For all the talk of the immemorial, Levinas never quite links or embeds that talk in a wider theory of living after the Shoah. So, what is the Shoah to Levinas, beyond terrifying autobiography?

Let me propose an answer by giving away, ahead of the analysis, a sort of conclusion: Levinas's account of beginning and futurity in *Totality and Infinity* is his one and most sustained exploration of the philosophical consequences of catastrophic loss. Levinas does not frame his analysis in that book with these terms, but, if read with catastrophic loss and its challenges to theorizing the future as a frame, *Totality and Infinity* begins to look like a book about beginning and disaster. Or at least one that formulates an important response to the problem. In that text, the name of the father – by which we mean here the surname, not the Lacanian motif – functions as something akin to a ruin after catastrophe, a cindered trace capable of carrying memory and identity into a future torn apart by violence. The fecundity of the (sur)name gives the future a meaning and continuity that survives loss. Very little, perhaps, but not nothing. The key for us will be how Levinas configures that fecundity in relation to the past, which, as I hope to show, exposes the hints and traces of atavism in his work.

To the text, then. Two sites form our initial reading of Levinas and the problem of beginning and futurity in *Totality and Infinity*. First, the opening passages in the Preface in which Levinas asks the larger question of the ethical, war, and the possibility of thinking otherwise – pages that in so many ways set his itinerary for the following two decades. Second, and perhaps most importantly, the concluding section of *Totality and Infinity* entitled 'Beyond the Face.' In that final section, the fecundity of the ruined past is transformed by the name, which, when read in the frame of catastrophe and living after, intertwines responsibility with the openness of the future. The son, whom Levinas describes as the paradoxical site of my subjectivity which is not one, bears this future in the surname. What sort of continuity does this suggest? And how is that continuity a remnant not just of a fracturing of the past, but of a loss of place and being? The frame of catastrophic loss helps us articulate this difficult problem.

The opening paragraphs of *Totality and Infinity* have occasioned more than a few comments, mostly concerning the elevated and historical terms of Levinas's programmatic motif. Levinas asks the biggest question, one to which *Totality and Infinity* by itself could never comprise a full answer: are we duped by morality? Levinas, in a tone wholly appropriate to the middle of Europe's twentieth century, wonders if the seeming permanency of war is inevitable and worthy only of calculation in response – after all, the millions dead in the wake of two world wars left the geography of Europe little changed, and so only atrocity and mass death stand as legacy. What are we to make of this 'legacy'? Is it simply a lesson for humanity, that war is intractable and we should merely calculate for victory? Levinas is right: morality is at stake in this wondering, for morality (desperately) holds out for another possible world. Or at least an interruption of war's dominance over the world and its transformation of human relations. Morality promises a repudiation of war, against the ongoing, shifting instrumentalization of violence. If war is the only possibility, then politics is nothing other than the calculation of the best possible means for the execution of violence, rather than the channeling of ethical sensibilities into the wider sense of human relations. In the opening section to *Totality and Infinity*, Levinas writes:

Does not lucidity, the mind's openness upon the true, consist in catching sight of the permanent possibility of war? The state of war suspends morality; it divests the eternal institutions and obligations of their eternity and rescinds *ad interim* the unconditional imperatives. In advance its shadow falls over the actions of men. War is not only one of the ordeals – the greatest – of which morality lives; it renders morality derisory. The art of foreseeing war and of winning it by every means – politics – is henceforth enjoined as the very exercise of reason. Politics is opposed to morality, as philosophy is to naiveté.[2]

Levinas's final remark on politics, which renders politics nothing but the management of war, conflict, and destruction, will be rewritten across the pages of *Totality and Infinity*, then many times thereafter, as the urgency of the ethical. Without the ethical, the intrigue of the interhuman is only disaster. But Levinas does not pose this problematic from historical reflection or mundane, speculative observations about states of nature. Rather, he arrives at those characterizations of politics first through provocative and radical characterizations of consciousness, knowledge, and the exercise of reason. Reason roots the self in the self, consciousness in consciousness. This changes everything about our relation to the world. The free and sovereign *I* – epistemological language that is at once ontological and political – constitutes the meaning of the world. Such constitution makes value out of a valueless plenitude. The Other, then, becomes only a fantasy and projection of the self, organized, in the context of war and violence, into conventional categories of conflict.

Under these conditions, the state of war is more than an event in which morality is suspended. War is simply the condition of being in Being. Totality cannot *become* moral or manifest a moral sensibility in order to mobilize against violence and conflict. The problem is neither with poorly reasoned calculation nor with an improperly calibrated ontology; tweaking the machine will not produce responsibility and peace. In other words, for Levinas, war is a *state of being as Being*, rather than the perversion or instrumentalization of a neutral commitment to identity for political ends. Indeed, identification itself lies at the root of morality's vanishing in politics. Totality sets the categories of social and cultural play, and when we are fixed in them we lose both our singularity and our capacity to encounter a face. We only encounter manipulable images.

Levinas's characterization of the state of war is quick, straightforward, and decisive. The equation of Being, politics, and war dominates so much of *Totality and Infinity* and after; such a massive theoretical and historical claim surely warrants a life's work to demonstrate. Levinas is remarkably plain in formulating his claim here, too. In the exclusivity of being and the wielding of violence, he sees not only the techniques of anticipating, then emerging as victor in, war, but also the epistemic and existential eclipse of unicity. Levinas writes, again in only the second paragraph of the book:

> But violence does not consist so much in injuring and annihilating persons as in interrupting their continuity, making them play roles in which they no longer recognize themselves, making them betray not only commitments but their own substance, making them carry out actions that will destroy every possibility for action. Not only modern war but every war employs arms against those who wield them . . . nothing henceforth is exterior.[3]

Totality is therefore akin to the transcendental of war – the condition for the possibility of making the Other the target of mass annihilation and liquidation. War as such *proceeds from* the annihilation of the exterior. And yet annihilation of the exterior is a peculiar act. Murder neither presupposes nor requires the eclipse of the exterior for its destructive act. In fact, exteriority may be the very condition of murder – I can only murder what I know to be and register as unique, singular, other, and so Other. War is something quite different. The soldier does not murder another soldier; the subject is not a murderer, the victim is not murdered. The soldier kills. The soldier kills a *category* 'enemy,' having given himself up, in the concession to war, to the category of warrior. Frenchman. Israeli. German. Vietnamese. Palestinian. Revolutionary. Patriot. In every case, war makes us play a role in which we no longer recognize ourselves. This is perhaps Levinas's deepest claim against Hegel, who in *Philosophy of Right* identified the critical moment of political formation as the habitual identification of subjectivity with the State. For Hegel, we become properly political when it becomes part of the animality of everyday life; no mediation is necessary or desirable. We simply are the state. And, for Levinas, this is war itself. Not the instrument of war – making us 'play roles' is not *preparation for* war – but *violence itself*. Identity makes war possible, violence inevitable. We are lost to ourselves and morality slips away. Playing roles in which we no longer recognize ourselves enacts epistemological and ontological violence, as we no longer know ourselves and others, and so are alien to the being of the self and the beings populating our world. It is also, and for that very reason, the very element and condition for the possibility of warfare.

What, then, has become of *Totality and Infinity*'s opening query? Are we duped by morality? If so, what does that mean? Where is the duplicity located and how is it possible to contest the state of war? And why this strange and hyperbolic beginning to *Totality and Infinity*?

The problematic of futurity emerges as crucial in the midst of these questions. Morality has duped us in so far as morality is inevitably, and perhaps even invariably, duplicitous when it operates under regimes of totality. Duty, virtue, and so on – all for Levinas fall under suspicion not only because he objects in simple principle to the occlusion of singularity, which is absorbed by generalities of law and habit, but even more importantly because conventional models of morality service totalitarian violence with barely a hiccup. Duty, after all, has long been identified by thinkers like Adorno, Horkheimer, Arendt, and others as a prominent feature of the National Socialist machinery of death. Part of Levinas's alternative evokes the language of first philosophy and what has been called the transcendental dimension of Levinasian ethics. For example, when he writes in *Totality and Infinity* that war 'presupposes peace, the antecedent and non-allergic presence of the Other; war does not represent the first event of encounter,'[4] we see that Levinas is committed to the idea of first philosophy, *even if that idea of first philosophy provides no stable foundation at all*. If peace is presupposed by war, then an appeal to the possibility of the ethical – however remote, with whatever tenor of desperation – has real grounds. The first grounds, in fact, anarchic and infinite as they may be. War is not the definition of intersubjective life, but rather a perversion – though a rather regular one – of the meaning of our interhuman intrigue. There is something beyond (and so before) war. First philosophy secures, however precariously, a sense of hope.

With this cast, Levinas has given the *history* of the West the form of ceaseless war and violence as a matter of knowing and being, not simply documentation of armed conflict and persecution. The disastrous violence of the twentieth century functions as a clue to a deeper philosophical and cultural form. Obsessions with being and knowing, those signature features of Western philosophy, explain war as a total cultural and historical event. An event of totality. War is not only possible, but wholly necessary. History could not unfold any other way. (This is what it means to call totality the transcendental of war.) Yet, hope does not disappear into the theory, then practice, of violence, for another world is possible – even if only in glimpses and occasional interruptions. *Only the future can save us.* That is, because peace is *before* war, and so infinity is *before* totality, the philosophical and cultural forms that sustain war and violence are always possibly thought otherwise. But even the future has been colonized by totality, as Levinas makes clear when he writes:

> The meaning of individuals (invisible outside of this totality) is derived from the totality. The unicity of each present is incessantly sacrificed to a future appealed to in order to bring forth its objective meaning. For the ultimate meaning alone counts; the last act alone changes beings into themselves. They are what they will appear to be in the already plastic forms of the epic.[5]

The struggle for a future otherwise than totality is posed here against a future that, from the outset, has objective meaning. In this passage, Levinas announces, in a precursory fashion, the important figurative distinction between the Homeric epic of Odysseus' return and the Biblical tale (epic?). Is time explained by arrival? Or is the moment punctured by what lies outside – and so not just ahead – of it? Indeed, only two years later in 'Trace of the Other,' this distinction will prove crucial in Levinas's ongoing attempt to break with totality. If the future is only sacrifice to a preconceived idea, then the future is no future at all. Everything is repetition.

Perhaps another future is possible. The block to another future, which would require a completely other sense of beginning again, is clear: the dominance of objective meaning. Totality, violence, and war are projective. The future is set out as repetition unless there is interruption. Levinas's central insight from the 1940s onward is that ethics and the face open the possibility of interruption. Interruption means the possibility of a different future, one that Levinas rewrites under the rubric of messianism and the prophetic. But those articulations of the future, even when they appear in *Totality and Infinity*, seem less attuned to life after catastrophe than reflective of the hopeless hope we find in late then post-modernity. That is, rubrics of messianism and the prophetic offer only interruption, never continuity, whereas life after catastrophe always keeps continuity in view *even as interruption works its deconstructive work.* Interruption tells us a hopeful story about violence in general, but never about catastrophe. Catastrophe, as a matter of material destruction and generational imperative, insists upon a radical beginning and different future;

interruption is not enough, for, after disaster, we begin with death and ruins. Levinas's work on the future at the close of *Totality and Infinity* maintains a sense of continuity across death, and so, for that reason, can be read as inseparable from the destruction and survival of Judaism in and after the Shoah. With this in mind, then: how does Levinas conceive futurity with remnants of continuity? And, thus, how can we read his account of futurity in the frame of living after catastrophe?

Catastrophe changes everything about beginning, initiating not just the urgency, but the necessity of beginning again after violence. Beginning again means beginning with a new relation to the Other and, in particular, with a new or renewed sense of how the various manifestations of otherness – the cultural Other, the political Other, the Other as neighbor, even familial – make futurity possible. Levinas's various names for this new relation – the ethical, justice, fraternity – are grounded in what is absolute and is itself groundless. And so the new relation is always fragile and precarious, subjected to the often dispiriting vicissitudes of action and commitment. Not even love is sufficient, for lovers shirk their responsibilities in the bordered intimacy of the one-to-one relation. Responsibility is difficult. It always exceeds what love finds and that to which love grafts itself.

But not all love is insufficient. In the final section of *Totality and Infinity*, Levinas's treatment of fecundity, paternity, and 'the son' rewrites love against propriety and borders. A future opens up in this rewriting of love, in its conceptual work and affective austerity, responds to the devastating work of disaster. It responds with a gesture of *creation* that works against despair and nihilism. That is, this rewriting re-imagines a future in which there is both continuity and disruption, identity and difference, borders and infinity. Time itself is exploded at the very same moment time keeps the past alive into the future. When we mark the interval between disaster's devastation of the past in death and the creative moment of remaking a future, we are stalled. What is this in between? How does this in between, this kind of existential and temporal interstitial, make becoming possible? Levinas's word for this interval is *fecundity*. Fecundity, in this interval of death and the future, creates in the sense of bringing into being. And so '[f]ecundity is to be set up as an ontological category.'[6] Levinas writes:

> The son is not only my work, like a poem or an object, nor is he my property. Neither the categories of power nor those of knowledge

> describe my relation with the child. The fecundity of the I is neither a cause nor a domination. I do not have my child; I am my child.[7]

The ontological moment in time lies in the identification of the I and the child, which is also a way in which the child renders the father in the accusative, setting up at the same time a relation, in reproduction, of the ethical: the Me and the child. Fecundity's future is, paradoxically, being and outside being without contradiction. Levinas locates this entwining of being and the outside in the subjectivity of the father and the son, declaring the paradox of the future when he writes that '[i]n this transcendence the I is not swept away, since the son is not me; and yet I *am* my son.'[8]

The fecundity of the father–son relation produces beyond what Levinas calls the *unique* son – the son who is only my own. My son is not my possession, even as I am my son. Rather, the chosenness of the son by the I and the I by the son is transformed into – or perhaps just already implicated in – the chosenness of fraternity. That is, the paradox of relation between father and son, fecundity *par excellence*, chooses the subjectivity of both and produces, in that chosenness, a different kind of time of the future: the infinite. Chosenness therefore moves the future from the model of sequentiality, and therefore countability, toward infinity. Difference is set out into the future without borders (it is infinite), but one that maintains the continuity of the paternal line in the name (a thread that gives identity to the anarchy of infinity). *Multiplicity, difference, and identity all at once.* Levinas writes:

> But the I liberated from its very identity in its fecundity cannot maintain its separation with regard to this future if it is bound to its future in its *unique* child . . . Paternity is produced as an innumerable future; the I engendered exists at the same time as unique in the world and as a brother among brothers . . . [F]raternity is the very relation with the face in which at the same time my election and equality, that is, the mastery exercised over me by the other, are accomplished.[9]

While quick and in many ways still suggestive, Levinas here weaves together fecundity, paternity, fraternity, and election in order to stake out a place for difference after death. Difference after death – which is here a matter of the death of the father and the life of the son, though I would write the same larger as the death of the past (catastrophe) and the life of the future (what persists after the disaster) – is crucial not just because death marks a break in time, raising the question of the interval, but also because the despair of loss so easily generates the desire for sameness. Nostalgia is no mystery, after all, even if it appears impossible and pathetic. I may *want* my son to be a reproduction of myself because I will die, but the onto-logical category of fecundity produces something different: difference that differentiates across time (my son will have a son – let us ignore the uncritical heteronormative thing here), while also, paradoxically, maintaining a thread of continuity. Equality and fraternity name this paradox, for, Levinas claims, they do not neutralize or overcome the asymmetry of difference in the ethical relation. Equality and frater-nity seem to be modes of sameness, yet, in the paradox of fecundity, they are also names for difference. In a peculiar twist of logic, and against the nostalgic desire for sameness after loss, the asymmetry of difference is given a future in fraternity, negotiated by way of the son and the strange temporality he opens up for the father.

What I find so interesting about this Levinasian claim is how it signifies an absolute break with the past. Levinas does not fold time across the interval, hiding the severity of the break between a full past and full future. He reckons directly with loss and a future built out of what little remains. Fecundity is an ontological category because my persistence in being is exposed as finite in the economy of reproduc-tion, meaning that the being of a being fails, dies, disappears. This is constitutive, or even just a bland factual characteristic, of the move-ment from father to son. I do not join my son in the future. I die and my son has his future, which is also, in some strange way, also mine, but not at all mine. An absolute gap is opened up. Equality and fra-ternity take up after that gap, pulling a thread across a time ruptured by death. But the thread is not bloodline, race, or ethnicity. That is, fraternity is not the same as filiation; this is why Levinas's rejection of the plastic forms of epic in the Preface to *Totality and Infinity* is so critical for the remainder of the book. The story of the ancient fathers and mothers is no longer necessary, on Levinas's account, for conceiving a community that functions as a kind of ante- and anti-community. So, in Levinas's hands, there is the possibility of a collec-tive identity as asymmetry of difference without the talk of filiation. A future that survives death.

In this account of fraternity and futurity, we can hear an echo of the problematic of beginning after catastrophe. Perhaps we could say that Levinas gives us something like a transcendental account of beginning again, laying out for us those conditions under which it is possible to make collectivity *again* after or without filiation. If we read Levinas on fecundity and futurity in this frame and register, then we can revisit the famous remark at the beginning of 'Signature' and reopen the problem of reading Levinas as (at least in part) a post-Shoah thinker. The Shoah was not just an event of singular or collective suffering. It was and is also a complete and total cultural loss. After World War Two, the category 'European Jew' – a category so constitutive of European history, across the whole range from intellectual production to political negation – ceases to exist in any significant way. Whatever the sedimentation in culture and history, whatever the remaining numbers, and whatever the fantasied version of Israel that remakes it into a kind of European nation, the Nazi genocide changes everything about history. An absolute gap opens up. And so beginning again cannot summon the fullness of the past to the present in order to give the future continuity. This is in many ways Levinas's moment of rewriting Heidegger's remarks on the Greek temple, where, on Levinas's account, the absent god of the Greeks is replaced with the absent community after catastrophe. Yet, as with Heidegger summoning the god at the temple, there is always the future. The future thinks with the ruin. The ruin is never the past in its fullness, but only a remainder or survivor of loss. A remnant. A trace. Very little, perhaps, but not nothing. Levinas, like Heidegger, begins after devastation, but devastation is never the abyss.

What can that future mean? Fecundity gives us just that clue and theoretical guide, if not a fully explicit treatment. What survives catastrophe, in the context of the Shoah, is *the name*. The name is the name of the father, which becomes the name of the son, which then becomes the name that makes fraternity and the infinity of time possible. The name survives catastrophe, exceeding genocidal violence with a fecund survival. With a name, a people survive with more than bodies; cultural forms and possibilities are carried with a name, even as both become traces or remnants in the wake of death, now mass death. Just as there is a son – or perhaps *because* there is a son – there is continuity *in name* for Judaism after the disaster. Not because the name wills the future to come or because the name functions as some sort of redemption of violence (it obviously does not), but because the future *happens to* subjectivity, collective or singular, in the interval named fecundity.

THE OTHER OTHER PAIN

In the very same year that Levinas published *Totality and Infinity*, the global south was galvanized by the publication of arguably the most important anti-colonial manifesto: Frantz Fanon's *The Wretched of the Earth*. It was also the penultimate year of Algeria's brutal struggle against French colonial rule (which claimed hundreds of thousands of Algerian lives) and, in particular, was the year French police murdered peaceful Algerian protesters in the so-called Paris Massacre of 1961. While many of the key figures in French intellectual life gave complicated and at times controversial thoughts on the Algerian situation (as well as the other colonies involved in anti-colonial struggle), Levinas seems to have been all but oblivious to the world-changing conflict surrounding France and other European powers. And by 1961, Fanon's home country of Martinique had been one of the newly established Départements d'Outre-Mer for a decade and a half. The entanglements of France in colonial empire were transforming not just the far-out margins, but the very heart of the country.

In other words, *Totality and Infinity* was published in interesting times.

Whatever the interesting times, Levinas's work shows no signs of engagement with these events; nor does his work seem especially attuned to the experiences of mass suffering just outside of (or technically within) French borders. I do not say this to shame Levinas somehow for his insularity or insensitivity (though such shame would be refreshing to read in Levinas scholarship from time to time), but rather to underscore the intimacy of the problem of beginning, catastrophe, and futurity with the *other* Other's moment on the world stage. Catastrophe *as such* dominates the middle of the twentieth century and, in the moment of anti-colonial struggle, the problems of beginning and futurity are raised with every bit the same urgency as those in a specifically European context. Colonialism devastates the past. The moment of postcolony life is saturated with the question of the future precisely because an absolute gap is opened up. What is the character of that gap? Especially: what is the character of that gap in the Caribbean context? And how does a response to that gap change how we think about fecundity, the future, and the forms of subjectivity – singular and collective – that emerge from a vision of the future? *How does this colonial difference decolonize Levinasian thinking about the future and beginning?*

Fanon's *Wretched of the Earth* plays an important role in thinking through the problems of beginning and futurity, especially when paired with the earlier articulation of a new humanism in *Black Skin, White Masks*. *Wretched of the Earth*, written in the very same year as *Totality and Infinity*, asks the question of beginning, wondering in a language both analytical and polemical how to begin after colonialism. What is national culture and consciousness after the colonizer leaves? What does it mean to think through the remnants of colonialism – ruins and remainders that only alienate – in order to begin again? History provides Fanon no real guide; one of the defining features of his work is a Sartrean-inspired rejection of history. Indeed, Fanon could not be more decisive than when he declares in the conclusion to *Black Skin, White Masks* that he is not a prisoner of history, even to the point of eschewing the pursuit of reparations. Questioning the place and function of national culture in postcolonial state-formation, for example, is posed as a problem of beginning in *Wretched of the Earth*, but always without appealing to the constitutive role of historical experience. Fanon's new humanism always starts *new*. And this is where Glissant's work becomes especially important. For Glissant, historical experience of catastrophe haunts the problem of beginning in the postcolonial moment – a moment exacerbated and prolonged by the arrangement of departmentalization in Martinique and Guadeloupe. Glissant's postcolonial question becomes how to re-render historical experience such that the pain of history becomes productive and not just debilitating. The abyss of beginning, as Glissant puts it, means that beginning has to be abyssal, but at the same time fecund. Put to Fanon, then, it is a matter of imagining the collective outside of the inferiority complex, affirming the abyss as a fecund moment, which then culminates in an affirmation of the Caribbean's composite cultural life. Glissant calls this affirmation the method of *Antillanité*, which thinks through beginning, abyss, and fecundity without recourse or return to an elsewhere. We need not return to an origin. In fact, as abyssal, beginning has already vanished the origin.

Beginning with historical experience therefore entails an honest reckoning with the pain of history. The abyss bequeaths affects of sadness and melancholia, while at the same time releasing the future from a fate of despair – that fate Fanon would seem to fear most. For Glissant, historical experience discloses a sense of futurity that translates pain, through an engagement with composite cultural forms, into another imaginary. The pain of history informs the imagination of the world – that way in which collective identities emerge by giving the world an infusion of subjective and intersubjective vision. The world *is* always imagined, no matter the pain. Pain exiles the imagination, traumatizing its link to roots of various sorts, but with Glissant, and here he crosses Bhabha's work in interesting ways, exile produces a different sort of imagination and imaginary. Exile becomes the fecundity of errantry, the rhizomatic character of a detour that refuses return. We see this most clearly in Glissant's *Poetics of Relation*, perhaps his greatest theoretical work. *Poetics of Relation* brings four decades of reflection in poetry, literature, and theory to bear on questions of beginning, globalization, and futurity. How does *Poetics of Relation* begin thinking about pain, trauma, and beginning?

'What is terrifying,' Glissant writes, 'partakes of the abyss.'[10] With that remark, Glissant initiates a long meditation on the relation between traumatic historical experience and beginning the creative and creolizing project of Caribbean identity. Creation and creolization form responses to the abyss produced by the Middle Passage, that traumatic event which opens an absolute gap between the past and the future. Glissant's sense of beginning is structured by a three-fold sense of this abyss. The abyss *generally* is produced in the trauma of the forced migration of the Middle Passage, but with specific, nuanced shifts in sites of trauma; the event is not single-sited. Glissant's account traces three moments of that migration: departure, passage, and arrival. The first abyss, the loss and vanishing of memory, is initiated when 'you fell into the belly of the boat . . . Yet the belly of this boat dissolves you, precipitates you in a nonworld from which you cry out. This boat is a womb, a womb abyss.'[11] With the sequence of belly, dissolve, nonworld, precipitate, and womb, Glissant brings the paradoxical swirl of trauma into focus. This first abyss, the spasm of violence that initiates departure from Africa, dissolves roots and origin, throwing the slave into the nonworld of the boat. The boat's belly is both the term for the holding place for slaves transported to the New World and an evocation of the terrible condition of birth. The abyss is a womb; the Middle Passage gestates and there is birth upon arrival in the New World, no matter how traumatic the effect on memory, history, and identity. Falling into the boat, there is the first moment in the womb. The first abyss.

> The next abyss [Glissant writes] was the depths of the sea. Whenever a fleet of ships gave chase to the slave ships, it was easiest just to lighten the boat by throwing cargo overboard, weighing it down with balls and chains. These underwater signposts mark the course between the Gold Coast and the Leeward Islands.[12]

The second abyss names passage itself and provides for Glissant the primary figure of loss: drown memory. The bodies thrown overboard carry with them the memory of passage and origin, marking the route of passage – literal and figurative – with signposts of radical absence. Abyssal absence. Drowned presence. We should note an important difference here between the figures of loss in European discourse on the Shoah and in theorizing the Middle Passage. Rather than ashen memory and the cinder, there is the ball and chain at the bottom of the ocean. At the bottom of the ocean, there is neither the body nor its remainder. Only that which drowned the body, the instrument of terror and violence, lies at the bottom of an unfathomable sea.

So, memory in the second abyss figures loss differently, and that figure is far from just literary. It is poetic in the sense of *poiesis*: it brings something into being. The drowning of memory is the drowning of the name, a loss that is perhaps more total than ashen memory because it leaves no ruin. The distinction here between ruin and abyss is critical for understanding the difference between Levinas and Glissant (and so the postcolonial difference in difference). In ruin and abyss, the interval functions as both the terms of catastrophe and the condition under which another time is brought into being. In other words, fecundity, that *making after loss*, is an ontological category. Glissant's second sense of abyss casts an importantly different problematic. Drowning memory leaves no ruin. Beginning is abyssal, and so begins without the thin, fragile continuity of the name. Drown memory seals namelessness as a condition of beginning.

But the Middle Passage and abyssal loss do not close or vanish time at the bottom of the sea. There is the third moment of abyss: the event of arrival. The event of arrival is defined by the disorientation and trauma of plantation violence, but it is also defined by the absoluteness of forgetting. That is, arrival is not a moment of reassembly, where the traumatic violence of departure and passage ruins, yet sustains, a beginning that recalls, gathers, and begins recasting the past. What is drowned in the second abyss arrives without name. The 'mass of water' becomes the nameless surge of arrival. Glissant writes:

> Paralleling this mass of water, the third metamorphosis of the abyss thus projects a reverse image of all that had been left behind, not to be regained for generations except – more and more threadbare – in the blue savannas of memory or imagination.[13]

Arrival confirms forgetting, setting exile as a material *and* memorial condition. The first two appearances of the abyss sever the memorial tie, which would *seem* to give nothing to the future except melancholic loss. Without the name, continuity is drowned rather than broken or made ashen. That distinction is critical, of course: ashes are remnants of the past, even if only cinders of what was. Ashes erase intelligibility, making that trauma both massive and generative of an absolute gap. But drown memory is really something different, as there is no remnant. Even Glissant's image of absence is late to the scene; the balls and chains, those 'underwater signposts,' are already absent corpses. What could remnant or ruin mean in this context? Yet, there is beginning. Arrival begins with the abyss of the shoreline, reckoning with drown memory and the persistence of the future. The very notion of retrieval is set in the blue savannas of memory – which is to say, no memory at all. And so arrival remaps a wholly new, wholly fractal geography of cultural production – that measurement of the irregular shorelines of composite culture – striking the final traumatic blow against the past. Arrival's disorientation does not re-root according to an atavistic logic of origins or the oblique version of the same in the form of ruins and remnants, but instead re-routes according to what Glissant describes as the nomadic and rhizomatic logic of Chaos. It would be enough to theorize the catastrophe as mass death and suffering. The Middle Passage is a disaster in numbers that tells a plenty catastrophic story. But for Glissant, the forgetting of origins widens and deepens disaster by tearing apart and dispensing with European narratives of loss, recovery, and futurity. In the European context, those ruins and remnants, as we see in Levinas with the function of the name, thread together what little remains when conceiving the future of a community or people. The Middle Passage does not offer that thread. The gap is absolutely absolute, rather than the somewhat restrained gap, compromised in its absoluteness, that we find in Levinas's appeal to the quiet continuity of the name.

Exile is the consequence of the Middle Passage, but it is not the end of time. Catastrophe always has a future, melancholic or otherwise. The abyss, in its three-fold claim on life, makes 'one vast beginning, but a beginning whose time is marked by these balls and chains gone green.'[14] *Time is marked.* That is, time is fundamentally transformed – to the point of curvature – by the catastrophe of the Middle Passage. By the curvature of time, Glissant, in appealing to Einstein's physics, wants to make an absolute break with those models of sequentiality that dominate the European model of trauma and loss. We can see this clearly in relation to Levinas's work, where even the traumatic break with atavism does not, in the end, dispense with the name. *That* beginning begins with the thread of the surname, the remnant or ruin that still breathes after death and loss, giving a future that is at once alienating and intimate, both wholly Other and wholly Me. The figure of drown memory changes this story dramatically and also underscores Glissant's great distance from that other theory of beginning in the Caribbean context: Negritude. Abyssal beginning is not simply a story of the first Africans in the Americas. Rather, abyssal beginning is *another* beginning, a first and new beginning of the history of *a new people* – albeit with a sense of collectivity that is hardly what is traditionally called 'a people.' Loss is just that total and absolute, rendering the past as blue savannas of memory and imagination. This would seem to be a sort of collective instantiation of the Levinasian (and Derridean) trace. And yet, again, there is an important nuance in Glissant's sense of the trace. Rather than a question of identity, the trace functions in the play of an imagination that *seeks* identity, but can never draw upon a past identity or the affects of lost identity (which, in the ruin and remnant, is still a kind of identity). This space of play is less *continuity* than it is a force without name, that none the less animates the world. Africanness is not a question of identity, for Glissant, but instead an imaginary component, animating what is *first* (and thus not secondary or tertiary) a composite culture and its productions. In other words, Africanness is an imaginative and imagined trace, which does not have to be present or have been present, but only enters, through the blue savannas of memory, into the play of history and the making of an identity, culture, and world *after the abyss*.

Abyssal beginning thereby changes the meaning of alterity in the New World context. Otherness becomes the foundational, rather than alienating or questioning, experience of arrival and after. So, we should not be surprised at the ethical language that comes to the fore in Glissant's later work. The Levinasian motifs in *Poetics of Relation* are evident from the tropes of 'the Other' and 'opacity,' both of which signify the ethical core of Glissant's theorizing the Caribbean, and are derived from the fundamental fragility and vulnerability of composite cultural forms. The historical experience of conquest and the slave trade, after all, seals fragility and vulnerability in the margins of the global system of cultural formation. On Glissant's account, production, reproduction, and transformation of composite cultural forms maintain fragility, rather than overcome it with meaning. Without atavistic roots, everything is precarious. As well, and this is crucial here, composite cultural forms are *ex vi termini* comprised of relations with 'the Other' that implicate Levinasian epistemological, ontological, and ethical themes.

Still, this is subtle conceptual space. Otherness, of course, can play many roles in which the Other is placed outside the peculiar economy of the Levinasian ethical. In this register, Glissant is careful to mark out the distinction between what he calls 'the thought of the Other' and 'the Other of thought.' The former is still bound by the structure of knowledge that circulates through a centered subject, suggesting the first position of knowledge as *comprendre*. Glissant employs *comprendre* as a troubled term in order to evoke senses of seizing upon or capture (*prendre*) at the rhetorical heart of conventional epistemology. Such rhetorical habits resonate with a terrifying historical specificity in an African context. Yet, seizing is the standard characterization of what it means to know. In the act of knowing, I seize upon the world, take it into my consciousness, and, in reflection, establish the worldly, objective meaning of that world. Terrifying indeed. This is precisely how the logic of colonialism and conquest is already present in habits of knowing and being; like Levinas, Glissant sees the imperialism of the West in the foundations of epistemology and ontology. But the Other as the Other of thought suggests something else, something that makes the work of composite cultural formation vital, intense, and imaginative rather than an alien and alienating difference to be overcome. Glissant is careful and deliberate when he writes that the

> thought of the Other is sterile without the other of Thought.
>
> Thought of the Other is the moral generosity disposing me to accept the principle of alterity, to conceive of the world as not simple and straightforward, with only one truth – mine. But thought of the Other can dwell within me without making me alter course . . .
>
> The other of Thought is precisely this altering. Then I have to act. That is the moment I change my thought, without renouncing its contribution. I change, and I exchange. This is an aesthetics of turbulence whose corresponding ethics is not provided in advance.[15]

For Glissant, then, the explosion of thought by the Other, which breaks alterity out of the seizing grasp of consciousness, sets thinking into the Chaos of Relation. From this sense of Relation, an 'imaginary [is] rekindled by the other of Thought.'[16]

With the term 'imaginary,' Glissant wants to retain the idea of knowing without putting the Other at risk in knowledge. Abyssal beginning, after all, changes so much of what it means to know.

Comprendre and comparison import both the figures and practices of imperial force. Seizing and grasping figure in the act of knowledge of what is and has long been political and cultural practice under colonialism. But there is also the composition of knowing and contact *outside* that totalitarian economy, a sense of relation that keeps the opacity of the Other safe without insisting on simple separation. Opacity, contact, *then* composition. The composition of knowing in a composite cultural context crafts meaning in the imaginary – that precarious aesthetic sphere of knowing and being that structures a relation to the world – out of fragments of the past and present that bear no atavistic relation to a rooted memory and history. The future is open in precisely this sense: unrooted and persistent. The Caribbean imaginary is this unrooted Chaos of knowing. Knowing, that is, which is never fixed and never a struggle for domination, but rather a constant figuration, *mise en question*, and refiguration – a knowledge that *becomes* in the fullest sense. The imperial and totalitarian are ultimately perversions and foreshortenings of becoming, whose open horizon – abyssal, searching, composite – does not congeal into seized and grasped forms. Indeed, the opening intertext to *Poetics of Relation* makes this clear when Glissant writes:

> Thought draws the imaginary of the past: a sense of knowledge as becoming. One cannot stop it to assess it nor isolate it to transmit it. It is sharing one can never not retain, nor ever, in standing still, boast about it.[17]

Glissant's vision of the Caribbean is that of a form of knowing as irreducibly becoming, moving across the dynamic space of thinking and its other without cessation. This dynamic space maintains, and is even kept vital and urgent because of, the opacity of the Other. The Other of thought makes thinking compatible with, if not dependent upon, a sense of radical alterity and an ethics thereof.

This vision of knowledge is crucial for understanding Glissant's conception of the future. Because becoming and knowing are generated in relation to the past (the space of beginning), the traumatic production of the abyss delinks the future from a rootedness in the past. For this reason, Glissant repeatedly turns to Deleuze and Guattari's figures of the rhizome and nomad in his later work when arguing against atavistic conceptions of culture and meaning. (This has political implications as well, which we explore below in the next chapter.) The abyss, informed by the rhizomatic and nomadic conceptions of relation and identity, gives becoming to Being, disassembling the totalitarian pretensions of identity with the historical experience of the other Other. After the Middle Passage, there is not even the continuity of the name. And yet there is knowing. In the opening section of *Poetics of Relation*, Glissant makes the relation between the abyss and knowledge clear when he writes:

> Thus, the absolute unknown, projected by the abyss and bearing into eternity the womb abyss and the infinite abyss, in the end became knowledge . . . For though this experience made you, original victim floating toward the sea's abysses, an exception, it became something shared and made us, the descendants, one people among others . . . This experience of the abyss can now be said to be the best element of exchange.[18]

This is a peculiar and even unexpected twist in the treatment of catastrophe. Not unlike Levinas's shift from the dispiriting philosophy of history as totality and war to the fecundity of the name and identity, Glissant sees the opening of the future as a break from catastrophe – not as redemption, but rather, and simply, as the persistence of time. The persistence of time manifests in the making of a people. A future is made out of the abyss, that womb which bequeaths no name, yet still bequeaths time. That is, it is not just that descendants survive. Descendants *become* a people, creating connections to place through contact and what Glissant calls Relation: a nomadic, rhizomatic identity, animated by Chaos and the open horizon of creolization and creolizing *knowledge*.

Without the persistence of the name, we get an important shift away from Levinas's response to our opening query: how to begin after catastrophe? The ashes of memory leave a certain (albeit nascent) continuity intact, so loss is not total *in so far as one retains rights to loss*. By 'rights to loss,' I here mean a sense of connection to the terms of loss and the narration of its meaning; rights to loss indicate a prior attachment, however fleeting, to the object or condition later subject to violent extraction or destruction. Loss registers as, in a rather conventional sense, the loss of something nameable (homeland, tradition, autonomy). The name therefore persists, which gives an important contour to loss; we can narrate the terms of loss, what it puts in crisis, and so what it means to begin again, after disaster. In a certain sense, we can again see Levinas's conception of futurity as a rewriting of Heidegger's conception of language and retrieval – loss *is* loss because we catch sight of continuity and its breaking up. The drowning of memory is very different, though, as what is lost is the name itself. Atavism vanishes in the second sense of Glissant's abyss; the balls and chains gone green at the bottom of the sea – this is Caribbean historical experience in its originary trauma. 'The sea,' as Glissant quotes the poem's title, 'is history.'[19] If we begin with Derek Walcott's claim that the sea is history, and the sea is the trauma of the Middle Passage's drowning of memory, then history is a total vanishing of memory and name; fragments and traces, in this catastrophic effect, bear no threaded relation to the past, nor to an original. Originless, beginning begins again without the rights to loss. Narrative fails before it begins. The word, and so too the name, is first, wholly new, and always *creolized.*

CREOLE TIME, AFTER EUROPE

What are we to make of this difference? And why would it matter to a rereading of *Totality and Infinity* on beginning and futurity? Or, maybe better, why would it *not* matter to a rereading of that text and that problematic? *Totality and Infinity* was of course written in interesting times. Let us revisit the radical meaning of those times by thinking just as France lived that moment in 1961: across borders, as a matter of Self.

Glissant's account of memory, history, beginning, and place gives the future the wholly elevated, perhaps impossible task of articulating a people. A people, that is, who emerge out of the historical experience of disaster – beginning with the abyss. Levinas tells so much the same story when read in the frame of the Shoah, a reading authorized (at least in part) by his remarks in 'Signature' and elsewhere. The continuity of the name says something important about the aftermath of catastrophe. There is the name, which means there is the possibility of fraternity in and through the fecundity of the paternal relation. Paternity functions as a literal and figurative source-point for reproduction, whether of the family or of the people. The border of disaster marks this conceptual moment with the urgency of everything: refusal of total destruction, survival, imagining life after catastrophe, and so a sense of future taken on as the consequence of both arrival on the other side of violence and the sheer persistence of time. After all, life goes on. The future is both the site of imaginary transformation and the pure passivity of time. The future *happens,* but is also *forged.* Work makes the future; the materiality of life is worked over by language, names, and the imagination. Levinas and Glissant articulate important conceptual tools for understanding this moment of forging, and the infusion of the ethical only deepens the significance further.

And yet there is a decisive nuance here, a subtle shift in meaning that underscores the postcolonial difference in the language of difference. What is the postcolonial moment between Levinas and Glissant? How do this particular transnational context of beginning, the encounter with Otherness, and the ethics of futurity critically engage with Levinas's work? It is important to note how, even as the irreducible opacity of the Other becomes central to his theoretical work, Glissant's work does not move in the direction of the language of the subaltern. As well, his insistence on creolization and the instability of identity, which places Chaos in the first position, does not turn to hybridity and interstitial space as an explanation of postcolonial identity. In fact, Glissant is explicitly critical of the applicability of hybridity in the Caribbean context when he distinguishes between *métissage* and creolization in *Poetics of Relation*. That is, Glissant's work is fundamentally different than that of Spivak and Bhabha, both of whom also think knowledge and identity in the context of radical difference. Perhaps a sense of place is the crucial concept here. For Spivak – and this is what generates the language of subalternity – the Other is produced through relations of conquest and occupation, which creates a certain epistemological abyss that no language crosses. *The subaltern cannot speak*. Bhabha's sense of the Other is generated by migration, the movement across borders in which different, hybrid identities are formed out of both engagement and traumatic loss. *Counter-narrative changes the meaning of subjectivity and nation*. Both thinkers begin with a sense of loss, but for neither is beginning an abyss. The meaning of place is altered in this very moment in the analysis.

Part of what is at stake in this parsing of the meaning of difference is the status of the name after catastrophe. Whether we have in mind the intra-European disaster of the Shoah, mass death, and genocide or the transnational violence of colonialism and migration, our sense of what loss means is largely tied a loss of place in space, time, and history. Something is *disrupted* by catastrophe, conquest, or, at times, traumatic transformative encounter. Levinas, Spivak, and Bhabha all frame trauma and beginning with the affect of anxiety – anxiety, of course, in the sense of not being at home with oneself and in one's surroundings. As a precondition of its meaning, anxiety supposes a prior experience and a right to place. Loss, we could say, is conditioned by a prior right to loss.

But, in *Poetics of Relation*, Glissant makes an interesting and subtle rephrasing of place. Glissant evokes the problematic of the imaginary in order to address the chasm opened up by the loss of name, home, and history. This loss recasts the problem of space and time, and so too place. Without the persistence of the name, what remains for a future? How can the future be navigated, beginning with the abyss, without the fold of the ruins of the past into the present-then-future? Again, Glissant turns to Deleuze and Guattari's figure of the rhizome, here explicitly (even wildly) translated from tactic to direct description. In characteristic fashion, Glissant poses the problematic as a question – not because he is evasive or uncommitted, but rather because the interrogative mode better captures the rhizomatic sensibility of the future-imaginary. He writes:

> I am doing the same thing in the way I way *we* – organizing this work around it. Is this some community *we* rhizomed into fragile connection to a place? Or a total *we* involved in the activity of the planet? Or an idea *we* drawn in the swirls of a poetics?[20]

Glissant's rendering of traumatic experience, and all of its various alterations of the movement of memory and history, shifts away from the language of the loss and remainder of the name (a meta-theory of ruins, perhaps), toward the rhizome as an *activity*. Rhizome deployed in its verbal sense, no matter how much that shift from noun to verb requires an abuse of language. That is, and to put it in direct terms, the trauma of the Middle Passage resets the question of place. Caribbean historical experience, catastrophic at the outset, makes place, people, and so future without a single-root. Levinas's conception of the future is similarly transformative of our notions of space and time, to be sure, yet there is also that quiet continuity across difference. The name as an ashen ruin, rather the vanishing of names in drowned memory. Again, what are we to make of this distinction in the interval of catastrophe?

For both Levinas and Glissant, the problem of beginning, then place, is set against the devastation of history. And yet, unlike, say, the historiographic argument of Walter Benjamin's 'Theses on the Philosophy of History,' which imagines telling (or the imperative to tell, then impossibility of telling) history from the perspective of the sadness of the victims, Levinas and Glissant emphatically turn to an analysis of the future. Neither Levinas nor Glissant produces a pessimistic or nihilistic philosophical vision – and the pain of history with which they are concerned surely invites such production. There is no redemption of the past and pain through retrieval, and in this sense both gain plenty of distance from Heidegger's account of loss and the task of thinking. For both Levinas and Glissant, the past is sealed in its immemoriality both in structure – neither thinker can theoretically justify awakening the absent – and by the complete urgency of the future. Survival is not enough. To have survived simply means that the immemorial is not all that remains, that something sits in the present *after* devastation in the interstitial space of post-Shoah Jewish Europe or the shoreline of the New World after passage. There is always the matter of *how* one is to survive, *how* the collective remains or is to remain across the interval between catastrophe and an accomplished living-after. How to begin, in other words, is a question of reckoning with the past while refusing to concede the future to the traumatic past with (or in) gestures of pessimism or nihilism.

This means in part that we read Glissant against the sorts of sentiments Aimé Césaire expresses in the famous line from *Discourse on Colonialism,* where he writes that what Hitler did to European Jews and other enemies merely 'applied' what Europe had been doing to Africans and indigenous peoples of the Americas for centuries.[21] To be sure, Césaire makes an important point. One ought not to be astonished at the severity of internal violence – genocidal and otherwise – in Europe across the two world wars. After all, Europe had already proven itself to be a machine of death and suffering in other parts of the globe. Nearly all of the globe, in fact, so the catastrophic violence in the first half of the twentieth century seems, with a bit of perspective, completely consistent with the internal character of European culture and habits. And there is a bit of unexpected continuity between Césaire and Levinas on this very point, in so far as both see a *form* across violence that points to an inner identity of the West. Just as Césaire writes the slave-trade and colonial violence across the collapse of Europe into internal spasms of mass-killing and genocide, Levinas gestures toward the inner identity of violence both in his account of totality as the transcendental of war. Glissant's critique of *comprendre*, for how it reveals the imperial character of knowing and being, gestures in this same direction.

The shift in figures of beginning changes everything, though. Beginning does not proceed from one and the same catastrophe, repeated, as Césaire would seem to suggest, across geographies. Rather, as we have seen, the figure of loss as cindered or drowned prefigures the terms of beginning – and so also of futurity. Consider how this difference is captured in Levinas's and Glissant's use the motif of *curvature*. For Levinas, curvature describes the transformation of space in the (non-)relation of separation. The 'truth' of exteriority produces a surplus exceeding all ideas, locations, and therefore any mapping of the relation(s) constitutive of moral consciousness; Levinas calls this the curvature of the space of relationality. Intersubjective life is transformed from a grid underpinning theories of objectivity – the service to which Husserl put intersubjectivity in V. *Cartesian Meditation* – into the strange, infinite quasi-space of obligation. In *Totality and Infinity,* Levinas writes:

> This 'curvature' of intersubjective space in which exteriority is effectuated (we do not say 'in which it appears') as superiority must be distinguished from the arbitrariness of 'points of view' taken upon objects that appear ... The 'curvature of space' expresses the relation between human beings.[22]

Separation is not perspectivalism infused with moral language, of course. This is such an important distinction in Levinas's work and the complexity entailed in it cannot be overstated. But here it is enough to say that Levinas conceives curvature as fundamentally spatial. If separation is documented in curved space, then it is immeasurable. It is immeasurable, not because of its extension or expanse, but because the idea of measurement is irrelevant to the kind of difference separation names. Difference as separation is therefore *otherwise than measure,* much as Descartes's idea of the Infinite (to which Levinas owes so much) is different in kind than the Indefinite.[23]

Glissant also turns to the motif of curvature in describing the relation of Same and Other in both *Poetics of Relation* and *Introduction à une poétique du divers,* but with an important shift. For Glissant, catastrophe produces a curvature of *time,* not space. The curvature of time breaks with sequentiality absolutely, without remainder or retention. And so memory functions otherwise than fracture and separation. Curvature evokes, again, Einstein's relativity theory, removing all senses of measure from the experience of historical time. Rather than being measured by a hastily universalized European experience of time, which has its own specific marks and fractures and fissures, and rather than the experience of the loss of the African root as the defining feature of Afro-Caribbean life, Glissant's account of the curvature of time clears the space for thinking trauma, beginning, and futurity on its own terms – by way of the method of

Antillanité. If living after disaster entails a certain bit of intractable melancholy, then the time and space of that melancholic resonance need accounting in specifically historical terms. Historical experience must be thought in specificity. That is, we need an accounting in terms of the decidedly *non-universalizable* sense of both a connection to and historical experience of place. Root or rhizome? And what kind of rhizome, for what sorts of reasons? The curvature of time, which Glissant describes in *Poetics of Relation* as what makes it possible 'to study Chaos without succumbing to a vertigo of disillusion over its endless transformations,'[24] lends temporal depth to the mobility of the rhizome and nomad. In so doing, with the curvature of that temporal depth as the analytical frame, Glissant sees separation as immeasurable to the point of a fecund, swirling Chaos.

We can now return to the opening remarks of the present essay. It is not enough simply to note that Levinas's work is exclusively concerned with European thinkers (true) or that he makes immensely troubling remarks when his thoughts wander outside the 'borders' of Europe (also true). Rather, it is necessary to think about Levinas's work as structured from within by his idea of Europeanness. In the case of the present reflections, this is another way of saying that Levinas's concern with the fecundity of the Jewish name and future fraternity of the Jews as a people turns on a Eurocentric concern with a certain kind of catastrophe, a particular problem of beginning, and so a very specific form of futurity. This concern is itself fecund. For atavistic cultural forms and traditions that bear the memory of disaster, Levinas's account of beginning and possible futurities conjoins questions of retrieval, productivity, and responsibility to wider issues of history and language. In certain colonial and postcolonial contexts, such as those explored by Spivak, Bhabha, and others, Levinas's work is both deeply connected and consistently important – even, as we have seen, when there are significant differences. But that very work presupposes continuity in order to address the *particular form* of discontinuity and fracture that too often gets discussed as a generalized sense of trauma, loss, and separation. Glissant's work on the same interval between catastrophe and fecundity exposes a fundamental monolingualism at the heart of Levinas's ethics of the future. We see this monolingualism in the function of the name as a thread of continuity and continuation, holding close to what is broken apart and the pain of history, while at the same time promising a future to the fraternity to come. *A future promised to a people who have been, suffer catastrophic loss, then begin again*. This sequence reveals an inner connection between Levinas's conception of time and a theory of ruins.

Glissant's commitment to Caribbeanness begins with a space already dispossessed of the kinds of ruins that, in the hands of Levinas and so many other thinkers, prove productive. Beginning without productive ruins (the ruins of the New World remind the colonizer of conquest, the colonized of the shoreline's abyssal beginning) initiates nomadic, rhizomatic movement without an initial rootedness in the past. The rhizome reterritorializes, marking place with contact and connection, but deterritorialization is simultaneous with the proliferation of difference in composite cultural forms; however precarious those roots become after catastrophic violence, there is only abyss where one might see foundation. The melancholic moment in this story is obvious and it leads Glissant to remind readers of the necessity to 'remember our boats.'[25] Memory of pain persists, without ruins, as drown memory, but so too does the future. The future is absolute mixture in that chaotic curvature of time Glissant calls creolization. Creolization mixes without circulating around a single root, and yet also and always mixes in order to set multiple roots – not one of which, of itself, can sustain the life of a people alone, but, as a de- and reterritorializing composite, polyrootedness does in fact give the identity of a people vitality, meaning, and possibility. *Rhizomatic imaginary*. The imagination unrooted, oriented by the Other of thought. 'Rhizome,' in Glissant's hands, is therefore at once a noun (the rhizome), adjective (rhizomatic), and verb (rhizomes), *entangled* with pursued, unexpected, and even haunting senses of the Other.

Entanglement means everything here. What Levinas calls Europe is famously composed of 'the Bible and the Greeks.' That formulation of European identity is as peculiar as it is common. For, though the Greek–Christian and Judaic elements of European culture certainly describe and account for much of what we call 'Europe,' there is also the now five-plus centuries-long entanglement of Europe with the Americas – and indeed the globe as such. What is Europe without this entanglement? How much entanglement is necessary before the object of entanglement – here, of conquest and domination – becomes part of identity? Part of what is entailed in these questions is the difficult matter of responsibility, as well as the meaning of historical experience. But what I want to underscore here in conclusion is how the question of beginning after catastrophe in Glissant's work is situated in the same entangled – to the point of *rhizomatic relation*

– historical experience as that of Levinas. Now, we might want to conclude that Glissant's work is just a matter of Caribbean singularity, and the fact that Levinas's analysis operates with the privilege of the name is just a matter of difference. Europe, we might say, has its own *histoire* and tells it according to those experiences of edification, struggle, trauma, loss, and so on. And yet we should be moved to reflection by Césaire's remark in *Discourse on Colonialism*. Césaire notes the continuity of Europe in its machinery of violence, which is convincing even when we pause, critically, before assertions of equivalence. Europe lived for centuries from and on the basis of a machine of violence, enslavement, unspeakable extraction and exploitation, and mass death. Indeed, Europe is unimaginable without empire. Empire is unimaginable without the machinery of catastrophe. In that sense, the deepest sense, the history of the Caribbean is immanent to the meaning of Europe, which implicates catastrophe across the spectrum of historical experience between Europe and the Americas. Beginning after catastrophe, from the ashes or the abyss, is therefore a matter for all thinking of beginning, even those sites of beginning that most put notions of fecundity, paternity, fraternity, and the name in question.

A last note: the entanglement of identity that underpins Glissant's conception of both Europe and the Americas allows us to pause and consider a different sense of globalization. Globalization rightly evokes images of imperial economic forces, perhaps connected to nation-states, perhaps quasi-autonomous powers severed from those roots, all brought to bear on so-called 'developing countries,' robbing those countries of their autonomy and sense of self-determination. A leveling of the very idea of social and economic organization. But entanglement in terms of historical experience – the incarnate historiography that bears mixed memory and mixed history on the body, in language, and so on – reminds us of a richer and more exploratory sense of globalization: the global multilingual. This is what Glissant calls the *tout-monde*. *Tout-monde* is a poetic and even ontological principle that spreads the problem of imagination and being out across the alterity of the entangled roots of a complex global Chaos of languages, memories, and histories.[26] In this Chaos, there is another globalization. Indeed, Glissant will go so far as *not* to identify himself as a poet and theorist of Martinique, claiming in an interview:

> No! I don't see myself as a Martinican writer. But the question of identity is important because I see myself as a writer of the

'tout-monde' in a world of global relations. The writer of the 'tout-monde' is the relational writer. He is the writer of rhizomatic identity ... Still, it is important to be a Martinican writer, because you have to bring something to the 'tout-monde' relation.[27]

Glissant's zigzag enacts the movement of deterritorialization and reterritorialization that comes with this richer sense of globalization. As globally entangled, Glissant is no longer bound to the site of Martinique, yet, as someone who engages and moves nomadically in the space of entanglement, he has to 'bring something' to that cluster of relations and roots and points of contact. (As well, Glissant is plenty cognizant of how uneven global entanglement proves for those on the margins of history, which grounds the need for 'bringing something' to Relation.)

This sense of globalization begins a counter-story to Derrida's worry in 'On Forgiveness' and elsewhere about *globalatinization* – the sense of cultural and aesthetic global movement that levels and makes uniform. The Caribbean already is, and has been since its historical founding, a site of global entanglement; Antonio Benítez-Rojo's patient conceptual study of the historical genesis of entanglement in *The Repeating Island*,[28] which tracks the movement of global entwinement through the plantation, developments of military technology, and increasing bureaucratization, demonstrates this, much like Glissant in *Caribbean Discourse*, in terms of rhizomatic principles and the play of Chaos. But thinking the global rhizome, this peculiar globalization without globalatinization, is fraught business. Glissant is clear in *Poetics of Relation* that the global margins risk so much in entanglement. The uneven distribution of political and economic power, while not precisely attached to poetics, is also not inseparable from the habits and seductions of domination. This is why the question of the Other – the precarious alterity of the face, the Other of thought – is so crucial for establishing a sense of the ethical in the heart of entanglement. Between Levinas and Glissant, there is at least the beginning of an ethics of entanglement. From Levinas and Glissant both, we get an account of how an honest reckoning with beginning and the future sets out from the encounter with the Other – perhaps an Other whom we cannot yet fathom. In fact, the unfathomable is precisely the moment of the ethical, where the refusal of *comprendre* is met with the urgency and inescapability of contact, connection, and, when the future of a collective is at stake, *production*. An ethics of entanglement, then, is tasked with a difficult, yet wholly fecund tension between imperatives: to withdraw the reach of knowledge *and* to create-with.

Notes

1. Emmanuel Levinas, *Difficile Liberté*. Paris: Livre de poche, 1991, 406; *Difficult Freedom*, trans. Séan Hand. Baltimore: Johns Hopkins University Press, 1997, 291.
2. Emmanuel Levinas, *Totalité et l'infini*. The Hague: Martinus Nijhoff, 1961, ix; *Totality and Infinity*, trans. Alphonso Lingis. Pittsburgh: Duquesne University Press, 1969, 21.
3. Ibid.
4. Ibid., 174/199.
5. Ibid., xi/22.
6. Ibid., 254/277.
7. Ibid.
8. Ibid.
9. Ibid., 255–6/279.
10. Édouard Glissant, *Poétique de la relation*. Paris: Gallimard, 1990, 18; trans. Betsy Wing, *Poetics of Relation*. Ann Arbor: University of Michigan Press, 1997, 6.
11. Ibid.
12. Ibid.
13. Ibid., 19/7.
14. Ibid., 18/6.
15. Ibid., 169/154–5.
16. Ibid., 170/155.
17. Ibid., 13/1.
18. Ibid., 20/8.
19. 'The Sea is History' is one of Glissant's epigraphs to *Poetics of Relation*, which refers to Derek Walcott's 'The Sea is History,' in *Collected Poems: 1948–1984*. New York: Farrar, Straus & Giroux, 1987.
20. Glissant, *Poétique de la Relation*, 222/206.
21. See Aimé Césaire, *Discourse on Colonialism*, trans. Joan Pinkham. New York: Monthly Review Press, 2000, 36.
22. Levinas, *Totalité et l'infini*, 267/291.
23. I take up the importance of this Cartesian distinction in terms of a theory of sense, which is a bit different than, yet related to the context here, in John E. Drabinski, 'The Enigma of the Cartesian Infinity,' *Studia Phaenomenologica* VI (2006): 201–13.
24. Glissant, *Poétique de la relation*, 150/136.
25. Ibid., 20/9.
26. On the problem of ethics and poetics, see Mary Gallagher, 'Relating (in Theory) in a Globalized World: Between Levinas' Ethics and Glissant's

Poetics,' in *World Writing: Poetics, Ethics, Globalization*, ed Mary Gallagher. Toronto: University of Toronto Press, 2008, 86–121.

27. Michael Dash and Quincy Troupe, 'Interview with Édouard Glissant,' *Black Renaissance*, vol. 6, no. 7 (2006): 53.

28. Antonio Benítez-Rojo, *The Repeating Island: The Caribbean and the Postmodern Perspective*, trans. James Maraniss. Durham, NC: Duke University Press, 1997.

CHAPTER 5

Decolonizing Levinasian Politics

> The sixth reflection traveled a lot, five times a thousand, to all the lands of those we call brothers. We asked of them; we listened to them. We held our word so that it would become fruitful and find its time.
>
> Subcomandante Marcos, 'Seventh Anniversary of the Zapatista Uprising'

To whom am I obligated? And in what sense am I obligated – to what end, with what severity, and with how much scope? Levinas's ethics induces plenty of vertigo in the face-to-face. The character of my relation to the Other forecloses the possibility of fully adequate response; the infinity of obligation overwhelms the finitude of my person and my place in the world. And yet that is my responsibility, which incarnates obligation in the same manner in which the Cartesian sense of the Infinite is thought: what comes to mind overflows consciousness as a matter of principle, not will or commitment. As well, I am responsible without the possibility of evasion, not just for the Other, but for all Others. My responsibility exceeds presence in multiple ways, from the infinity of the singular Other to the signification of humanity *as such* in the ethical encounter. Infinity, multiple ways. How we get to that severe and seemingly preposterous claim is a long story, some of which is recounted in the preceding chapters, but even after that story is told, there is more obligation for which we must account. As we have seen in the preceding chapters, the ethical takes on a different register in the postcolonial context, a shift in frame that widens our language of difference and implicates a new sense of responsibility, new senses of the impossibility of action, and therefore new conceptions of epistemology, ontology, and philosophy of history. Those multiple senses of the Other, generated by the experiences of race and nation, complicate the letter of Levinas's thought, while at the same time extending Levinasian thinking through engagements with companion discourses of otherness. The transnational transformation of

Levinasian thinking also changes the social, cultural, and political character of Levinas's work. Signification is already enmeshed in race and nation, something attested to in the phenomenology of incarnate historiography, and so the very beginnings of Levinasian thinking about difference and responsibility are already politicized. We quite naturally arrive at the political question.

Levinas's work on politics and the political – a distinction to which he pays only a little attention – is always guided by the ethical question. That is, responsibility is paramount. The face-to-face sets relationality in the singularity of signification. But there is always more. What about my political responsibility? What about the others who populate my community, my surrounds, my state, or even perhaps the globe? Does responsibility for 'all of the Others' make me a peculiar kind of political animal?

This shift from ethics to politics is complicated for Levinas, not just because it intensifies the field of responsibility, but also, and perhaps foremost, because politics alters the dimensionality and space of obligation from *Otherwise Than Being* to *being*. That is, whereas the ethical names a relation of singularities outside the economy of being and comparison, the political proceeds from relations comprised of belonging and not-belonging, inclusion and exclusion, friend and enemy, and so principles of comparison that lie at the heart of rights, goods, power, and justice. In politics, being and knowing are paramount. Principles of comparison proceed from the notion of occupying space, the right to that space, and the capacity to debate, determine, then choose the proper course of action. From the otherwise than being to being, without question. The ethical is of course so very different, and thus in conflict as a matter of form. My obligation to the Other is singular and neither of us can be replaced, but at the level of politics, our language is always of interchangeability – you and all others possess (or should possess) rights, the rights to goods, and a sense of protection under various notions of just law. Our lives move between these two planes of obligation. That is indisputable, though the meaning of that movement between is both evasive and fraught with tensions, contradictions, and betrayals. Such movement between is perhaps the greatest anxiety of moral consciousness, putting us out-of-home with ourselves and others just at the moment we experience responsibility. As I come to myself in proximity to the neighbor, denucleated and yet a creature of obligation, I am immediately transitioned into political terms – a new kind of ontology, less fractured – that both obligate me otherwise and betray the intimacy of the ethical. In recurrence to self (the ethical), there is also the dispersion of *conscience* across social and political space. The for-the-Other subject is, in so many ways, the movement across this interval. And Levinas's work seems to stall and defer in this moment of transition, unsure of precisely how we ought to think responsibility across the border of ethics and politics.

This is not to say that the issue passes by Levinas's critical eye unnoticed. Quite the contrary, the question of the relation between ethics and politics in Levinas's work has occasioned a good number of reflections, many of which revolve around the central concept in his articulation of the political: *le tiers*. This notion of the 'third party' proposes to resolve what is at first glance an unsolvable contradiction between the singularity of the ethical and the compulsion of the political into languages of universality and common space. The resolution is quirky, though, as the third-party *tends* to function more as a phenomenology of how the political is signified in moral consciousness than an actual clarification or exploration of the meaning of political responsibility. For example, Levinas writes in a now famous remark that in the relation of passivity and disinterestedness, obligation that is both ethical and political flows from a common event. Politics does not supplement ethics, but rather draws from the same source in the creatureliness of the responsible subject. That is, we are subjected to ethical and political obligation in one and the same moment. Levinas writes:

> In this disinterestedness, when, as a responsibility for the other, it is also a responsibility for the third party, the justice that compares, assembles and conceives, the synchrony of being and peace, take form.[1]

The *also* in this passage takes note of the common site of signification; in the disinterested relation, subjectivity is stretched across obligations. And yet, in that very same context in *Otherwise Than Being*, Levinas will remark that '[t]o be on the ground of the signification of an approach is to be with another for or against a third party, with the other and the third party against oneself, in justice.'[2]

The very moment in which Levinas describes the simultaneity of forms of responsible subjectivity, he arrives at the perhaps intractable difficulty of creaturely politics. I am called against myself in the moment of justice, seeing my place in the world as an ethical and political usurpation; the Other and the third put that usurpation in question and denucleate me otherwise than within the plane of being.

I am called to the site of outrage, where the Other is victimized by the third. This leads Levinas to suggest – and most of his work on politics and the political is suggestive – a sort of ethical solidarity, an obligation not just to the Other whom I have harmed, but also to the Other harmed by the other Other. Levinas's famous comment that the Palestinian does not fall under the category of neighbor has to be read under this rubric.[3] And yet that other Other is still an Other, who, in the ethical relation, demands my responsibility. *His work stalls in this moment of transition.*

Or alternatively, Levinas renders the question in messianic terms, marking the impasse of ethics and politics with a sense of the future that is, if anything, unsatisfying for those of us with a materialist sensibility. With the messianic, Levinas makes time and history central to the problem of politics, but always as a sort of pure futurity. A future with hope, to be sure, but a future whose relation to the present and past is at best tenuous, at worst wholly unrelated. Messianism postpones the meaning of ethics and politics; the moment of hope appears in the interruptive moment of the messianic vision – the way in which the present practices, ideological formations, and distributions of goods and right are exposed as violence by a vision of another, perhaps infinitely deferred, future. Saturated with the ethical, there *might be* or even *will be* a reconciliation of the ethical and political, but such a moment, while critical and diagnostic of the present in its illumination of *injustice*, does not lend itself to prescribing just political action. In fact, it barely lends itself to regulation, except in so far as the ethical – in this other sense of the messianic – puts politics always in question. So, in *Totality and Infinity*, Levinas writes of the time, historical or otherwise, when 'the eschatology of messianic peace will have come to superpose itself upon the ontology of war.'[4] Eschatological and messianic, Levinas's vision of the political future, the one that makes sense of the movement from ethics to politics, sees a relation only to come. *His work defers in this moment of transition.*

Ethics and politics therefore pose a conceptual problem for Levinas. But it is also, at the same time, a concrete problem. The movement from the otherwise than being to the plane of being raises the question of action, mobilization, and resistance; the materiality of political life, even in its suggestive and gesturing register, begins to make new demands on Levinasian thinking. Levinas has said a decent bit about these sorts of relations, tensions, impasses, and messianisms. The secondary literature has said considerably more. And of course I want to say a bit about the same, but with what is to my mind a decisive shift. I want to suggest turning our focus away from Levinas's own formulation of the problem of ethics and politics and toward a *Levinasian thinking* about that same problem. This turn in focus itself turns on a certain decolonizing work, much of which has been accomplished in the previous chapters. As it stands, Levinas's conception of the plane of being presumes uniformity in space, barely beginning an interrogation of the asymmetry of political space and the complexity of bordered and unbordered relations. Movement, migration, and entanglement draw on incarnate historiography, and in a postcolonial context, offer another sort of ethical politics.

The aim of the following reflections, then, is to navigate the question of a Levinasian politics critically after the work of decolonization – that is, to reread Levinas's outline of a theory of the political in a postcolonial context. In particular, I want to address the now familiar impasse of ethics and politics in the frame of another conception of singular and political subjectivity: the rhizome. The rhizome, I want to argue, offers a figure of difference that sustains the sorts of alterity and obligation we find in Levinas's work, while simultaneously making it possible, through a reconfiguration of the structure of being, to navigate a different sort of passage from ethics to politics in both theory and practice. Rather than Gilles Deleuze and Felix Guattari's notion of rhizome developed in the opening chapter of *A Thousand Plateaus*, however, I would like instead to reread the Levinasian impasse in the context of Glissant's radical rewrite of the rhizome in his *Poetics of Relation* and elsewhere. In that rewriting, postcolonial through and through, Glissant is able to merge the singularity of rhizomatic subjectivity with a collective sense of the same through a robust notion of historical experience. Glissant's rendering of the historical experience of the New World – its traumas, its machinery, and its subjectivities – deepens the sense of rhizome, moving it away from the experimental character it displays in Deleuze and Guattari's work and toward the important relation such identity questions bear to memory, history, and political formation.

This excursus into Glissant's work has two functions. First, with his articulation of rhizomatic sensibility, Glissant is able to mix the question of the Other (opacity, respect, responsibility) with the non-identity of the self-differentiating rhizome in ways that make it possible to transition better from ethics to politics. Indeed, my central claim here is that Glissant's postcolonial rethinking of the rhizome overturns Levinas's impasse by articulating the *necessity* (and so not the *logical impossibility*) of an ethical politics. Second, with this sense of rhizome and ethical politics made *in theory*, particularly with reference to Glissant's notions of solidarity and building-with (*donner-avec*), I want then to turn briefly to the post-Sixth Declaration political vision of Subcomandante Marcos. Marcos's work, which is really just a reflection on Zapatista political action in the southern Mexican state of Chiapas, merges rhizomatic thinking about ethical politics with a practice of interstitial social, economic, and political transformation. Laboring in the shadow of the state, perhaps even outside of that shadow, Marcos offers action to ethical politics. This sense of action, as we will see, contests Levinas's impasse and fretting about difference and being, while at the same time keeping the problem of alterity prominent and always problematized. Lastly, and by way of conclusion, I will return, as always, to the question of historical experience and revisit how the postcolonial *moment* and *imperative* shifts the geography of reason and revitalizes, in such important ways, what it means to think the relation of ethics and politics.

THE POSTCOLONIAL RHIZOME

Though less known and read in postcolonial theory circles than folks like Said, Bhabha, and Spivak, Glissant has written extensively on the very same notions of difference, trauma, and identity since the early 1950s. Celia Britton, in *Édouard Glissant and Postcolonial Theory*, makes an extensive argument for the relevance of Glissant's work for Anglophone postcolonial theory, drawing on his literary work to establish important points of contact with notions of subalternity and the language of difference.[5] And, as we saw in the previous chapter, Glissant's postcolonial theory draws on both the power of the ethical – placing the opacity of and respect for the Other at the center of his work – and the distinctive experience of the Middle Passage to forge a new sense of beginning and identity, much of which has implicit political significance. Across those writings, whatever the shifts in emphasis and language, his central task has been to think through the experience of diversity in the Caribbean on its own terms. Against the assimilationist tendencies in the immediate aftermath of Europe's withdrawal from strict colonial relations in the West Indies, and in contradistinction to the Negritude movement of the 1940s and 1950s, Glissant engages and affirms the cultural complexity and composite character of the Caribbean. 'Caribbeanness' – that key term from the 1970s forward in Glissant's work – signifies not so much a state of being or style of existence, but rather a *methodologi-*

cal approach to questions of difference and identity. The question is plain: how can the Caribbean signify a collectivity when the historical experience of the archipelago offers fragments of what Derek Walcott famously calls 'epic memory'?[6] There is no grand story that establishes the identity of the people. There is rather the machinery of the Middle Passage, global trade routes, and the Plantation, all of which produce an irreducibly chaotic mixture. Interrogating this chaotic mixture, Glissant produces the method of Caribbeanness as a way of understanding the distinctive metaphysical, epistemological, and aesthetic issues of New World historical experience and the production of unprecedented forms of diversity.

Those issues gather most concretely and most urgently around matters of identity. How are we to think identity after the abyss? What sort of identity emerges from what, in the preceding chapter, we called shoreline thinking – the thinking after arrival?

The problem of identity animates Glissant's earliest work, which is at first informed by a post-Negritude rewriting of Surrealism that recasts problems of exoticism, otherness, and the unknowable as productive, excessive positivities. His concerns in the 1980s and after, however, take on a decidedly more postmodern tone. By 'postmodern,' I here mean that Glissant is increasingly attentive to the problem of thinking without meta-narratives and taking the problem of fragmentation seriously as a foundational, and so not occasional, theoretical concern. This has enormous consequences for thinking about identity, ethics, and politics. In particular, fragmentation blends the ethical question with the problem of incarnate historiography; history is written on the Caribbean body as a story about difference, fragmentation, and opaque alterity. How can identity be conceived without eclipsing the fragmentation that comes from the abyss? We have Glissant's most sophisticated answer in *Poetics of Relation*, a text in which he revisits the conception of Caribbeanness in light of Deleuze and Guattari's work on rhizome anti-identity and nomadology in *A Thousand Plateaus*. Whereas previously Glissant had proposed his notion of Caribbeanness in *Caribbean Discourse* and elsewhere in the context of largely critical discussions of Negritude and Surrealism – those massive movements in the anti-colonial, then postcolonial Francophone Caribbean – *Poetics of Relation* seizes upon a whole different set of possibilities through an appropriation of *A Thousand Plateaus*. Deleuze and Guattari propose the rhizome as a model for subjectivity that both reflects a certain postmodern moment and provides a sense of resistance to the microfascism of everyday life. In his appropriation of the rhizome, Glissant is able to take up the problem of resistance to root-identity – a resistance that signals a deep break with Negritude and other single- and hybrid-identity projects – while at the same time capturing something important and difficult about Caribbean history: the Middle Passage as abyssal beginning. The rhizome, in other words, allows Glissant to think identity with the method of *Antillanité*.

This shift is significant for a number of reasons. To begin, it gives Glissant a new vocabulary for what he calls *archipelagic thinking*, an engagement with fragmentation and difference that literally and figuratively takes account of the geography of the Caribbean without reference to an elsewhere. Against *continental thinking*, Glissant's archipelagic thought sees the identity of fragmentation, paradoxically, in the reproduction and persistent differentiation of difference. *A thinking about identity which does not assemble or reassemble.* But how do we understand relationality in this context? Fragments, after all, have chaotic dis-assortment, a falling apart that does not refer back to an original unity, but instead repeats dispersal and differentiation without single-origin, nostalgia, or *telos*. Being is fragmentation. So, if we rewrite the Parmenidean claim here, both ironically and with philosophical depth, being *and* thinking are fragmentation. The enigma is two-fold. First, there is the peculiar sense of place, for Glissant will insist both that Caribbeanness is defined by fragmentation and that archipelagic thinking articulates an authentic sense of home and place; Caribbeans are not a lost, alienated, or estranged people. Second, there is the strangeness of a thinking that is itself fragmented. Fragmentation is not a theme for thought, but rather a way of beginning a theoretical apparatus for identity.

The importance of Deleuze and Guattari now comes into some focus. For a thinking *as* (and so not just *about*) fragmentation, Deleuze and Guattari's rhizome (and also, at times, nomad) help Glissant underscore a sense of connection to place – the rhizome has roots – while at the same time insisting on persistent movement. Mobility makes and unmakes place. The rhizome deterritorializes, but only to re-root and poly-root in the multilingualism of the archipelago. Glissant's rhizome marks the composite, rather than atavistic, character of both subjectivity and collectivity; given their common origin in historical experience, Glissant thinks subjectivity and collectivity at one and the same time, while nevertheless refusing, in the figure of the rhizome, to ascribe a fixed essence. His dilemma is clear and comes in three parts. The task of articulating an identity in the Caribbean context cannot appeal to the single root of Africa (assuming even that a whole continent could be reduced to a single identity), yet does not embrace the characterization of the African diaspora as lost or alienated. As well, in thinking the Caribbean context, Glissant insists on beginning with, as an originary condition, the diversity of the archipelago. The question of rootedness and roots resolves this dilemma. He writes in *Introduction à une poétique du divers*:

> [T]he thought of the root and the thought of the rhizome . . . I apply this image to the principle of identity. And from this, we can make a sort of 'categorization of cultures,' which, for me, is properly a division between atavistic and composite cultures.[7]

This is not merely a distinction of kind. It would be enough, I think, to make a metaphysical distinction between cultural formations produced by distinctive historical experiences, or to mark the limits of knowledge and empathy through the marking of historical difference. But Glissant pushes the question of culture – always composite, never fixed or single-rooted – into matters of identity. Composite culture produces composite identity, which is, in the end, nothing other than an identity formed in the chaos of difference. A poetics of the diverse, as the book title reads, is akin to a full rendering of that identity – not just expressing the *object* called rhizomatic identity, but also a practice of the *verbal* sense of the same: *rhizoming* identity into being, differentiating and fragmenting the fragments. The distinction between atavistic and composite cultures is therefore a comment on the possibility of conceiving both subjectivity and collectivity, which, in turn, is a recasting of the problem of the plane of being.

For Glissant, the distinction between the atavistic and the composite is also a commentary on the possibilities of violence. Violence in Glissant's work – and this brings him into important proximity with Levinas – circles around the problem of identity. Attribution of a single root commits violence against composite culture and subjectivities by eliminating, either through the construction of mythic and epic stories or material genocidal violence, the Other of that privileged root. The single root can only maintain its dominance through elimination of difference. Atavistic and composite cultures therefore have very different senses of the Other, with the former constructing otherness as an enemy, the latter seeing the entanglement of One with the Other to the point of shared construction of meaning. In *Poetics of Relation*, Glissant writes:

> Roots make the commonality of errantry and exile, for in both
> instances roots are lacking. We must begin with that . . . The root
> is unique, a stock taking all upon itself and killing all around it. In
> opposition to this, they [Deleuze and Guattari] propose the rhizome,
> an enmeshed root system, a network spreading either in the ground
> or in the air, with no predatory rootstock taking over perma-
> nently. The notion of the rhizome maintains, therefore, the idea of
> rootedness but challenges that of a totalitarian root.[8]

Errantry and exile move to the center here in order to make the claim
for difference. If errantry and exile are common, so not exceptional
or an aberration, then difference *begins* identity. The archipelago
figures the distribution of difference in being *without assembly*.
Difference, fragmentation, being, place. And for that reason, the
simultaneity of rootedness and non-predatory roots is crucial. For,
in this simultaneity, Glissant is able to forge a different sort of relation between thinking and otherness, affirming how the Other sets
out a particular and always new (or renewed) sense of exile *without
loss*. In other words, the rhizome can be read in the Caribbean – and,
perhaps more generally, the postcolonial – context as an ethics of
thinking and cultural contact that sustains, rather than threatens,
the identity of thought and culture. For example, entwined and creolized multilingualism – as one element of composite culture – only
threatens that which holds fast to mythic conceptions of the monolingual and the single root. Glissant proposes multilingualism as the
originary situation, not an epiphenomenon of combined, distinct,
single-rooted languages. In that way, we can say that the rhizome
says *yes* to diversity and what it offers as connection to place, which
fundamentally transforms the sense of entanglement with alterities
and the opaque character of the Other, whereas monolingualism is
necessarily predatory and destructive of the original entanglement.
The rhizome is *with* the Other in the relation of building and becoming place, rather than struggling, as with the single root, against what
usurps place. We can already see some important conceptual distance
from Levinas's conception of difference. Glissant's is an ethics of
building-with and solidarity, rather than an ethics of welcoming and
hospitality. Indeed, in a context of composite, rather than atavistic
cultural formation, an ethics and inkling of an ethical politics could
not unfold otherwise. Errantry and exile function as the condition
of responsibility, rather than, in an atavistic context, a threat to the
continuity of the self and place. The rhizome rhizomes into place.
Without the competing economies of usurpation and rights to place,

we can begin thinking differently about ethics, being, politics, and practice, while keeping the transcendence of the Other at the center of our theorizing.

Glissant's reading of Deleuze and Guattari reroutes the language of rhizome through a different sort of historical experience. Composite cultures *begin* with the rhizome. Atavistic cultures *dismantle* with the rhizome. We can begin to see here how Glissant's appropriation of Deleuze and Guattari is far from a straightforward adoption of language and concept. It is, rather, a creolization of theory that generates a new sense of the rhizome by placing it at the *beginning* of the question of identity, not as a creation for the sake of resistance. To wit: whereas *A Thousand Plateaus* is written against the hegemony of certain metaphysical and epistemological habits – such that the single-rooted fantasy of identity is described by them as *predatory* at the level of everyday life (microfascism) – Glissant's appropriation of the language of rhizome is less revolutionary than it is a straightforward description of Caribbean history and memory. The fantasy of single-rooted identity is plainly absurd in the Caribbean context; across islands, there are not only racial and linguistic differences, but also (and as the efficient cause of those differences) profoundly different experiences of the plantation, colonialism, and then independence. Resistance lies in the anti-colonial assertion of *difference first*, rather than, as the colonial fantasy would have it, a sameness by which the colonized are measured. The origin of Fanon's famous account of the inferiority complex shows itself here, surmounted by a reorientation and proper account of composite cultural complexity.

Further, when Glissant critiques the single-rooted identity, it is not simply for the sake of articulating a more appropriate ontology of the collective Caribbean subject (though that would surely be plenty). Rather, and this is something his work throughout the 1990s insists upon with increasing intensity, the fantasy of the single root lies at the heart of eliminationist and assimilationist notions of politics. The single root, Glissant claims along with Deleuze and Guattari, is *predatory*. The single root consumes or eliminates difference in order to establish itself as single and the source of life. Diversity and difference are givens, so the single root can only stake its claim or tell its story if the Other and others are eliminated. Such a mythic conception of collectivity is inherently political, given that it is a claim about being as uniformity; the single root is a vision of being (both in particular and in general), which is a plane of possible and imperative actions, which, in the end, is the politics of territory.

The single root proclaims itself as the sole root, a source of self-legitimating legitimacy, and so also claims the space it occupies and shadows as its own. This is a familiar politics, of course: occupation and displacement. Too familiar. The rhizome forges a very different cluster of chaotic, indeterminate paths, questioning the very idea of the possession of exclusive and excluding rights, place, and territory. For Glissant, again following Deleuze and Guattari, the rhizome deterritorializes and opens being, practice, and the political field with an originary difference. Fragments as fragments, not fragments as lost origins. But, because he does not want to concede the sense of connection to otherness that comes with roots, Glissant's treatment of the rhizome places the ethical question at the center of the problem of identity. Fragments do not lead to estrangement or despairing disconnection and solitude. Polyrootedness is still contact and connection – that enigmatic sense Glissant calls Relation. Difference without reconciliation in identity is identity itself – a for-the-Other subject as rhizome, in so far as identity answers to irreducible differentiation. This is an ethical question, for, as Glissant writes in *Poetics of Relation*, in rhizomatic identity

> I thus am able to conceive of the opacity of the other for me, without reproach for my opacity for him. To feel in solidarity with him or to build with him or to like what he does, it is not necessary for me to grasp him. It is not necessary to try to become the other (to become other) nor to 'make' him in my image. These projects of transmutation – without metempsychosis – have resulted from the worst pretensions and the greatest of magnanimities on the part of the West.[9]

One can surely hear the resonance of Levinasian thinking here, especially around the notion of the opacity of the Other. Opacity is not simply the unknowable. Opacity is the condition for the possibility of another sort of contact, one that says *yes* to the rhizome without consuming the Other or committing to the leap of identification. And yet Glissant goes a significant bit further than Levinas. At the moment he extends the relation of contact to feeling solidarity and building-with, Glissant repeats, with a decisive difference, the problem of the third party. In solidarity and building-with, there is the signification of a collectivity, but that collectivity becomes the meaning of subjectivity on the plane of being *as differentiation itself*, rather than, as for Levinas, a relation to the uniform (and enormously important) conception of humanity as such. The rhizome makes this possible, as we have seen in the previous chapter, by re-entangling the subject in being-as-difference, rather than the unicity-to-unicity-to-generality schema in Levinas's work. Politics as being as difference.

As well, and perhaps most important for our reflections here, Glissant's exploration of the rhizome against single-rooted identity functions as an implicit argument against nationalism and the nation-state. Part of this is due to the peculiar and specific character of Caribbean historical experience, where the multilingual character of each island and the archipelago more widely forbids the terms of nationalism. How could one conceive an inner nature of a people without a shared language, race, or even fixed borders? The archipelago and its diverse historical experience already labor against national or racial identity, suggesting creoleness against what Wilson Harris calls the 'involuntary associations' handed down by colonial history.[10] Thinking the rhizome in the Caribbean context, then, says yes to the composite complexity of place and the paradoxical identity-as-differentiated-difference such a place manifests. But Glissant also thinks the rhizome more widely, and in that more suggests a wider vision of mixture and the deconstruction of borders. In a globalized and globalizing world, one defined not just in part, but as a totality, by its entanglements, the nation-state becomes more and more a matter of fantasy and myth. A violent and imperial one, for sure, but a myth nonetheless. The myth is exposed in a global migration of cultures and cultural forms that, unlike globalizing economic hegemony, know no center, origin, or purity. Globalization *in this sense* is errant and exilic as a matter of first and originary principle: rhizomatic and rhizoming, always initiating contact with otherness and, in the wake of that contact, bringing opacity and polyrootedness as a form of both resistance and identity formation.

Glissant's rhizome therefore does not concede the world to predatory single roots and epic stories of filiation that underwrite violence and persecution. If we are to write the epic at this moment of globalizing contact and creolization, then we write the anti-epic against the nation-state. Perhaps there is still the state, with its civil and more broadly political infrastructure, or perhaps not, but if we conceive it this way, then it is a state without the affective or metaphysical inner identity of a people. Difference and differentiation, as a property of the rhizome and being more broadly, labor against this inner identity, which, in turn, deterritorializes all claims to place. The language of national and sovereign space gives way to solidarity and building-with. The Same and the Other – which interestingly form the basis of both Levinas's and Carl Schmitt's political theory (and thus shows the precariousness of any Levinasian claim) – cease to be the dyadic ground for the construction of a politics and, instead, become items in the element of creolized and creolizing space – rhizoming a fragile connection. Fragile connections derive their moral force from fragility itself; there is never hegemony-over, but only the creative, unexpected building-with that begins with respect for the opacity of the Other. The rhizome is always a fragile connection to place and also an identity in being as difference and differentiation. Yet, Glissant is also worldly and worldly-aware; in a global space dominated by Western predation for over five centuries, the ethics of building-with, drawn from a felt and transformative solidarity, has to remake the world with the composite and the creolizing in view. Actually, it is more urgent: not just in view, but as the foreground that then becomes the background, remapping relations as fractals and indeterminate movement. The rhizome becomes, then, not just a noun, but a verb. 'We,' Glissant writes, 'who rhizomed this fragile connection to place.'[11]

ZAPATISMO AND THE DETERRITORIALIZATION OF ACTION

Glissant's rhizome operates according to the anti-law of primary difference. Rhizome identity is regulated by the proliferation of difference, rather than the constraint or elimination of the Other. The opacity of the Other sustains, rather than repels, entanglement. Indeed, the ethics of deterritorialization, which suggests a politics of the same, is just that: the affirmation of the Other's place in the sun, perhaps even at the expense of my own, while still holding fast to the notion of building-with such that we can think rhizomatically about place without re- or dis-placement. This generates a peculiar notion of being – not one interrupted by the Other, but rather a space of totality that is diffracted and differentiated by the diversity and multiplicity of beings. An ethical *and* political sense of being. Still, Glissant's work is in large part a theoretical exploration of difference, with only a hint or two about the political meaning of such work. Concerned with creole quasi-linguistics, history, and the function of poetics in the *chaos-monde*, Glissant's work can only gesture at how rhizomatic subjectivity might change the meaning of praxis. Except we do know at least this much: the praxical meaning of rhizome and entanglement must exceed the posturing and positioning of the European articulations of the same. The Caribbean context – or perhaps more broadly the New World context – begins with entanglement, rather than experimenting with the rhizome as a political strategy. If the New World context begins with the rhizome as a site of being (both in particular and in general), then such a context reconfigures the ontology of political space in such a way that it is possible to think – and perhaps, then, to act – difference and differentiation without the recurrence of the general and the neutral. A different kind of solidarity, one without inner identity and nation-feeling.

With this in mind, it is worth beginning again with the epigraph above from Subcomandante Marcos. In commemoration of the anniversary of the Zapatista uprising – that insurgency against the Mexican state in the name and body of the subaltern indigenous class – Marcos appeals, not to a moral or political posture against the machinery of the state, but to travel, listening, speaking, keeping one's word, and the patience of time. The shift away from polemic and anti-state mobilization, even as that remains important work, and toward projects of solidarity as difference and differentiating adds a dimension of praxis to thinking through the rhizome as a figure of ethical politics. In so doing, Marcos marks ethical space in political thinking with the affects of contact. This is not to say that such affects are disconnected from larger institutional or ideological concerns. The Zapatista movement is of course deeply engaged in anti-capitalist struggle and mobilizing against the reach of neo-liberal economic imperialism, but, at the same time, much of Marcos's writing since 2005 has been concerned with the theory and practice of an ethical politics. Ethical politics, in Marcos's account, is concerned firstly with the crossing of borders – or even the elimination of them – while at the same time maintaining a sense of connection. A rhizomatic relation that refuses to oppose difference and contact. It is worth recalling this passage:

> The sixth reflection traveled a lot, five times a thousand, to all the lands of those we call brothers. We asked of them; we listened to them. We held our word so that it would become fruitful and find its time.[12]

Now, in this sense of travel and listening we see an expression or even a general characterization of the well-known Zapatista principle of revolution and leadership from below. Marcos's various explorations of the meaning of authority and organization bear this out, for the Zapatista movement has from the beginning sought to rethink the function of power in subaltern political organization. But travel and listening also name something enigmatic about identity. With 'travel,' Marcos dislocates and deterritorializes the meaning of political identity by infusing movement and contact with ethical language – listening *after* travel is akin to, if not an outright example of, the seeking of the Other and otherness we find in Derrida's Levinasian rereading of reason in *Rogues*.

With that seeking-of-the-Other, we catch sight of a cluster of features of difference in Marcos's thinking. First, the territory across which political obligation de- and re-territorializes is asymmetrical and already plural. If politics is being, then being is difference and all sorts of responsibilities follow. That is, I am compelled to travel out of an ethical imperative, drawn by the Other out of the comforts of my place in the sun in search of modes of solidarity and practice; there is no appeal to *my* territory in the first place, but only the asymmetry of, first, ethically deterritorialized space. Second, the asymmetry of space, deterritorialized from the outset, locates its gravity outside the center of the political subject and, in that gravitation-from-the-outside, *makes* political subjectivity. I am drawn to the Other because the Other *comes first*, even as alterity sits in the margins of the geography of reason and action. Third, deterritorialized space is nevertheless the space of roots, meaning, and historical experience. On the model of Glissant's rhizome, polyrootedness keeps the idea of place in place, as it were, making it possible to think simultaneously about the mobility of obligation without the imposition of borders first, then welcoming across those sites of violence and exclusion. Entangled as an originary condition, travel and listening operate outside the dyadic conception of the border in the interest of a minimal violence. This minimal violence, and the kind of rhizomatic political identity and practice it implicates, infuses practice with a theoretical sensibility dedicated to difference and differentiation – to the point of seeking and cultivating difference, rather than simply negotiating the proximal, factical difference of the neighbor. With the multilingualism and polycultural conception of the plane of being in Marcos's work, perhaps we could say that he *creolizes* the idea of political space – or, perhaps even better, responds responsibly to an already creolized distribution of meaning. Difference and differentiation sustain at the very same moment they devastate with obligation; this is the crossing of the political and the ethical, both directed by the Other. In a certain sense, then, the gathering point of difference is in the moment of political vision that *is not vanguardism*. There is no single idea in and through which Zapatismo happens. Instead,

Zapatismo is an identity which is not one, forged and shed in the movement against borders that none the less proceeds with respect for the alterity of the Other. Traveling. Listening.

The figure of the rhizome helps organize this sense of differentiation. To begin, the struggle itself moves against rootedness. In turning away from (or at least setting aside) direct action against the state, and moving back toward the material labor of justice in 'the other possible world,' Marcos unroots the very idea of struggle. Practice deterritorialized becomes a practice of deterritorialization. The practice of deterritorialization becomes a practice deterritorialized. This zigzag relation between territory and practice confirms the non-centered site of beginning for politics. And like Glissant's theorization of the same, Marcos's rhizome is fundamentally committed to roots as *non-predatory*. Rhizomatic roots are open and spreading across what *should* be borders and sites of exclusion, as per the predatory practices of colonial history and the memory of that predation, but, under the rubric of the polyrooted, roots are instead points of ethical political contact. Such points of contact – the just work of solidarity and building-with – are moments of transgression against race, nation, and cultural habits of constructing problematic notions of otherness. Deterritorialized and deterritorializing practices *decolonize* the relation to the Other, transgressing the borders prescribed by the territorializing gaze, which then transforms political space into plurality, a morally gravitational Other, and differentiating work of solidarity.

The transgression is motivated by the vulnerability of the Other; it is instructive to consider one of Marcos's earliest dispatches, 'Dying in Order to Live,' where the rationale for sacrifice is precisely the vulnerability of the Other. 'During these past ten years,' Marcos writes in early 1994, 'more than 150,000 indigenous have died of curable diseases . . . We are ready to die, 150,000 more if necessary, so that our people awaken from this dream of deceit that holds us hostage.'[13] Indeed, even the location of struggle in the southernmost state of Mexico, Chiapas, is its own geography of reason. Situated at the literal and figurative borders of the Mexican state, Zapatismo responds to the Other with a *political action* that is firstly a call of *ethical responsibility*. That is, it is the singularity of suffering that prompts attention, a call, a putting in question. But that is never enough. The vulnerable Other is a *political Other*, an alterity or outside of political space, and so the gravitational moment initiates political duties, service, sacrifice, and, ultimately, a (re)building-with the Other. Marcos writes in the 'Sixth Declaration':

> We are going to try to build, or rebuild, a different way of doing poli-
> tics, one that again has the spirit of serving others, without material
> interests, with sacrifice, with dedication, with honesty, which keeps
> its word, whose only payment is the satisfaction of duty performed.[14]

The 'different way of doing politics' proclaimed in this programmatic
statement is enacted in material struggle. That is, it is not a theorization of the political alone – though it is plenty engaged with such a
theorizing – but also a moment of praxis in the plane of being. That
plane is what bears a moral call precisely because being is asymmetrical, differentiating, and so comprised of radical, irreducible
difference. Such difference grounds, but does not forbid, the practice
of solidarity. So, material struggle is here first a different kind of
solidarity, one motivated by the shared experience of victimization,
fragility, and obligation. That shared experience does not reduce
plurality to a unity of the victim; rather, it roots without territoriali-
zation and is a call for travel, listening, and so on. For, the opacity
of experience does not limit contact, but instead reminds of the
necessity of differentiation and solidarity at one and the same time.

Marcos's sense of transgressive justice – that is, a justice that
operates against borders – is oriented by travel, listening, and this
enigmatic 'keeping of one's word.' There is Levinasian teaching here,
for sure; to listen is to be taught, to have one's prerogative denucleated, and to be then prompted to action. Marcos regularly appeals
to sacrifice, but always as a moral call and practice, never in the
sense of self-glorifying martyrdom. Action is never final or resolved,
precisely because Zapatismo is not identity-making. Rather, action
takes place in a space opened up between the state and Other – an
interstitial space of justice made ethical by the urgency of suffering
and a history of persecution. This interstitial space is constructed by
way of the asymmetry of political relationships, the wealth of one
whose enjoyment displaces the other who dies of a curable disease
or infection, but, importantly, this is never on the model of charity.
Charity, after all, functions as a moral center in the ethical and
political relation, neutralizing asymmetry. The rhizome, on the other
hand, (re-)entangles this asymmetry and generates a potent sense of
political responsibility modeled at once on socialism and anarchism
– redistributive, but without center. Rhizomatic identity makes this
possible by mapping, without territorial claim, the flow of capital,
power, and possibility *at the very same moment* that the ethical call
rewrites the map with a different sense of difference and differen-

tiation as morally gravitational. Traveling, asking, listening, and holding to words are tactics, but tactics that generate an emergent identity. *Onto-tactical* actions – a making of being, always nomadic, out of tactical and strategic work in a Levinasian sense of passivity, then action. Given the irregularity of the map of political responsibility and solidarity, perhaps we should nuance the action one more time: *onto-fractal-tactical* action. Is an-archy not always a form of chaos? Responsibility, in a rhizomatic, fragmented plane of being, maps political subjectivity in the moment of the call, never before. This is not an a priori science. Marcos's is an onto-fractal-tactical praxis, producing that very kind of political subjectivity.

In this context, Simon Critchley's short and suggestive remarks in *Infinitely Demanding* regarding Zapatismo, indigenous rights, and most importantly the practice of an interstitial politics are relevant. Critchley is drawn to this political site because it shares with him an enigmatic blend of anarchism and socialism – a Levinasian politics without center, but oriented toward generosity. To be sure, his concern is not much with the Zapatista movement and Marcos's theorization of an ethical politics, but both the common concerns and the fact that Critchley is one of the few to take up the anarchic dimension of Levinas's thought in a political context make a brief remark or two instructive. The Zapatista shift of emphasis from armed struggle to ethical politics relocates itself from a concern with the center (state power, representation) to a responsive praxis on the margins and borderlands of the state. In other words, an interstitial politics. And this is where Critchley's work is particularly interesting for making connections. For Critchley, the first question of an interstitial politics is that of territory or the space of encounter and practice. Critchley writes:

> this distance from the state is within the state, that is, within and upon the state's territory. It is, we might say, an interstitial distance, an internal distance that has to be opened from the inside.[15]

And further, with a quick reference to Marcos and Zapatista resistance, Critchley writes:

> the task of radical political articulations is the creation of interstitial distance within the state territory. The Mexican example of indigenous identity discussed above is a powerful instance of the creation of such a distance, an act of political leverage where the invocation of an international legal convention created the space for the emergence of a new political subject.[16]

The turn toward indigenous identity in Mexico offers Critchley an example of *created* interstitial space, a way of making the Other's place on the margins of the state, but still close enough to the interior of the state so that the Other puts something of political power into question. My hesitation here with Critchley's position should be clear, though. He wants to make the move from an ethical sensibility oriented toward the Other to a politics that does not enter the plane of being *as* the state, but instead generates a different sense of being, one placed outside the state, and so a sense of anarchic action outside totality that is responsive to the material conditions of suffering. And puts the state in question, from this marginal between. A doubling of being, perhaps, in which the interstitial plays an insurgent role at the level of ideas, revolutionary praxis, or even just alternative space for the political work of justice.

I appreciate the impulse and the intuition. Still, such a conception of ethical politics remains too closely tied to notions of fraternity, to the proximity of me to the community for whom I am. That is, interstitial politics, while it takes (or can take) measured account of the place of excluded and persecuted indigenous communities, keeps political space local and tempered, because of that locality, in its asymmetry. But this need not be the case and it in fact overstates the meaning of 'indigenous,' concealing the internal differences in that too-broad term. Interstitial space, when withdrawn from revolutionary struggle for state power, is still itself asymmetrical, so identity is just as perplexing in southern Mexico as in any other locale. Indeed, one of the innovations of the post-Sixth Declaration Zapatista movement is the diffraction of the question of identity, moving away from the traces of *indigenismo* of the early armed struggle and toward the entanglement of difference constitutive of southern Mexico as a region of radical differences. Identity is not made out of indigenousness, but rather from a shared commitment to justice – the love and politics (in the widest sense) between neighbors *and* communities at the margins of neo-liberalism and the nation-state. The puzzle for Marcos, then, is how to conceive and mobilize love and justice without surmounting the diffraction of identity with a hegemonic vanguard. It is no coincidence, of course, that Subcomandante Marcos renames himself Agent Zero at this very moment, erasing himself in the movement at the moment the movement takes on another, internally differentiated character. Agent Zero prunes the remnants of vanguardism in order to make the rhizome *work and live*. The being of the rhizome is enacted in this tactic and its consequences – the name Agent Zero as identity-maker performs this onto-fractal-tactic – and such rhizoming of rhizomes is expressed concisely in the language of traveling, listening, duty, building, and of course solidarity.

This politics can be characterized as indigenous and interstitial, then, only in so far as we understand both indigeneity and interstitiality to be fully ethical political spaces of identity and praxis. As fully ethical political sites, difference and differentiation comprise what Critchley calls a 'new political subject' to the extent that we read subjectivity in the frame of the rhizome.

How, then, are we to reread Levinas's conception of the ethics–politics relation after Glissant, Marcos, and the rhizomatic transformation of being and action? Critchley's blending of interstitiality and anarchic justice begins that conversation for Levinasian thinking, but the repudiation of roots and the Same–Other dyad in the rhizome raises new, unexpected questions for Levinas and Levinasian thinking. In particular, the infusion of the problem of ethical politics with a more robust historical experience of difference and differentiation changes the meaning of being as the plane of politics and the political. What remains of Levinas's thought after this postcolonial context rewrites his central ideas? And what has been transformed and translated into another conceptual language?

BORDERS AND DECOLONIZATION: LEVINAS, *OTRA VEZ*

I have taken this lengthy excursus into a decolonized and decolonizing rhizomatic theory and practice in order to return to the impasse of ethics and politics in Levinas's work that began the present reflections. The rhizomatic recast of being opens up new possibilities for an ethical politics, but only if some fundamental elements of Levinas's theorizing of the same are rewritten. And, of course, only if Deleuze and Guattari's rhizome is overwritten by the ethics of the Other in the postcolonial context. In Levinas's formulation, no matter the crossing of them in signification, the singularity of the ethical and the generality of the political remain, as a matter of principle, stuck in opposition. This impasse is not merely conceptual. It alters how we conceive the possibility of justice and a just practice of lesser violence. Levinas's first commitment is always to the singularity of the ethical in which my obligation is mine alone (I am *chosen* by responsibility), and this obligation is solely connected to the irreducibly incomparable singular face. Politics betrays this obligation, for, in a uniform conception of being, political life must proceed from comparison. State power, in this configuration, is not so much a betrayal of politics as it is a fulfillment and expression of one of the most basic impulses of political life: domination of the uniformity of being.

Singularity and being form an impasse in the political moment. This moment is fraught precisely because singularity and being cross in politics and the political. That is, both singularity and being make a claim in the space of politics without being resolved in a third conceptual space; paradoxically, crossing and hiatus are simultaneous, and Levinas does not turn to dialectics to resolve the problem. In politics, there is already ethical sense, just as in the ethical, there is already the political. When I am called to political responsibility by an Other who faces me, two forces fundamentally structure that call. The singularity of the face calls me (singularity writ across subjectivity and the Other) to the one and only moment of obligation, the moment that surges as the accusing face sets subjectivity in the accusative. I come to myself as singular, having already been made a direct object. I am obligated. That obligation is to *this Other elsewhere*, the Other who accuses and is located in the non-locatable site; all of those qualifications on what Levinas means by 'the Other' only make (necessarily) complex the straightforward claim that responsibility is always responsibility for a unique Other. The second force in the sign, which Levinas calls simply 'the third,' is the political moment in this same event of the face. Levinas reminds us on occasion that every face-to-face implicates the third – a sort of co-signification. We can say, then, that what is meant by the third is not an extraneous or additional concern of the ethical encounter. We are always already both ethical and political, assuming, with Levinas, that we limit the political to the question of the third and the economy of signification. There is nothing extraordinary about political obligation at the level of the sign. In the hyperbole of the ethical encounter, supplemented to even more excess in the political, there is already too much ethics and too much politics.

And yet this is an impasse. The co-signification of the Other and the others, the sign of the neighbor and humanity in one and the same event of responsibility, is a fundamentally incompatible signification. That is, the *intimacy* of the Other and the third in the sign of the face notwithstanding, the shift from the singular to the political marks a dramatic shift in plane, fracturing responsibility. Ethical life is no life at all; subjectivity is denucleated, fractured, and, as with Spivak's subaltern, is faced with a sense of otherness that ciphers itself before approach, concern, care, or any other sort of way in which an *ethics* might take hold. As a matter of foundational theoretical claim, politics asks something different. To be sure, the signification of the third provides a certain phenomenological context for Levinas's well-known expansion of responsibility to 'all the others,' but signification left to itself is misleading. Politics moves to the plane of being; political life is shared space between agents, subjects with interests and freedom, and therefore concerns competing claims to a place in the sun *even as the place in the sun is called in question by the ethical.* If we recall Bhabha's long reflections on Fanon and agency, for example, we can see how political life bears a relation to the ethical while at the same time trafficking in the political value of self-possession. Fanon's subject, Bhabha claims, takes up the problem of agency in the name of the political and historical other in a gesture of redemption and solidarity. For better or worse, Levinas's movement from the otherwise than being of the ethical to the plane of being in the political is *always* an act of violence. The very items called into question in the ethical are deployed as matters of legitimate, even obligating, concern in the political. In that sense, Levinas is not being hyperbolic when he describes politics as a kind of betrayal of the ethical. So long as being is uniformity, we cannot have politics and the political without calculation and comparison, whereas the ethical as such proceeds from the first position of the incalculable and incomparable. Politics transgresses this boundary, and yet we cannot have the ethical without the political. A necessary, inevitable violence.

This impasse has specific, limited positivity for Levinas, as well. The formulation of *Totality and Infinity*, which declares that politics left to itself is tyranny, seems fundamentally *right*. The exercise of power, whether through the authoritarian personality of a figure of the hegemony of one class over another, is tyrannical as a matter of essence, not just as a perversion or exceptional occasion. Levinas therefore begins *Totality and Infinity* with the humbling evocation of the history of war and violence, seeking, in the ethical, a glimpse of something that is not contained by that history and its repetition in the philosophical trajectory of politics against ethics. For this reason, perhaps, the ethical plays a primarily interruptive role in relation to politics. The tyrannical character of political life – the life of comparison, judgement, distribution of rights and goods – is both exceeded by the ethical (we are called to the Other outside political structures and prescriptions) and put in question by it (the fragility and precarious life of the Other expose the violence of politics, law, and the state). In that sense, we can say that the ethical *resists* politics and the political with the singular, though never in the name of an alternative political vision or ideology. The vulnerability of the face alone undercuts the totalizing desire of the political. Moral consciousness refuses to give in to the commandments of politics, and in turn, in that audacious Levinasian claim, the categories of political life owe their very being to the event of the ethical. If we are creaturely as a condition of the possibility of responsibility *and* response, then being begins after the creative event of moral consciousness. Paul Celan's short lines, quoted at the heart of *Otherwise Than Being*, are instructive: *ich bin du, wenn ich ich bin.*

The problem for Levinasian thinking, then, lies in this conflict and separation. What are we to make of the exclusion of the ethical from politics, except as an interruptive force? Is Levinas simply articulating the tension constitutive of being human? We are, after all, constantly torn between our obligations as actors and citizens, so perhaps Levinas is observing something rather banal. It is certainly a familiar and terrifying experience. Or, alternatively, can we say that Levinas produces conceptual tools for thinking the relation between ethics and politics differently? How can we reconfigure the relationship between ethics and politics, such that the ethical intervenes in a productive register, rather than simply interrupting, then withdrawing, from political life?

Consider for a moment Derrida's work from the middle 1980s and after. That work, so consistently provocative and unexpected, explores the ambivalent possibilities for thinking a Levinasian politics and, in doing so, exposes both the limits and futures for such a politics. Beginning, perhaps, with the 'Force of Law' essay, Derrida revisits the animating spirit of Levinas's work across themes of memory, justice, democracy, and law. Across all of those themes, Derrida is able to track the double movement of the ethical and the political, seeing first how the ethical (justice, futurity, and so on) seizes up the totalizing pretensions of political life, but then also how dimensions of justice are opened up that enact the ethical in the plane of being (hospitality, cosmopolitanism, and so on). For example, it is noteworthy in this context how the function of hospitality and welcoming in *Adieu*, a work occasioned by Levinas's death in late 1995, underpins the conceptual work and moral claim of cosmopolitanism and the deconstruction of borders in later essays. If the boundary of the subject, the site of an originary violence that also imposes responsibility on me, is also the boundary of home and my place in the sun, then the consequent relation of obligation – the command to welcome and host the widow, orphan, and stranger – is already implicated in a political world. The home is like the state: a site of exclusion that, on reflection, points to a resulting excessive responsibility for s/he who is excluded. The refugee is produced by the border of the state, which then marks the excluding state with the political responsibility of refuge and repair. The positivity of the Levinasian ethical therefore leads Derrida to a theoretical position that Levinas himself could not conceive: the asymmetry of political space and the moral call issued from that space, within that space, and toward another configuration of space in which there is always the beginning of a political response. Justice becomes less an abstract interruption, complicated signification, or messianic deferral than a concrete practice of welcoming, hospitality, refuge, and ethically infused cosmopolitanism. The plane of being becomes, under Derrida's rewrite of the Levinasian position, a site of intensified obligation, rather than simply betrayal or interruption.

Whatever Derrida's creative advance on Levinas's thinking about ethics and politics, he is also attentive to that very same moment of impasse in the extension of Levinasian thinking. The presupposition – and it is irreducibly a presupposition, rather than a problem to be explained away – is always the border. The ethical intervenes in the political and opens a horizon of justice both *inside* and *outside* the plane of being, but, in the same way that the position of the ethical subject enacts the violence it is called to address, the problem of political justice proceeds from a prior violence. In other words, like the ethical, a just politics begins with the problem of borders. We see this in Derrida's work when the problem of, say, the city of refuge is offered as an occasion of a just – by which Derrida means, in the end, a less violent – politics. Derrida's story of the city of refuge follows a Levinasian script, for sure, where the city or state plays the political role of the host. The host is constituted *as* the host, as the one capable of welcoming, by the refugee. The one excluded exercises a certain ontological gravitation, pulling the origin of the being of a city of refuge away from the self-constituting and self-legitimating state, and relocating the meaning of refuge, host, and welcome to the one excluded. The state is chosen by the excluded; the border marks, literally, the difference between refuge and refugee, and, in so doing, prescribes the flow of ethical, political, and ethical political meaning.

In this sense, then, the ethical and the possibility of an ethical politics presuppose, or even depend upon, the persistence of borders. But this is precisely what limits Levinas's articulation of a politics or political theory (and perhaps too Derrida's account of the same). The border is the condition of violence; this is an intractable problem for a theory rooted in the relation of singularities and the problem of separation. The presupposition of the border or borders is further sustained by Levinas's conception of being as uniformity and totality without difference; even as we have been able, in the preceding two chapters, to begin reclaiming the idea of ontology as fracture, Levinas's work on subjectivity's political moment does not take fracture into the space of collectivity. Being is always uniform in politics, on Levinas's account, and most of his best words for political practice concede some goodness in uniformity (liberal notions of law, human rights, democracy, and so on). The Other is interruptive for this very reason – from outside, transgressive of the border, always putting the political in question because of the conflict between difference and uniformity. It is difficult, if not impossible, to fathom the Other as such a particular interruptive, transgressive force without the bordering of two sites and signification. And yet there is the *call* of the ethical in political space beyond the common, uniform protection of law and rights. This is the call to which Derrida, in those moments in which he appeals to the *least* violence, draws our attention and with which Levinasian thinking about politics must proceed. If we proceed with this call, then we see an ethically infused responsiveness at the political level, beginning with the asymmetrical political space of wealth, representation, and national and transnational violence – those first questions of social justice. At the same time, the problem of borders remains a presupposition for this kind of ethical politics.

What would it mean to rethink the structure of being, moving away from Levinas's claim of uniformity and Derrida's nuanced critique in the name of political asymmetry? That is, to rethink being with another, more fractured sense of border. Glissant and Marcos, as we have read them above, begin such a rethinking. Rhizomatic identity, especially when that sense of identity is saturated with the force of the Other, opens up an important new vocabulary for thinking about ethical politics. The fidelity to borders limits Levinas's conception of politics with the characterization of being as sameness, whereas the rhizome captures the entanglement of the ethical in a political context. As well, and this is crucial, the rhizome also carries with it the language of being *without concealing or canceling out the notion of a moral outside or margin*. This distinction is important and points, again, to the critical place of fractured ontology in moving Levinas across geographies; the rhizome has differentiation, fracture, and fragmentation as constitutive of being, rather than the contradiction of it. If we return to Levinas with this conception of being, while remaining in search of his sense of the ethical in the political, then politics as being is not contrary to the ethical, but rather a translation of it into another sort of asymmetry. With that asymmetry, we can begin (or rejoin with Marcos) another discourse of obligation that retains all the force, imperative, and sense of infinite work.

The objection from Levinas, of course, would be that this sounds a bit too much like political community. Community – not unlike war, ironically – is problematic for the very reason that it solicits (if not imposes) roles for singular subjects that commit them to forms of epistemological and ontological violence. A singularity, after all, cannot be classified or grouped under a shared identity, so even in its interstitial formulation one has to ask the Levinasian question about collectivity and collective action and responsibility. That is, Levinas's suspicion, and it is a righteous and important one, would surely be that identity-talk absorbs the singular in a gesture of liberation and action in solidarity, which, in the end, only repeats the violence. Can we say that building-with and traveling, as the practice of political solidarity, risk too much usurpation of the Other's place in the sun (the risk of identification) and absorb singularity with identity? That would certainly read the rhizome too strongly. Those sorts of Levinasian concerns would overstate or even misunderstand the too-rootedness of the political rhizome; the purchase of rhizomatic political thinking lies in its ability to set roots *and* live without fixed, tree-like roots. Rhizome identity names the *finitude* of community identification. Roots are not set deeply or exclusively. Mobile polyrootedness expresses a kind of responsiveness to the politically vulnerable (traveling, listening, creating with) that commits more profoundly to solidarity, more justly and with a deeper sense of transformation than a politics and ethics of charity. Solidarity and the risks of identity are crucial for radical politics; the play of de- and re-territorialization is critical for critical practice. The rhizomatic finitude of political identity minimizes the risk and violence of solidarity, while ceding the gravity of our moral life in being to the Other. Finite identification – the ethical sense of building-with and solidarity – moves against calcification of identities (the rhizome is never identified with a single root or set of roots) and allows solidarity and building-with without risks of identification, 'becoming the

Other,' and other sorts of usurpation. The rhizome is anti-predatory. Rhizomatic identity entangles obligation in multiple places, differentiating the plane of being in which politics and the political are enacted. The ethical haunts this differentiated space without straightforward contraction, saturating instead each of the moments of encounter – the singular, the third, and so on – with affects of responsibility that are both ethical and political. For me, this is a fundamentally Levinasian gesture, widening and deepening obligation. But it requires a break with the uniformity of conceiving culture as Bible–Greeks, moving instead toward composite notions of cultural formation, meaning, and identity.

In the end, this shift from the bordered dyad of Levinas's ethics and politics toward an ethics, then politics, of entanglement suggests a movement away from the language of welcoming and hospitality. In fact, such a language is largely unsustainable in the rhizomatic space of interstitial politics and the question of justice in that space. The European center of Levinas's discussion is all the more evident in this context, as well. Languages of welcoming and hospitality presuppose borders as a matter of general conceptualization, but there is more to it than just theory. There is also the practice of the center, which is deeply sedimented in felt and habitual assumptions about cultural and political formations. On the one hand, Levinas puts difference at the heart of his theory. This is what marks his work with an innovative and at times radical character. On the other hand, Levinas does not see diversity in difference. The difference of singularity conceals how incarnate historiography carries multiple, entangled differences across histories of colonialism, class oppression, sexual difference, and so on. In the context of the present reflections, of course, it is the failure to see the implication of European subjectivity in a transnational crossing of historical experience and responsibility that keeps Levinas's sense of difference so tamed. The anarchy of history is borne on the body, for Levinas, but never gives birth to the political subject proper. This is why the rhizomatic reconfiguration of being is so important for decolonizing Levinasian politics. With the rhizome, we get a stronger sense of how there is differentiation in difference, how difference is dimensional and fractal, making unexpected turns and twists that, when we arrive at the asymmetry of political space, are capable of sustaining multiple languages of moral call, obligation, and the just work of solidarity.

How do we ground this sense of ethical politics that thinks against the rigidity of borders in the anarchy of rhizomatic identity?

How do we transform the uniformity of being in Levinas into an ethically informed, wholly fractured relation to the transnational in Levinasian thinking? In a certain sense, the preceding chapters offer the beginning of an answer to those questions. The subaltern silence, mobile and hybrid identities, entangled beginnings, and rhizomatic transformations of ethical and political subjectivities all decolonize Levinas's ideas in order to deformalize them in new geographies. Across all of these shifts in the language of difference, there is incarnate historiography. So, a word or two more about history and how historical experience initiates languages and practices of difference.

*   *   *

What does historical experience change about our thinking the relation between ethics and politics? And how does historical experience bring race and nation to bear on the language of otherness, being, and obligation?

This is of course a peculiar question. Indeed, at first glance, the question of historical experience is alien to Levinasian thinking. Levinas's work is first dedicated to the interruption of history with the immemorial; the face and my incarnation of obligation are singular in every sense. It would seem that historical experience, which inscribes the sense and significance of the event with memory of the past, runs contrary to the enigma and surprise of moral consciousness. This is not to say that Levinas understands the ethical as ahistorical, but rather that the relation to history is always one of interruption (on the model of the messianic). The ethical proper comes from outside the synchrony of time, whether that is the synchrony of lived subjective experience or the fantasied, ideological continuity of cultural forms. But Levinas never conceives history as constitutive of the ethical encounter as such.

And yet Levinas's work makes a consistent appeal to at least one form of historical experience, in so far as even the possibility of a language of 'same' and 'other' draws on an idea of the meaning of history and its work in the constitution of culture. Again, I of course have in mind Levinas's claim that Europe is composed of the Bible and the Greeks, the Hebraic and Hellenic cultural forces that comprise the tension we call 'the West.' This account of historical experience is remarkable for its simplicity (one I hope to have contested in the preceding chapters) and the rather transparent way in which such a rendering of history and culture serves the Levinasian prerogative. 'The Bible and the Greeks' is already a peculiar formation and formulation, premised as it is on the implicit claim that such 'traditions' are single-rooted and not already excessively syncretic. Indeed, were we to take seriously the idea of the Hebraic as a rooted culture, we would be immediately placed in that peculiar intersecting of cultural hybridity with an epic storytelling that reduces the complexity of hybridity. Even more so if we were to consider the Hellenic, where the ancient mixing of cultures blurs any honest rendering of the term 'Greek.' Both the Bible and the Greeks, and so both founts of historical experience, carry with them such immense sedimentations of difference that only the power of epic and myth can overcome the fact that 'the Bible and the Greeks' express an imagined single culture (a project) whose origin is in fact not one, but many. After all, the Mediterranean world is inconceivable without the crossroads of cultures. In Levinas's work – and he is not alone in this, indeed far from it – a thorough exploration of the consequences of reclaiming the *syncretic* origins of the West has yet to happen. What does it mean that Levinas has essentially reified the *project* of the West, even as he claims to rupture it with the thought of the Other?

Drawing from our opening comments on Europe and identity in the Introduction above, I think we can say a few words about the problem of origins in the context of the discussion of ethics and politics. If Levinas's thought is dedicated to the problem of difference, then his eclipse of the self-differentiation of Western origins is, as a matter of principle, a Levinasian problematic. And yet it is an exceptionally productive eclipse at the very same moment that it undermines certain pillars of Levinasian thinking. The pillars gather around Levinas's articulation of the interval between ethics and politics, where the singularity of the Other is put at risk in the political commitment to the plane of being. For Levinas, there is always the originary border between the singular and the collective, the outside and being itself. At best, the generosity of welcoming, hospitality, and a deconstructed cosmopolitanism opens a border. Rhizoming identity changes something fundamental here and proves entirely more attuned to – even responsible to – self-differentiating historical experience. The ethical in politics is not a gesture or opening, bur rather an already entangled network of opaque sites of contact. These sites of contact open the thought of difference to senses of building-with and solidarity for which there are no borders across which to welcome; the nation-state is already late to the scene. The thought of the rhizome, which in Glissant's words and Marcos's practice becomes a thought of the other and other others, puts difference into being; indeed, this is part of Deleuze and Guattari's original claim, that the rhizome threatens the predatory character of single-rooted being, not in an exit of being, but in the internal differentiation of being itself. The advance of Glissant is straightforward: the infusion of multiplicity with historical experience, putting the strategic and insurgent work of Deleuze and Guattari back into contact with the material conditions of postcolonial life. And the advance of Marcos is to see the possibilities in this differentiation for another kind of justice. Race and nation differentiate the sense of otherness, not just as a matter of ontic, mundane, or mere worldly life, but as a constitutive moment of ethical and political responsibility itself. The phenomenological basis for this claim lies in the account of incarnate historiography. The ethical politics that responds to such historical experience lies in the rhizomatic entanglement with racialized and transnational senses of obligating otherness. The place of Europe as an operative concept in Levinas's thought conceals this historiography and entanglement, and so conceals the conception of being capable of sustaining an ethical politics.

So, at a certain point, one might ask: why think about Levinas at all, especially if his fantasied notion of historical experience eclipses what is most radical and reorienting about rhizomatic difference and entanglement? This question arises for me whenever I think about Levinas's relevance (or lack of relevance) in a world more complicated than any depicted in his work. It is a legitimate question, really, because there are plenty of discourses of the Other and responsibility in contemporary philosophy and political theory. The present study has of course only begun a conversation with a few postcolonial theorists. Why Levinas? The answer, I think, is really quite simple and a recurring one when offering hesitations about Levinas's work: the persistence of the ethical and its interruptive power remains crucial for understanding *why* and *how* politics *must* be committed to justice, that tense and precarious entwinement of love and political praxis. That is, without the recurrence of the ethical in being, without the interruption of political uniformity by the ethical *call* or *signal* of difference, we are left with a problematic conception of politics reduced to strategy and calculation. It is exactly that conception of politics which led Levinas to set out the project of *Totality and Infinity* and after in the starkest of terms: we must decide whether the world is simply the war of one against another *or* if a beauty still adorns the earth and can yield, with all caveats in place, some sense of hope.

Notes

1. Emmanuel Levinas, *Autrement qu'être ou au-delà de l'essence.* The Hague: Martinus Nijhoff, 1974, 19; *Otherwise Than Being or Beyond Essence,* trans. Alphonso Lingis. Dordrecht: Kluwer Academic, 1991, 16.
2. Ibid.
3. On this problem in Levinas's work, see Howard Caygill's reflections on Levinas, the third, and the problem of exclusion in his *Levinas and the Political* (New York: Routledge, 2002), especially Chapter 2.
4. Emmanuel Levinas, *Totalité et l'infini.* The Hague: Martinus Nijhoff, 1961, x; *Totality and Infinity,* trans. Alphonso Lingis. Pittsburgh: Duquesne University Press, 1969, 22.
5. Celia Britton, *Édouard Glissant and Postcolonial Theory: Strategies of Language and Resistance.* Charlottesville: University of Virginia Press, 1999.
6. Derek Walcott, 'The Antilles: Fragments of Epic Memory,' in *What the Twilight Says.* New York: Farrar, Straus & Giroux, 1998, 65–84.
7. Édouard Glissant, *Introduction à une poétique du divers.* Paris: Gallimard, 1996, 59. Translation mine.
8. Édouard Glissant, *Poétique de la relation.* Paris: Gallimard, 1990, 23; *Poetics of Relation,* trans. Betsy Wing. Ann Arbor: University of Michigan Press, 2000, 11.
9. Ibid., 207/193.
10. Wilson Harris, 'Creoleness: The Crossroads of a Civilization?,' in *Selected Essays of Wilson Harris.* New York: Routledge, 199, 237–47.
11. Glissant, *Poétique de la relation,* 222/206.
12. Subcomandante Marcos, 'Seventh Anniversary of the Zapatista Uprising,' *The Speed of Dreams,* ed Canek Peña-Vargas and Greg Ruggiero. San Francisco: City Lights, 2007, 36.
13. Subcomandante Marcos, 'Dying in Order to Live,' in *Our Word is Our Weapon,* ed Juana Ponce de León. New York: Seven Stories, 2001, 17.
14. Subcomandante Marcos, 'The Sixth Declaration of the Lacandon Jungle,' in *The Speed of Dreams,* 282–3.
15. Simon Critchley, *Infinitely Demanding.* New York: Verso, 2006, 113.
16. Ibid., 114.

Concluding Remarks

Let me begin this ending in the first person.

In the final quarter of my Great Books program in college, I took my first course in contemporary philosophy. Though the course dealt a bit with Heidegger, it primarily concerned French philosophy, and in particular the work of Gabriel Marcel and Maurice Merleau-Ponty. The course changed everything for me about my interests. I became, in many ways, a little philosopher for the first time. The professor, Robert Cousineau, pushed us to think *with* the ideas, rather than imitate the texts and language. That was difficult. And yet it continues to be the most important philosophical lesson I have learned in the over twenty years since.

But Professor Cousineau taught me something else. We used to have one-on-one sessions with professors after turning in drafts of final essays, and they were terrifying. It felt like an unscheduled oral exam. In our session, Cousineau asked me a simple question: 'do you believe what you've written here?' I answered honestly, saying that I believed my essay to be a fair reflection of one of Marcel's arguments in *Creative Fidelity* in relation to a passage in Karl Marx's *1844 Economic and Philosophical Manuscripts*. There was of course a follow-up. Cousineau wanted to know if I believed the *ideas to be true* or at least *a legitimate and justifiable account of the world*. It was a shocking question to field as a student. After all, schooled as we were in the idea of the 'great thinker' (a sensibility to which I still largely subscribe), our own particular sense and judgement of those ideas seemed better suited for dorm study hall than a formal essay. At the same time, I was moved by its imperative, an imperative made all the more urgent when Cousineau filled the silence of my non-response with another question: 'why would you write about something you did not believe?' He actually seemed a bit angry at the suggestion that I would write an indifferent, if writerly sharp, piece of work.

I am still moved by that imperative. In this work, I have tried to say something about the problem of difference, moved as I am, authentically, by both the power of the Levinasian ethical and the limits of the ethical in a transnational context. For the past dozen years, I have been increasingly unnerved by the tension between those two sentiments, those two beliefs about the world and what it means to philosophize, and so I wrote this book. This is such a critical problematic for those of us so taken by Levinas's work and the transformative effect of his account of for-the-Other subjectivity. We no longer live in insular places, if we ever did. We live in a world formed by the entanglements of empire, colonialism, and all the violences of slave trading, cultural decimation, and institutions formed entirely to destroy the human being from the inside out, outside in. That world is not a world from the past; historical experience is not really even historical. Historical experience saturates the present and gives content and orientation toward the future. This is the enduring truth of Merleau-Ponty's claim that the body has a history and motivates the first chapter of the present project, delineating the terms of what I called *incarnate historiography*. To Professor Cousineau, I would say simply, yes, I believe historical experience to be formative of our sense of self and world. And I also believe that the singularity of the ethical and the ethical more widely registered names the beauty that still adorns the earth after so much disaster and all of this sadness of history. So we need to think them together. The chapters above start that thinking along what I hope is an interesting and productive path. I surely have no pretensions to having solved the important problems of ethics, the geography of reason, and postcolony life. That is neither the aspiration of this book nor my place in the world as a thinker.

Professor Cousineau's remarks to me helped me understand what is at stake in writing, especially when writing about important, pressing ideas. Those remarks are about forming sentences and making sense of one's own thoughts with some integrity and deep moral, political, and intellectual attachment. There is of course another side to all of this, and it is how Cousineau's comments have been reinvented in my own path as a writer. One must also ask about what it means to be writing a book. For this, I have written, edited, revised, and rethought this project also from a displaced position: what would I think of this book were I a reader, not a writer, of it? That is of course an altogether more difficult question. It means, among other things, taking seriously the idea that the book might not be convincing at all or that it might be written – perhaps the greatest fear of a philosophical writer! – purely from within the conceptual and affective space of the author's mind. I hope this book is more than just me talking to myself, of course, and so I have wondered how this book will sound to other readers. What are the suspicions? What are the moments of overstep? Where is analysis left wanting? What remains to be said?

There are two sites for these questions, at the very least.

First, there is the question of Levinas scholarship. What will Levinas scholars think of this work? How will it challenge them? What part of that community do I hope to have troubled? And what do I think that they will find most problematic and even suspicious about my claims? When I put myself in that place, I am struck by one anticipated, and wholly fundamental, impasse. The foundation of the chapters assembled above is a robust, constitutive notion of historical experience. History is formative of our language, and so of our place in the world, of our sense of being, and so, ultimately, the terms of our obligations to others. In a transnational context, this history carries with it transgenerational culpability and the effects and affects of centuries of pain. Europe lived from violence for so many centuries. In European philosophy, scholarship has barely begun to reckon with how Europe was an enormous machine of death and suffering for nearly five centuries. Nearly five damn centuries. Incalculable, yes, but the incalculable only intensifies the imperative to reckon honestly. Outside Europe, as the object of that machine, living under violence for so many centuries was the condition of being itself. And so I have tried to bring that experience, in both registers, to bear on the language of difference and the ethical. But that places Levinas in a philosophical context to which he was, perhaps from the beginning, completely resistant: the worldliness of the world. The ethical is otherwise than being. Outside knowing. Beyond essence. Even when he reads Heidegger in the early essays and *Theory of Intuition* book, Levinas seems hardly moved by the problem of history. So, reading Levinas with history and all of the attendant characteristics of worldliness in view – or even as a frame – already intervenes in Levinas's thought against Levinas's terms. Singularity, after all, is singularity *because* it gains distance from the terms I have introduced in the preceding chapters.

To this worry or criticism, I would offer two intertwined responses. There is of course the question of method posed above in the opening chapter. For Levinas, if I read him correctly, philosophy becomes capable of documenting the wisdom of love when it becomes phenomenological. We have to describe the world and subjectivity as they appear to us in reflection. For me, and this is the entry-level critique I have of Levinas's work, the Other and my sense of responsibility are deeply embedded in the historical character of the encounter. The Other's body and my own body bear history in signi-fication. Historical experience is not a construction. The body has a history, which means obligation outstrips the terms of my action as well as the terms of the present moment. The orientation and meth-odology of Levinas's work lead us to this insight. As well, to be plain and blunt, it is just an obvious part of being in the world. Historical experience terrifies and haunts us. Levinas's commitment to thinking through haunting, the ghosts of the Other and others, is quite com-patible with this conception of the ethical, even as it requires us to temper his critique of worldliness more than a little bit. As well, to add a second, intertwined response to anticipated criticism, Levinas's thought is so deeply committed to the idea of Europe that only by breaking him free of that commitment, and exploring the conse-quences, can we ensure (or begin to ensure) that his work remains relevant into the twenty-first century. Levinas's thought is already naïvely unworldly in its Eurocentrism. As readers, we are obligated to reorient elements of Levinas's thinking by drawing out some of the implications of his Eurocentrism and the consequent fantasies of insularity, bordered culture and politics, and constrained senses of obligation. In the end, I truly believe Levinasian thinking is all the better for having undergone such fundamental, immanent critique.

Second, there is the question of the postcolonial. What are we to make of Levinas and the postcolonial thought together, even as that thinking remains in tension? What does the postcolonial mean in contact with Levinas? In this regard, my aims in this book have been considerably more modest, especially in comparison to the work I hope to have done in the context of decolonizing Levinasian think-ing. This is partly due to the orientation of the book, focused as it is in recurring tensions in Levinas's work, but it is also inherent in the term postcolonialism itself. Indeed, the term 'postcolonial' implies many already canonical thinkers not considered in this work, from Edward Said to Partha Chatterjee to Achille Mbembe and others. So, the scope of any claim regarding a field as varied – in terms of thinker, colonial experience, or intellectual tradition – as what we call postcolonial is necessarily narrow and ought to be constrained. I have tried to be modest in my aims by offering readings of particular ideas found in particular thinkers, rather than venturing claims about historical movements or intellectual trends and groupings.

At the same time, there are important philosophical moments that, while not absolutely identical, surely have some family resemblance. For, the postcolonial moment is always a matter of beginning again, after a disaster that, for all of its pain, is at once memory, resistance, retrieval, and creation of what Glissant calls the imaginary. An imaginary of life *after*. The imagination of a future. The imagination is always creative, to be sure, but imagination also begins on the basis of certain epistemological conditions, ontological formations, ethical concerns, and fraught political imperatives. To the extent that every postcolonial project is an interval for the imagination, I hope that the reflections above have something to contribute to theorizing the interval and the tiny bit, but not nothing, that a Levinasian notion of the ethical has to contribute to that moment. To recall the epigraph to the present project, Bhabha's remark that historical freedom and cultural survival require the inscription of a powerful, transformative silence into the 'raveling and unraveling between the psychic body and its political weight' evokes an ethics of the interval. Given that Levinas's work has been dedicated to the enigma of a companion – again, not identical – interval, this is a theoretical conversation, or, perhaps better, a conversation about theory, that is worth having. No matter the risks.

In the present project, the chiasm of Levinasian thinking and certain strands of postcolonial thinking can only be utopian. The project can only ask questions about the future in search of hope, imagining the terms set out by Fanon at the close of his famous 'Racism and Culture' essay, delivered in Paris at the 1956 1st International Congress of Black Writers and Artists, where he fantasized, just for a moment, what the new humanism might look like. 'Universality resides in this decision to recognize and accept the reciprocal relativism of different cultures,' Fanon writes, 'once the colonial status is irreversibly excluded.'[1] Fanon crosses the interval of past and future in this imaginative leap. The Levinasian ethical does not quite cross that interval, instead postponing the pure future on the basis of an irreconcilable past, sealed in diachrony, pain, and loss. The postcolonial reawakens the future, but without forgetting pain and loss, beginning again with multiple kinds of diachrony. In this collage of difference, time, memory, and history begin to bend, curve, and fracture. What does it mean to know, be, create, and act not *in* that collage, but *as* that collage and its swirl of difference? It means, in the end, to think race, nation, and Other at one and the same time.

Note

1. Frantz Fanon, 'Racisme et culture', in *Pour la révolution africaine*. Paris: Découverte, 2006, 52; 'Racism and Culture', in *Toward the African Revolution*, trans. Haakon Chevalier. New York: Grove, 1988, 44.

Index